Third Workshop on Text Simplification, Accessibility and Readability (TSAR 2024)

Miami, Florida, USA
15 November 2024

ISBN: 979-8-3313-0854-4

Printed from e-media with permission by:

Curran Associates, Inc.
57 Morehouse Lane
Red Hook, NY 12571

Association for Computational Linguistics
209 N. Eighth Street
Stroudsburg, Pennsylvania 18360

Phone: 1-570-476-8006
Fax: 1-570-476-0860

acl@aclweb.org

Additional copies of this publication are available from:

Curran Associates, Inc.
57 Morehouse Lane
Red Hook, NY 12571 USA
Phone: 845-758-0400
Fax: 845-758-2633
Email: curran@proceedings.com
Web: www.proceedings.com

TSAR 2024

The Third Workshop on Text Simplification, Accessibility and Readability

Proceedings of the Workshop

November 15, 2024

Order copies of this and other ACL proceedings from:

Association for Computational Linguistics (ACL)
317 Sidney Baker St. S
Suite 400 - 134
Kerrville, TX 78028
USA
Tel: +1-855-225-1962
acl@aclweb.org

Table of Contents

Introduction

The organisers are pleased to present the proceedings of the 3rd edition of the Workshop on Text Simplification, Accessibility and Readability (TSAR), hosted at The 2024 Conference on Empirical Methods in Natural Language Processing (EMNLP 2024), in Miami, Florida, USA.

This year the workshop was organised around two key tracks. The main track was of general interest to the audience and covered topics surrounding empirical research on text simplification, accessibility and readability. The special track encouraged participants to focus on the evaluation of systems with relevance to the workshop. In total, the workshop received twenty-eight submissions split between twenty submissions for the main track and eight submissions for the special track; special track sumbissions are indicated by * in the table of contents. These submissions covered a variety of current topics of interest to the TSAR community. In the main track, four papers considered simplification at the full text and lexical level, three papers presented work to identify various aspects of complex vocabulary and one paper considered accessibility through image generation. In the special track on evaluation two submissions focussed on the introduction of new evaluation methods, whereas three papers presented work with a particular focus on the evaluation of text simplification systems. All papers are listed below.

Main Track

- MultiLS: An End-to-End Lexical Simplification Framework
- OtoBERT: Identifying Suffixed Verbal Forms in Modern Hebrew Literature
- CompLex-ZH: A New Dataset for Lexical Complexity Prediction in Mandarin and Cantonese
- Images Speak Volumes: User-Centric Assessment of Image Generation for Accessible Communication
- Cochrane-auto: An Aligned Dataset for the Simplification of Biomedical Abstracts
- Considering Human Interaction and Variability in Automatic Text Simplification
- Society of Medical Simplifiers
- Difficult for Whom? A Study of Japanese Lexical Complexity

Special Track (*)

- Lexical Complexity Prediction and Lexical Simplification for Catalan and Spanish: Resource Creation, Quality Assessment, and Ethical Considerations
- SciGisPy: a Novel Metric for Biomedical Text Simplification via Gist Inference Score
- EASSE-DE & EASSE-multi: Easier Automatic Sentence Simplification Evaluation for German & Multiple Languages
- Evaluating the Simplification of Brazilian Legal Rulings in LLMs Using Readability Scores as a Target
- Measuring and Modifying the Readability of English Texts with GPT-4

All submissions were peer-reviewed by the members of the program committee which includes distinguished specialists in text simplification, accessibility, and readability. Out of the twenty-eight submissions to the workshop, two were desk-rejected, thirteen were rejected after review, eleven were accepted unconditionally and two were accepted subject to improvements in line with reviewer feedback. Out of thirteen accepted papers, five were selected to be presented orally and eight as posters, which were also presented during a lightning-talk session. We additionally invited three non-archival poster presentations from relevant EMNLP Findings papers.

The workshop is held in-person, with online attendance for authors who were unable to attend due to constraints beyond the organisers control. The program encompasses: two invited talks, first by Dr. Iria Da Cunha, National Distance Education University (Spain) and secondly by Walburga Fröhlich, CEO and Co-Founder of Capito; two oral sessions, comprising five presentations; a round of lightning talks to introduce the poster presentations; and a hosted discussion session on current issues and trends in text simplification, accessibility and readability research.

We would like to thank the members of the program committee for their timely help in reviewing the submissions and all the authors for submitting their papers to the workshop. We also thank the EMNLP 2024 workshop chairs for their kind support in delivering the workshop and producing these proceedings.

TSAR Organizing Committee
Matthew Shardlow,
Fernando Alva-Manchego,
Kai North,
Regina Stodden,
Sanja Štajner,
Marcos Zampieri,
Horacio Saggion

Organizing Committee

Organizing Committee

Matthew Shardlow, Manchester Metropolitan University, UK
Horacio Saggion, Universitat Pompeu Fabra, Spain
Fernando Alva-Manchego, Cardiff University, UK
Marcos Zampieri, George Mason University, USA
Kai North, Cambium Assessment, USA
Sanja Štajner, Karlsruhe, Germany
Regina Stodden, Heinrich Heine University Düsseldorf, Germany

Program Committee

Program Committee

Rémi Cardon, UC Louvain
Richard Evans, University of Wolverhampton
Joseph Marvin, University of Bath
Yingqiang Gao, University of Zurich
Mounica Maddela, Bloomberg
Jan Trienes, University of Marburg
Freya Hewett, Univesity of Potsdamm
Liana Ermakova, Université de Bretagne Occidentale
Andreas Säuberli, University of Zurich
Piotr Przybyła, University Pompeu Fabra
Sowmya Vajjala, National Research Council, Canada
Emad Alghamdi, King Abdulaziz University
Silvana Deilen, University of Mainz
Sandaru Seneviratne, The Australian National University
Tadashi Nomoto, National Institute of Japanese Literature
Gustavo Paetzold, Federal University of Technology - Paraná
Tomoyuki Kajiwara, Ehime University
Claire Gardent, CNRS/LORIA
Sweta Agrawal, Instituto de Telecomunicações
Jaap Kamps, University of Amsterdam
Zihao LI, University of Manchester
Raquel Hervas, University Complutense of Madrid
Michael Gille, HAW Hamburg
Sarah Ebling, University of Zurich
Tannon Kew, University of Zurich
Giulia Venturi, Istituto di Linguistica Computazionale "Antonio Zampolli"
Natalia Grabar, University of Lille
Anna Dmitrieva, University of Helsinki
Laura Vásquez-Rodríguez, IDIAP
David Kauchak, Pomona College
Margot Madina, Darmstadt University of Applied Sciences
Jipeng Qiang, Yangzhou University
Lourdes Moreno, Universidad Carlos III de Madrid
Jasper Degraeuwe, Ghent University
Michael Ryan, Georgia Tech
Itziar Gonzalez-Dios, University of the Basque Country
Reno Kriz, John Hopkins
Yannick Parmentier, LORIA
Akio Hayakawa, University Pompeu Fabra
Oliver Alonzo, Rochester Institute of Technology
Patrick Haller, University of Zurich
Thomas François, UC Louvain
Susana Bautista, Universidad Francisco de Vitoria
Christina Niklaus, University of StGallen
Núria Gala, Aix Marseille Université
Maja Popović, Dublin City University

Tomas Goldsack, University of Sheffield
Diana Galvan-Sosa, University of Cambridge
Daniele Schicchi, CNR-ITD
Dennis Aumiller, Cohere

Keynote Talk
Artificial Intelligence and Plain Language

Iria da Cunha
National Distance Education University
November 15, 2024 –

Abstract: Natural Language Processing (NLP), a branch of artificial intelligence, has evolved significantly over recent decades. Broadly speaking, three main paradigms have been employed: rule-based systems, machine learning, and, more recently, language models. Simultaneously, the international - plain languagemovement emerged, advocating for specialized texts addressed to the general public to be written in a simpler, more accessible manner. Over the past decade, a synergy has developed between these two fields—NLP and plain language— which has led to the creation of technological tools aimed at producing clearer texts. These tools follow the aforementioned NLP paradigms and can be classified, according to their function, into clarity testers, writing assistants, and clear text generators.

This presentation will offer an overview of the available tools, outlining their functionalities as well as the advantages and disadvantages of each NLP paradigm. Particular attention will be given to tools developed for the Spanish language, with a specific focus on the arText system (https://sistema-artext.com/), the first writing assistant for Spanish designed to help public administration staff draft texts in plain language addressed to citizens. This system has been developed with funding obtained through various competitive grants, in collaboration with different Spanish governments, and is available online free of charge.

Bio: Iria da Cunha is a lecturer at the National Distance Education University (Spain). She holds a PhD in Applied Linguistics from the Universitat Pompeu Fabra. Her research lines are Plain Language, Natural Language Processing, Terminology, and Specialized Discourse. She is the director of the arText team.

Keynote Talk

Easy-to-Understand Writing with AI Assistance

Walburga Fröhlich
CEO and Co-Founder of Capito
November 15, 2024 –

Abstract: Easy-to-understand language is not only needed by people with learning difficulties and disabilities. International studies show that many more people have difficulties understanding serious information from public authorities or companies.

In this presentation we will introduce rules and criteria for easy-to-understand language and show some good examples from companies and public authorities.

Since most people who are responsible for writing and providing information do not know how to write easy-to-understand texts, AI-based writing assistance can be very useful.

In the talk, we will show how we can analyze and simplify complicated information very easily with an AI-based writing assistance.

Bio: Walburga Fröhlich is Co-Founder and CEO of "capito". For 30 years, she has been concerned with the question of how the potential of disabled people can be made visible and developed in our society and what accessible communication does for our society. Together with her team, she has developed AI-based digital tools for easier comprehensible information.

Walburga was born in 1966 in Austria, she studied first social work and has in addition a Masters degree in Social Management. She has already received many awards for her work, including the European Woman Innovator Prize or the European Innovation Council "Seal for Excellence".

MultiLS: An End-to-End Lexical Simplification Framework

Kai North[1], Tharindu Ranasinghe[2], Matthew Shardlow[3], Marcos Zampieri[1]
[1]George Mason University, USA
[2]Lancaster University, UK
[3]Manchester Metropolitan University, UK
knorth8@gmu.edu

Abstract

Lexical Simplification (LS) automatically replaces difficult to read words for easier alternatives while preserving a sentence's original meaning. Several datasets exist for LS and each of them specialize in one or two sub-tasks within the LS pipeline. However, as of this moment, no single LS dataset has been developed that covers all LS sub-tasks. We present MultiLS, the first LS framework that allows for the creation of a multi-task LS dataset. We also present MultiLS-PT, the first dataset created using the MultiLS framework. We demonstrate the potential of MultiLS-PT by carrying out all LS sub-tasks of (1) lexical complexity prediction (LCP), (2) substitute generation, and (3) substitute ranking for Portuguese.

1 Introduction

Despite the importance and growing popularity of LS (Paetzold and Specia, 2016b; Yimam et al., 2018; Shardlow et al., 2021a; Saggion et al., 2022), all publicly available datasets, regardless of language, fail to cover all sub-tasks within the LS pipeline: lexical complexity prediction (LCP), substitute generation (SG), selection (SS), and ranking (SR) as depicted in Figure 1.

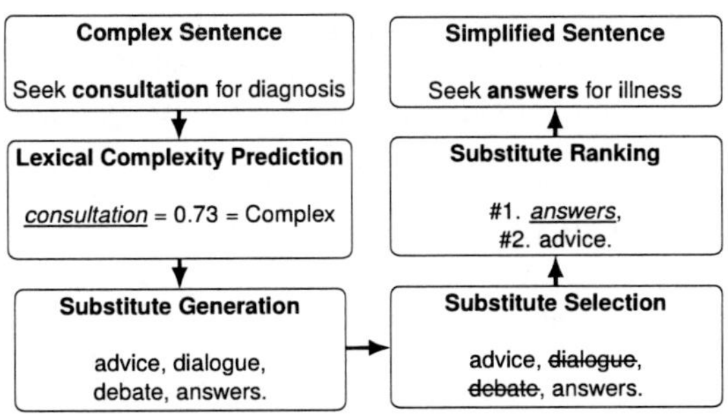

Figure 1: LS Pipeline. Example shows LS pipeline applied within the biomedical domain. Original figure adapted from (Paetzold and Specia, 2015)

End-to-end LS frameworks (McCarthy and Navigli, 2007; Specia et al., 2012; Horn et al., 2014; Hartmann and Aluísio, 2020; Saggion et al., 2022) have collected gold simplifications needed for SG, SS, and SR, but have excluded LCP. In contrast, lexical complexity datasets (Maddela and Xu, 2018; Shardlow et al., 2020) refrained from collecting gold simplifications. Each of these LS frameworks also annotated different target words meaning that their subsequent datasets cannot be combined to provide all the necessary information for LS.

In this paper, we introduce MultiLS, the first multi-purpose end-to-end framework for the creation of all-in-one LS datasets by providing target words with lexical complexity values required for LCP and gold candidate simplifications needed for SG, SS, and SR. MultiLS is an extensible framework allowing the creation of datasets in various languages. We use MultiLS to create MultiLS-PT, the first multi-task and multi-genre dataset for Portuguese LS. Portuguese is one of the ten most spoken languages in the world with over 250 million speakers (Eberhard et al., 2023). Many countries where Portuguese is spoken (e.g., Angola, Brazil, Mozambique) have low literacy rates. We chose to include texts from the Brazilian variety in MultiLS-PT as this is the most widely-spoken variety of Portuguese. While Brazil is one of the largest economies in the world, a large part of its population are either illiterate or functionally illiterate worsening existing socio-economic challenges (Ireland, 2008). As such, there is ample motivation for the development of assistive reading technologies for Portuguese.

The main contributions of this paper are:

1. **MultiLS**: the first multi-purpose framework for the full training and evaluation of all LS sub-tasks (Sections 2 to 3).
2. **MultiLS-PT**: the first Portuguese multi-genre dataset for LS to contain both continuous complexity values and ranked gold simplifications (Section 4).

Proceedings of the Third Workshop on Text Simplification, Accessibility and Readability (TSAR 2024), pages 1–11
November 15, 2024 ©2024 Association for Computational Linguistics

3. **Evaluation**: the performance of multiple state-of-the-art models for LCP, substitute generation and ranking (Sections 5 to 7).

2 Related Work

Complexity Prediction The first-step within the LS pipeline is the identification of complex words (North et al., 2022d). There are two approaches to this task. Complex Word Identification (CWI), a binary classification task which assigns each target word with a non-complex (0) or complex (1) label (Paetzold and Specia, 2016b; Zampieri et al., 2017). LCP is a regression-based task that assigns a complexity value on a continuum often using a Likert-scale, including such labels as very simple (0), neutral (0.5), to very complex (1) (Shardlow et al., 2020). Words that have an assigned complexity value substantially greater than 0.5 are considered to be complex words, such as the word "*consultation*" within Figure 1. LCP datasets have employed the use of human annotators to assign gold complexity values (Horn et al., 2014; Paetzold and Specia, 2016b; Yimam et al., 2018).

Substitute Generation and Selection SG is the second-step within the LS pipeline and it aims to produce a pre-defined number: k candidate substitutions that are easier to understand than the original complex word while persevering its meaning (North et al., 2023b). SS filters these generated candidates to find the best possible simplification, commonly referred to as the top-k candidate substitution. For example, given the sentence: "*Seek consultation about your diagnosis*", and the target word: "*consultation*" within Figure 1, SG would produce k candidate substitutions, such as "*advice*", "*dialogue*", "*debate*", and "*answers*". SS then removes those generated candidates that are more complex, semantically dissimilar, or do not fit into the provided context resulting in the *top-k* candidate substitutions: "*advice*" and "*answers*". While SG and SS datasets provide gold candidate substitutions, these datasets are independent of CWI and LCP as they do not include annotated complexity values per target word. Examples of SG and SS datasets include the ALEXSIS datasets for English, Spanish, and Portuguese (Saggion et al., 2022; Ferres and Saggion, 2022; North et al., 2022b) and SIMPLEX-PB 3.0 for Portuguese (Hartmann and Aluísio, 2020). These datasets, however, do not include complexity values required for LCP.

Substitute Ranking SR is the final step within the LS pipeline and it sorts candidate substitutions from the most to the least appropriate simplifications. It arranges candidate substitutions based on their complexity and their semantic similarity to the target word and context (North et al., 2023b).The example shown in Figure 1 ranks "*answers*" as being a more appropriate simplification than "*advice*" for the target word "*consultation*". This may, in part, be due to "*answers*" having a higher frequency within a reference corpus or being more frequent within a training set. Alternatively, "*answers*" may have a lower age of acquisition, higher familiarity score, or even concreteness (abstractness) rating (North et al., 2022d).

End-to-End Frameworks The few previous end-to-end LS frameworks have focused on substitute generation, selection and ranking and not on LCP. In fact, traditional notions of LS consider the identification of complex words a precursor and a separate task to LS (Paetzold and Specia, 2017). BenchLS (Paetzold and Specia, 2016c) provided a suitable framework for the training and evaluation of substitute generation to ranking. BenchLS (Paetzold and Specia, 2016c) contains sentences, target words, and several candidate substitutions ranked per their simplicity, but does not supply the continuous complexity values needed for LCP. PLUMBErr (Paetzold and Specia, 2016a), an automatic error identification framework for LS, demonstrated its potential by assessing several LS systems that conducted CWI alongside all other LS sub-tasks. Nevertheless, its CWI component was trained on a dataset different from that used to evaluate its overall performance. FLELex (Tack et al., 2016) caters for LCP by aligning two datasets of authentic and simplified texts and providing continuous complexity ratings for each target word. However, only a portion of their target words were labeled with a maximum of one candidate substitution per target word limiting its usefulness.

3 MultiLS Framework

As discussed in the last section, LS datasets often have a narrow specialization focusing on one or two tasks. They only include lexical complexity values, candidate substitutions, or candidate features, restricting their use to either LCP or substitute generation, selection, or ranking (Table 1). Unlike previous frameworks, the MulitLex framework supplies all the necessary data required for

		Original Datasets (English)				MultiLS Framework (New MultiLS-PT Dataset)			
						Step 1 →	*Step 2 →*	*Step 3 →*	*Step 4*
T.	D.	Token	Context (Sentence)	Val.	Substitutions	Selection	New Context (Sentence)	New Val.	New Substitutions
Task 1: LCP	**CompLex**	colleagues	pointed out colleagues	0.26	–	colegas	controlado por colegas	0.13	amigos (friends),.
		uncertainties	uncertainties in the	0.37	–	incertezas	influenciada por incertezas	0.08	dúvidas (doubts),.
		gentiles	teacher of the gentiles	0.26	–	gentios	doutor dos gentios	0.46	multidão (crowd),.
		prophet	raise up a prophet	0.27	–	profeta	um profeta semelhante	0.21	mensageiro (messenger),.
		maximum	a maximum of two	0.14	–	máximo	máximo corrigido	0.32	extremo (extreme),.
Tasks 2-3: SG & SS	**ALEXSIS-EN**	observers	the number of observers	–	watchers, spectators,.	observadores	observadores que tiveram	0.19	examinadores (examiners),.
		authorities	assistance to authorities	–	officials, powers,.	autoridades	alegando que as autoridades	0.23	forças (forces),.
		condolences	sincere condolences to	–	sympathy, comfort,.	condolências	suas condolências pedindos	0.21	compaixão (compassion),.
		regime	between Assad's regime	–	government, rule,.	regime	aregime do presidente	0.11	governo (government),.
		monitoring	it was monitoring the	–	watching, observing,.	monitoramento	sistema de monitoramento	0.32	acompanhamento,.
	ALEXSIS+	criteria	meet the criteria	–	requirements, standards,.	critério	critério de visão pública	0.24	normas (standards),.
		pledges	the agreement pledges	–	promises, guarantees,.	promessas	faz promessas e	0.11	compromissos,.
		acquisition	the acquisition announced	–	transaction, purchase,.	aquisição	local de aquisição	0.33	obtenção (obtaining),.
		residence	the residence next door	–	house, apartment,.	residência	tenham residência habitual	0.17	casa (house),.
		inclusion	ensure the inclusion	–	participation, presence,.	inclusão	inclusão das opções	0.12	inserção (insertion),.
Task 4: SR	**CompLex-BC**	exchange	(exchange, brains)	1	–	intercâmbio	intercâmbio efetivo das artes	0.21	troca (replacement),.
		sight	(sight, implants)	0	–	vista	agradável à sua vista	0.12	visão (view),.
		wisdom	(wisdom, women)	1	–	sabedoria	na muita sabedoria há	0.13	conhecimento (knowledge),.
		sword	(sword, densities)	0	–	espada	ferimentos por espada	0.07	faca (knife),.
		spirit	(spirit, Mesopotamia),.	0	–	espírito	há um espírito	0.08	almas (souls),.

Table 1: Illustrates the creation of MultiLS-PT. "–" indicates missing data in previous datasets. **T.** stands for sub-tasks within the LS pipeline that the corresponding dataset could be used for prior to MultiLS expansion. **D.** is Dataset. **Val.** represents assigned complexity value. Only a snapshot of contexts and candidate substitutions are shown.

the training and evaluation of the entire LS pipeline, including LCP. We use the MultiLS framework to guide the creation of the first multi-purpose, and multi-genre LS dataset, named MultiLS-PT (Table 1). The MultiLS framework consists of the following summarized steps.

Selection We identified target words from four pre-existing English datasets: CompLex (Shardlow et al., 2020), ALEXSIS-EN (Saggion et al., 2022), ALEXSIS+ (North et al., 2023a), and CompLex-BC (North et al., 2022c). Only words with a similar use and meaning within both English and Portuguese were hand-selected to provide comparable data for future multilingual and cross-lingual experiments (Section 8.1). Selection was done by a trained linguist fluent in both languages.

Context Retrieval Once target words had been identified, we automatically scraped several genres (bible extracts, news articles, and biomedical papers) to obtain new and varied sentences, hereby referred to as contexts, for each target word ready for annotation. Bible instances were obtained from Portuguese translations of the King James Bible. News instances were scraped from the PorSimplesSent dataset (Leal et al., 2018) as well as from the CC-News (Common Crawl-News) corpus (North et al., 2023a). Biomedical instances were extracted from abstracts of biomedical literature supplied by WMT-2019 (Bawden et al., 2019).

New Complexities (Val.) We presented target words in bold within the scraped contexts to annotators and asked annotators to rate their perceived difficulty using a 5-point Likert-scale: very easy (1), easy (2), neutral (3), difficult (4), to very difficult (5) (Shardlow et al., 2020, 2022). Each target word was annotated by 25 crowd-sourced Amazon Mechanical Turk (MTurk) workers located in Brazil. Table 2 shows an example Human Intelligence Task (HIT) presented to each of the 25 annotators. We selected a high number of annotators in order to get a representative gold complexity value for each target word by averaging the returned labels. Annotators were paid 2 cents of US Dollar per annotation allowing them to surpass the minimum hourly wage in Brazil.

New Substitutions Additionally, we asked annotators to suggest a valid simplification to the target word that fits within its surrounding context. Generated candidate substitutions were ranked per their suggestion frequency providing a list of gold simplifications.

4 MultiLS-PT Dataset

The uniqueness of the MutliLex framework is the collection of both continuous complexity values and gold candidate substitutions. This is what gives MultiLS-PT and future datasets that follow the MultiLS framework their distinctive multi-task functionality. The resulting MultiLS-PT dataset is unlike any other prior Portuguese dataset for LS. As referenced in Section 2, only two datasets exist made specifically for Portuguese LS: SIMPLEX-PB (Hartmann and Aluísio, 2020), and ALEXSIS-

Example MTurk HIT for Annotation	Difficulty
Identify the word ***authorities*** in the sentence below:	1. Very Easy
	2. Easy
"One of the greatest ***authorities*** on the subject, says	3. Neutral
that the destruction of the biome is irreversible."	4. Difficult
	5. Very Difficult

Tasks
(1). In your opinion, how difficult is the word in bold in this sentence? Select from 1 to 5.
(2). Write a simpler alternative to the word in bold (if any). Your suggestion must maintain the meaning of the sentence above and be easier to understand than the word in bold.

Table 2: An example HIT provided to the annotators. The HIT asks for both a continuous complexity rating and a suggested simplification. Each HIT was provided in Portuguese. Example has been translated for illustrative purposes.

PT (North et al., 2022b). However, these datasets only contain candidate substitutions without complexity values for target words. Moreover, both datasets are restricted to a specific genre. MultiLS-PT, on the other hand, contains 5,165 Portuguese target words annotated with complexity values in context taken from the Bible (2,321), news articles (1,817), and biomedical texts (1,237) with each target word also having an average of two gold candidate substitutions. Table 3 shows a direct comparison between MultiLS-PT and existing Portuguese datasets for LS.

	SIMPLEX-PB	ALEXSIS-PT	MultiLS-PT
Genre	children's books	newspapers	multi-genre
# Annotators	5	25	25
# Target Words	730	387	5,165
# Complexity Vals.	-	-	**5,165**
# Substitutions	**3,650**	**9,605**	**9,932**

Table 3: Comparison of Portuguese datasets for LS. MultiLS-PT is the first LS dataset to contain both gold complexity values (vals.) and candidate substitutions.

5 Tasks

We showcase three applications of the MultiLS-PT dataset for LS. We believed substitute selection to be conducted simultaneously during substitute generation and ranking, and therefore have only focused on LCP, substitute generation, and substitute ranking in the form of binary comparative LCP (North et al., 2022c). Each task was defined as follows: *LCP:* a regression-based task. Models were trained to automatically identify complex words by predicting their complexity value, between 0 (very easy) and 1 (very hard), of a target word in context. *SG:* a text generation task. Models were set to generate top-10 (k) candidate substitutions. *Binary Comparative LCP (BC-LCP):* a binary classification task used for substitute ranking (North et al., 2022c). Models were trained to rank candidate substitutions by assigning either 0 or 1 labels; 0 indicated that candidate 1 has a greater complexity than candidate 2 and 1 denoted the opposite.

Data for each task was formatted differently for model training. Example instances with gold labels are provided below (Table 4). Gold labels for the three tasks were averaged complexity values, most frequently suggested simplifications, and a binary label showing which of two candidate words was more complex, respectively.

Task	Example Instance with Gold Label(s)
LCP	"Procure **consulta** para diagnóstico" <\t> 0.73 (Gold) (Translation: Seek **consultation** for diagnosis) "Múltiplas feridas de **espada**" <\t> 0.08 (Gold) (Translation: Multiple **sword** wounds)
SG	"**consulta**" <\t> **respostas, conselho**, ... (Gold) (Translation: **consult** <\t> **answers, advice**) "**espada**" <\t> **faca, lâmina** ... (Gold) (Translation: **sword** <\t> **knife, blade**)
BC-LCP	"**respostas**" <\t> "**conselho**" <\t> 1 (Gold) (Translation: **answers** <\t> **advice**) "**lâmina**" <\t> "**faca**" <\t> 0 (Gold) (Translation: **blade** <\t> **knife**)

Table 4: Example instances with gold labels used for training each task. Only a snapshot of gold simplifications for SG are shown. For BC-LCP, a gold label of 1 shows candidate word 1 as being less complex than candidate word 2; i.e. "answers" is less complex than "advice", whereas 0 shows the opposite.

#	Task	Train	Dev	Test	Total
1	LCP	3,615	516	1,034	5,165
2	SG	-	-	462	462
3	BC-LCP	20,113	2,873	1,029	24,015

Table 5: MultiLS-PT's train, dev, and test splits per task. No training was conducted for the SG task.

MultiLS-PT was divided to have a 70/10/20 corresponding train, dev, and test split for the LCP and binary comparative LCP tasks, whereas the SG task had no train, dev, and test split since it was conducted in a zero-shot setting (Table 5). The test set of the binary comparative LCP task was also reduced by removing candidate substitution pairs that contained unrelated words and therefore were unsuitable for candidate ranking. Each task used a different number of total instances. The LCP task leveraged all 5,165 instances. The SG and BC-LCP tasks, on the other hand, utilized smaller subsets of the MulitLex-PT dataset. The SG task used a total of 462 instances that had a minimum of 5 gold simplifications in order to conduct meaningful eval-

Sub-Task	Num.	Name	Prompt
LCP	1	ZeroShot-5-Likert	On a scale from 1 to 5 with 5 being the most difficult, how difficult is the "target word"? Answer:
	2	Context-5-Likert	On a scale from 1 to 5 with 5 being the most difficult, how difficult is the "target word" in the above sentence? Answer:
	3	ZeroShot-10-Likert	On a scale from 1 to 10 with 10 being the most difficult, how difficult is the "target word"? Answer:
	4	Context-10-Likert	On a scale from 1 to 10 with 10 being the most difficult, how difficult is the "target word" in the above sentence? Answer:
	5	Ensemble-5-Likert	Average returned complexity from prompts 1 to 2.
	6	Ensemble-10-Likert	Average returned complexity from prompts 3 to 4.
SG	1	ZeroShot	Find ten easier words in Portuguese for "target word". Answer:
	2	Context	Find ten easier words in Portuguese for "target word" in the above sentence. Answer:
BC-LCP	1	Difficulty	Which word is more difficult "target word1" or "target word2"? Answer:
	2	Frequency	Which word is less common: "target word1" or "target word2"? Answer:
	3	Context	Which sentence is more difficult: (a). "sentence1" or (b). "sentence2"? Answer:
	4	Ensemble	All of the above.

Table 6: Prompts used per task.

uation. The BC-LCP task used a total of 24,015 instances comparing words of similar meaning and usage per a substitute ranking scenario.

6 Models

Multiple approaches using state-of-the-art models were applied to all three tasks. These approaches ranged from prompt-learning, regression, masked-language modeling (MLM) to binary classification depending on the task. Several LLMs were chosen to perform various prompt learning experiments given their high performance on a variety of NLP-related tasks. These LLMs, all of varying sizes, included GPT-3.5 (text-davinci-003) from OpenAI's API, alongside Mistral (Jiang et al., 2023), Llama-2 (Touvron et al., 2023), Falcon, and MPT avialable on Hugging Face. The prompts fed into these LLMs for LCP, substitute generation, and binary comparative LCP are shown in Table 6. These prompts were designed to artificially replicate answers provided by human annotators by copying the instruction supplied via MTurk.

We also experimented with several pre-trained transformers and feature engineering models such as support vector machine (SVM) and random forest (RF). Transformers and feature engineered models are currently state-of-the-art for LCP and binary comparative LCP, respectively (Shardlow et al., 2021a; North et al., 2022c). Transformers trained with a MLM objective were also state-of-the-art for substitute generation and selection prior to the arrival of recently proposed LLMs (Saggion et al., 2022; North et al., 2022a). MLM models replace the target word with a "[MASK]" special token and then attempt to provide a suitable simplification based on the masked target word and its surrounding context (Qiang et al., 2020).

We selected several transformers pre-trained on English and/or Portuguese data. These included BERT, mBERT (Devlin et al., 2019), RoBERTa (Zhuang et al., 2021), XLM-R (Conneau et al., 2020), BR-BERTo[1], Albertina PT-BR[2], ALbertina PT-PT[3] (Rodrigues et al., 2023), RoBERTa-PT-BR[4], and BERTimbau[5] (Souza et al., 2020) and were also obtained from Hugging Face. Each transformer was fine-tuned on the LCP and binary comparative LCP data supplied by MultiLS-PT as shown in Table 4. Fine-tuning was conducted over 5 epochs with a learning rate of 2e-5, a batch size of 8 and a max sequence length of 256 using a NVIDIA GeForce RTX 3060 GPU. No fine-tuning was conducted for substitute generation given that it is a zero-shot text generation task. Feature engineered approaches were trained on features previously shown to be indicative of lexical complexity (Desai et al., 2021; Shardlow et al., 2021b). Training was conducted over 5 epochs on features ranging from word length, syllable count, frequency, prevalence, and age-of-acquisition (AoA). Our SVM was set to have a sigmoid activation function and our RF was set to have 100 trees. Frequencies were calculated using the Exquisite Corpus[6] for Portuguese. English prevalence and AoA values were taken from Brysbaert et al. (2019) and Brysbaert and Biemiller (2017), respectively. These values were mapped to Portuguese due to the limited availability of Portuguese psycholinguistic datasets.

Evaluation Metrics Tasks were evaluated using their respective evaluation metrics found through-

[1]huggingface.co/rdenadai/BR_BERTo
[2]huggingface.co/PORTULAN/albertina-ptbr
[3]huggingface.co/PORTULAN/albertina-ptpt
[4]huggingface.co/josu/roberta-pt-br
[5]huggingface.co/neuralmind/bert-base-portuguese-cased
[6]https://github.com/LuminosoInsight/exquisite-corpus

out LS literature (Štajner et al., 2022). Mean squared error (MSE), Pearson Correlation (R) and Spearman Correlation (ρ) were used to evaluate LCP, with lower MSE values correlated with greater performance (Shardlow et al., 2021a). Weighted average recall, precision, and F1-score were used to assess binary comparative LCP (North et al., 2022c). However, substitute generation was evaluated using a alternative set of evaluation metrics introduced in the TSAR-2022 shared-task (Štajner et al., 2022; Saggion et al., 2022), including potential and accuracy at top-k = 1. Potential is the ratio of the predicted candidate substitutions that match the most frequently suggested gold label. Accuracy at top-k = 1 (A@1@Top1) is the ratio of best predicted candidate substitutions at rank #1 that are equal to the most appropriate gold simplification also at rank #1. It is important to note, A@1@Top1 is different from ACC@1 that is reported alongside A@1@Top1 at TSAR-2022 (Saggion et al., 2022). ACC@1 takes into consideration multiple generated candidates, whereas A@1@Top1 only considers the top-k = 1 candidate generated. We decided to use A@1@Top1 as it is a more competitive evaluation metric.

7 Results

In this section we present the results for each task using the MultiLS-PT dataset. We report model performances on LCP (Table 9 in the Appendix) before moving to substitution generation (Table 8 in the Appendix), and finally substitute ranking via binary comparative LCP (Table 7). For each task, we look into LLM versus transformer performance, impact of genre and context, and compare model performances on MultiLS-PT to prior datasets.

7.1 Lexical Complexity Prediction

Pre-trained transformers outperformed our LLMs for LCP, regardless of genre or prompt (Table 9). Transformers fine-tuned on all of the instances from MultiLS-PT, depicted lower MSE values alongside higher R and ρ values compared with our prompt learning approaches. The highest performing models were BERTimbau (#1) and XLM-R-L (#3) having achieved R values of 0.8423 and 0.8295, ρ values of 0.8081 and 0.8054, and MSE values of 0.0664 and 0.0698, respectively. In comparison, our best performing LLMs achieved noticeably worst performances when asked to rate the complexity of the target word in a zero-shot setting (ZeroShot-5-Likert, Table 6). Mistral-8X7B (#8) achieved a R value of 0.1810, a ρ value o 0.4816, and a MSE value of 0.1810. Llama-2-13B (#13) produced a R value of 0.2249, a ρ value o 0.3441, and a MSE value of 0.2249. All other prompts that took into consideration context or had their answers averaged within an ensemble resulted in worst performances. Without prior exposure to gold complexity ratings, our prompts were ineffective at modeling the complexity assignments of Portuguese speakers.

Differences in LCP performance per genre were observed by both transformers and LLMs. Transformers fine-tuned and evaluated on biomed instances returned the best results followed by Bible and news extracts. BERTimbau (#1) produced R values of 0.8959, 0.8260, and 0.7244 on biomed, Bible, and news instances, respectively. Likewise, XLM-R-L (#3) achieved R values of 0.8907, 0.8055, and 0.0.7212 on biomed, Bible, and news instances, respectively. Interestingly, Mistral-8x7B performed best on Bible instances having achieved a R value of 0.5608, followed by news instances attaining a R value of 0.4663, and lastly biomedical instances scoring a R value of 0.3762. Varying performances between genre can be seen throughout the remaining tasks.

7.2 Substitute Generation

Simplifications generated by LLMs were of a greater quality compared to those generated by the majority of MLM approaches for all instances (Table 8). The best LLM, being Falcon-40B (#1), achieved an A@1@Top1 of 0.01708 and a potential of 0.5291, closely followed by Mistral-8x7B (#3) having obtained an A@1@Top1 of 0.1375, and a potential of 0.4083. (Table 8). The majority of MLM approaches, including transformers such as XLM-R (#12), RoBERTa-PT-BR (#13), mBERT (#14), and so on, produced less suitable candidate substitutions with A@1@Top1 scores of 0.0458, 0.0333, 0.0229, respectively. However, the best performing MLM model, being BERTimbau (#9), achieved an A@1@Top1 of 0.0916, that surpassed the performance of smaller LLMs, such as Mistral-7B, and Llama-2-7B. A direct correlation was therefore observed between LLM size and overall performance.

Context influenced prompt performance. The three best performing LLMs, Falcon-40B (#1), Mistral-8x7B (#3), and Llama-2-13B (#5), produced their best simplifications across all genres when fed prompts referring to the target word's context. Their Zero-shot counterparts, on the other hand, performed noticeably worst. Falcon-40B scored a A@1@Top1 of 0.1708 with context dropping to 0.1375 without context. Mistral-8x7B achieved a A@1@Top1 of 0.1375 with context falling to 0.1125 without context. Llama-2-13B showed the greatest decrease in performance having fell from a A@1@Top1 of 0.1104 with context to a much lower A@1@Top1 of 0.0520 without context. This signifies the vital role context plays in substitute generation.

Substitute generation performance also varied between genres. Falcon-40B (#1), Mistral-8x7B (#3), and Llama-2-13B (#5) achieved greater A@1@Top1 and potential scores for Bible instances when compared to biomed and news instances. Falcon-40B Mistral-8x7B, and Llama-2-13B produced candidate substitutions with A@1@Top1 scores of 0.2086, 0.1695, and 0.1260 for Bible instances, respectively. However, the same LLMs produced inferior candidate substitutions for news extracts with A@1@Top1 scores of 0.1329 by Falcon-40B, 0.1040 by Mistral-8x7B, and 0.0867 by Llama-2-13B. We observed little variation between these LLMs performance on the biomedical extracts with Mistral-8x7B and Llama-2-13B achieving the same A@1@Top1 of 0.1168.

Performances on the news genre were lower than those achieved at the TSAR-2022 shared-task (Saggion et al., 2022). The wining system of TSAR-2022's Portuguese track was an BERTimbau-based system that achieved an A@1@Top1 of 0.2540 on the shared-task's news extracts (North et al., 2022a). Our best performing model, being Falcon-40B (#1), achieved an A@1@Top1 of 0.1329 for news instances. We attribute this performance to how MultiLS-PT's news instances were collected. Target words within MultiLS-PT's news genre were taken from CompLex's European Parliamentary proceedings (Parl) genre (Shardlow et al., 2020). This was done to maintain a level of similarity between the two datasets as described in Section 4. However, as a consequence, this resulted in more nuanced and complex sentences being present among MultiLS-PT's news instances in comparison to TSAR-2022's news extracts making substitute generation a more challenging task.

7.3 Binary Comparative LCP

GPT 3.5 achieved the best performance for binary comparative LCP. For the majority of instances, GPT 3.5 (#1) and Mistral-8x7B (#2) were able to predict which of two target words were more or less complex having achieved F1-scores of 0.7064 and 0.6992 for all instances, respectively. Unlike for LCP, no clear distinction was observed between the performances of several LLMs and transformers. For example, mBERT achieved an F1-score of 0.5223, whereas other larger LLMs, such as Llama-2-13B (#8), Falcon-7B (#6) and Falcon-40B (#11) attained F1-scores of 0.5043, 0.5097, 0.4737, respectively. This was likely due to the difficult nature of the task.

		F1-Score			
#	Model-Prompt/Features	All	Bible	News	Biomed
1	GPT 3.5-Frequency	0.7064	0.6555	0.7474	0.6063
2	Mistral-8x7B-Frequency	0.6992	0.5907	0.6986	0.6087
3	Mistral-7B-Difficulty	0.6276	0.6556	0.5989	0.6516
4	Llama-2-7B-Ensemble	0.6015	0.6168	0.5826	0.5984
5	mBERT	0.5223	1.0000	0.5932	0.3213
6	Falcon-7B-Frequency	0.5097	0.4771	0.2536	0.4781
7	RF-all	0.5044	0.5472	0.4938	0.3999
8	Llama-2-13B-Difficulty	0.5043	0.5225	0.6493	0.5986
9	SVM-all	0.4995	0.5030	0.4721	0.4875
10	MPT-7B-Difficulty	0.4789	0.5212	0.5633	0.5085
11	Falcon-40B-Sentence	0.4737	0.4692	0.4684	0.6355
13	XLM-R	0.4434	0.3995	0.4111	0.4579

Table 7: Shows weighted average binary comparative LCP F1-scores on instances separated by genre and language. Performances are shown as weighted averages. Models are ranked (#) from best to worst F1-Score for all instances. LLMs are separated by inputted prompt.

Features known to correlate with complexity were embedded within several prompts to better understand the thought process of our LLMs (Table 6). It was discovered that LLMs performed differently when taking into consideration different prompts. GPT 3.5 (#1) and Mistral-8x7B (#2) achieved their greatest F1-scores of 0.7064 and 0.6992 respectively when being asked to determine which target word was more or less complex based on its frequency. In contrast, these same models achieved noticeably worst F1-scores when being fed prompts that explicitly referred to word difficulty (Table 6). When inputted difficulty-based prompts, GPT 3.5 produced a F1-score of 0.6273 and Mistral-8x7B achieved a F1-score of 0.6154 amounting to a -0.0791 and -0.0838 decrease in performance respectively. Therefore, it would appear that our best performing LLMs considered frequency as being a highly influential factor in determining a word's overall complexity.

On several occasions, prompt performance varied between genres for binary comparative LCP. GPT 3.5 (#1) and Mistral-8x7B (#2) were able to use frequency-based prompts to differentiate the complexities of words taken from the news genre more easily than they were for words taken from the Bible or biomed genres. For the news genre, GPT 3.5 attained a F1-score of 0.7474 and Mistral-8x7B produced a F1-score of 0.6986. However, for the Bible and biomed genre, GPT 3.5 produced F1-scores of 0.6555 and 0.6063 respectively, whereas as Mistral-8x7B achieved F1-scores of 0.5907 and 0.6087 respectively. Interestingly, Falcon-40B (#12) produced it's highest F1-score when using sentence-based prompts (Table 6) for ranking words from the biomed genre. A probable explanation likely stems from the varying lexical diversity of each genre. The news genre was found to contain a greater combination of everyday and jargon-specific vocabulary making its complex and non-complex words easier to differentiate. The vocabulary of the Bible and biomed genres, on the other hand, were more jargon-specific making binary comparative LCP a harder task when considering word frequency, yet an easier task when comparing two target sentences since surrounding words are also taken into consideration.

8 Conclusion

The MultiLS framework provides a guide for the creation of a multi-purpose and multi-genre LS dataset. The MultiLS framework is unique in that it provides gold continuous complexity values and gold candidate substitutions, a feat not achieved by previous LS datasets (Sections 2 and 4). The resulting dataset can be used to train and evaluate all LS sub-task, including LCP.

We introduce MultiLS-PT, the first Portuguese LS dataset to be created using the MultiLS framework. By experimenting on MultiLS-PT, we were able to theorize the optimum LS pipeline for Portuguese given current state-of-the-art models and make several observations regarding the impact of genre and context on LS. Performances indicate that LLMs are incapable of rating lexical complexity for a specific target demographic, but are able to generate and rank possible simplifications. This provides insight into the role LLMs will have in future LS systems.

8.1 Future Work

In this paper, we provided empirical evidence of the MultiLS framework's potential to be used as an all-in-one simplification framework. We have trained models and conducted several experiments using MultiLS-PT. However, there are multiple research questions left outstanding that the MultiLS framework and MultiLS-PT can be used to answer. Future work will utilize the MultiLS framework to explore three open research areas as follows.

Full Pipeline Evaluation LLMs are able to simplify an entire text as a response to a single prompt and are even state-of-the-art for substitute generation (Section 7). This questions the need for models trained on individual sub-tasks of the LS pipeline. Comparisons need to be made between the readability and accessibility of texts simplified by a general LLM compared to texts simplified by end-to-end LS systems. To make this possible, we aim to perform an empirical comparison of the performance of a LS pipeline trained on a MultiLS dataset to a generalized LLM for text simplification.

Multilingual LS and Cross-lingual Transfer Cross-lingual models with transfer learning from a high-resource to a low-resource language is a successful strategy widely used in various NLP tasks. However, there is conflicting evidence regarding the performance of cross-lingual models for LS (North et al., 2022a; Štajner et al., 2022; North, Kai and Zampieri, Marcos, 2023). Further research is needed to establish whether cross-lingual transfer is viable for LS, especially for which LS sub-tasks. In this endeavour, we plan to apply the MultiLS framework to other languages whereby the complexities of shared and hand-selected words can be used to research the effects of multilingual LS and cross-lingual transfer on LS performance.

Domain Generalization LS systems are commonly trained on a single dataset containing either a specific genre, including newspaper extracts (Leal et al., 2018; North et al., 2022b) or educational materials (Hartmann and Aluísio, 2020; Merejildo, 2021), or for an undefined mix of genres, such as Wikipedia extracts on a range of topics (Shardlow, 2013; Horn et al., 2014). The lack of datasets containing multiple types of texts separated by genre limits the development of LS systems capable of domain generalization. The results presented in this paper account for different genres. As such, researchers can see what does and does not work well for specific genres and use this information to develop their LS systems accordingly. We aim to continue to experiment with MultiLS-PT developing a fully generalizable LS system for Portuguese.

Lay Summary

Lexical Simplification (LS) is the task of automatically replacing difficult words for easier ones while preserving a sentence's original meaning. LS is an important component of text simplification system that are developed to simplify texts aiming to improve accessibility to various populations such as individuals with learning disabilities.

Datasets containing hundreds or thousands of excerpts of texts annotated with human judgments are needed to train LS systems. Several datasets exist for LS but each of them specialize in a step of the traditional LS pipeline such as recognizing complex words, generating substitute words, or selecting the best substitute word. To the best of our knowledge no single LS dataset represents all steps of the pipeline.

To address this limitation, we propose MultiLS, the first framework that allows for the creation of all-in-one LS datasets representing all steps of the pipeline. We present MultiLS-PT, a Portuguese dataset dataset created using the MultiLS framework. MultiLS-PT contains texts from the Bible, news articles, and biomedical texts. Finally, we carry out various experiments that demonstrate the potential of the MultiLS framework and the MultiLS-PT dataset of improving LS systems and related assistive technologies.

References

Rachel Bawden, Kevin Bretonnel Cohen, Cristian Grozea, Antonio Jimeno Yepes, Madeleine Kittner, Martin Krallinger, Nancy Mah, Aurelie Neveol, Mariana Neves, Felipe Soares, Amy Siu, Karin Verspoor, and Maika Vicente Navarro. 2019. Findings of the WMT 2019 Biomedical Translation Shared Task: Evaluation for MEDLINE Abstracts and Biomedical Terminologies. In *Proceedings of WMT*.

Marc Brysbaert and Andrew Biemiller. 2017. Test-based age-of-acquisition norms for 44 thousand English word meanings. *Behavioural Research*, 49:1520–1523.

Marc Brysbaert, Pawel Mandera, Samantha McCormick, and Emmanuel Keuleers. 2019. Word prevalence norms for 62,000 English lemmas. *Behavior Research Methods*, 51:467–479.

Alexis Conneau, Kartikay Khandelwal, Naman Goyal, Vishrav Chaudhary, and Others. 2020. Unsupervised Cross-lingual Representation Learning at Scale. In *Proceedings of ACL*.

Abhinandan Desai, Kai North, Marcos Zampieri, and Christopher Homan. 2021. LCP-RIT at SemEval-2021 Task 1: Exploring Linguistic Features for Lexical Complexity Prediction. In *Proceedings of SemEval*.

Jacob Devlin, Ming-Wei Chang, Kenton Lee, and Kristina Toutanova. 2019. BERT: Pre-training of Deep Bidirectional Transformers for Language Understanding. In *Proceedings of NAACL*.

David M. Eberhard, Gary F. Simons, and Charles D. Fennig, editors. 2023. *Ethnologue: Languages of the World*, twenty-sixth edition. SIL International, Dallas, Texas.

Daniel Ferres and Horacio Saggion. 2022. ALEXSIS: A dataset for lexical simplification in Spanish. In *Proceedings of LREC*.

Nathan Siegle Hartmann and Sandra Maria Aluísio. 2020. Adaptação lexical automática em textos informativos do português brasileiro para o ensino fundamental. *Linguamática*, 12(2):3–27.

Colby Horn, Cathryn Manduca, and David Kauchak. 2014. Learning a Lexical Simplifier Using Wikipedia. In *Proceedings of ACL*.

Timothy D. Ireland. 2008. Literacy in brazil: From rights to reality. *International Review of Education*, 54(5/6):713–732.

Albert Q. Jiang, Alexandre Sablayrolles, Arthur Mensch, Chris Bamford, Devendra Singh Chaplot, Diego de las Casas, Florian Bressand, Gianna Lengyel, Guillaume Lample, Lucile Saulnier, Lélio Renard Lavaud, Marie-Anne Lachaux, Pierre Stock, Teven Le Scao, Thibaut Lavril, Thomas Wang, Timothée Lacroix, and William El Sayed. 2023. Mistral 7B. *arXiv: 2310.06825*.

Sidney Evaldo Leal, Magali Sanches Duran, and Sandra Maria Aluísio. 2018. A Nontrivial Sentence Corpus for the Task of Sentence Readability Assessment in Portuguese. In *Proceedings of COLING*.

Mounica Maddela and Wei Xu. 2018. A Word-Complexity Lexicon and A Neural Readability Ranking Model for Lexical Simplification. In *Proceedings of EMNLP*.

Diana McCarthy and Roberto Navigli. 2007. SemEval-2007 Task 10: English Lexical Substitution Task. In *Proceedings of SemEval*.

Borbor Merejildo. 2021. Creación de un corpus de textos universitarios en español para la identificación de palabras complejas en el área de la simplificación léxica. Master's thesis, Universidad de Guayaquil.

Kai North, Alphaeus Dmonte, Tharindu Ranasinghe, Matthew Shardlow, and Marcos Zampieri. 2023a. ALEXSIS+: Improving Substitute Generation and Selection for Lexical Simplification with Information Retrieval. In *Proceedings of BEA*.

Kai North, Alphaeus Dmonte, Tharindu Ranasinghe, and Marcos Zampieri. 2022a. GMU-WLV at TSAR-2022 Shared Task: Evaluating Lexical Simplification Models. In *Proceedings of TSAR*.

Kai North, Tharindu Ranasinghe, Matthew Shardlow, and Marcos Zampieri. 2023b. Deep Learning Approaches to Lexical Simplification: A Survey.

Kai North, Marcos Zampieri, and Tharindu Ranasinghe. 2022b. ALEXSIS-PT: A New Resource for Portuguese Lexical Simplification. In *Proceedings of COLING*.

Kai North, Marcos Zampieri, and Matthew Shardlow. 2022c. An Evaluation of Binary Comparative Lexical Complexity Models. In *Proceedings of BEA*.

Kai North, Marcos Zampieri, and Matthew Shardlow. 2022d. Lexical Complexity Prediction: An Overview. *ACM Computing Surveys*, 55(9).

North, Kai and Zampieri, Marcos. 2023. Features of lexical complexity: insights from L1 and L2 speakers. *Frontiers in Artificial Intelligence*.

Gustavo Paetzold and Lucia Specia. 2016a. PLUMBErr: An Automatic Error Identification Framework for Lexical Simplification. In *Proceedings of LREC*.

Gustavo Paetzold and Lucia Specia. 2016b. SemEval 2016 Task 11: Complex Word Identification. In *Proceedings of SemEval*.

Gustavo H. Paetzold and Lucia Specia. 2017. A Survey on Lexical Simplification. *J. Artif. Int. Res.*, 60(1):549–593.

Gustavo Henrique Paetzold and Lucia Specia. 2015. LEXenstein: A Framework for Lexical Simplification. In *ACL 2015 System Demonstrations*, pages 85–90.

Gustavo Henrique Paetzold and Lucia Specia. 2016c. Benchmarking Lexical Simplification Systems. In *Proceedings of LREC*.

Jipeng Qiang, Yun Li, Zhu Yi, Yunhao Yuan, and Xindong Wu. 2020. Lexical Simplification with Pretrained Encoders. In *Proceedings of AAAI*.

João Rodrigues, Luís Gomes, João Silva, António Branco, Rodrigo Santos, Henrique Lopes Cardoso, and Tomás Osório. 2023. Advancing Neural Encoding of Portuguese with Transformer Albertina PT-*. *arXiv: 2305.06721*.

Horacio Saggion, Sanja Štajner, Daniel Ferrés, Kim Cheng Sheang, Matthew Shardlow, Kai North, and Marcos Zampieri. 2022. Findings of the TSAR-2022 Shared Task on Multilingual Lexical Simplification. In *Proceedings of TSAR*.

Matthew Shardlow. 2013. The CW Corpus: A New Resource for Evaluating the Identification of Complex Words. In *Proceedings of ACL*.

Matthew Shardlow, Michael Cooper, and Marcos Zampieri. 2020. CompLex — a new corpus for lexical complexity prediction from Likert Scale data. In *Proceedings of READI*.

Matthew Shardlow, Richard Evans, Gustavo Paetzold, and Marcos Zampieri. 2021a. SemEval-2021 Task 1: Lexical Complexity Prediction. In *Proceedings of SemEval*.

Matthew Shardlow, Richard Evans, and Marcos Zampieri. 2021b. Predicting lexical complexity in english texts. In *Proceedings of LREC*.

Matthew Shardlow, Richard Evans, and Marcos Zampieri. 2022. Predicting Lexical Complexity in English Texts: The Complex 2.0 Dataset. *Language Resources and Evaluation*, 56(4):1153–1194.

Fábio Souza, Rodrigo Nogueira, and Roberto Lotufo. 2020. BERTimbau: pretrained BERT models for Brazilian Portuguese. In *Proceedings of BRACIS*.

Lucia Specia, Kumar Jauhar, Sujay, and Rada Mihalcea. 2012. SemEval - 2012 Task 1: English Lexical Simplification. In *Proceedings of SemEval*.

Sanja Štajner, Daniel Ferrés, Matthew Shardlow, Kai North, Marcos Zampieri, and Horacio Saggion. 2022. Lexical Simplification Benchmarks for English, Portuguese, and Spanish. *Frontiers in Artificial Intelligence*.

Anaïs Tack, Thomas François, Anne-Laure Ligozat, and Cédrick Fairon. 2016. Evaluating Lexical Simplification and Vocabulary Knowledge for Learners of French: Possibilities of Using the FLELex Resource. In *Proceedings of LREC*.

Hugo Touvron, Louis Martin, and et al. Kevin Stone. 2023. Llama 2: Open foundation and fine-tuned chat models. *arXiv: 2307.09288*.

Seid Muhie Yimam, Chris Biemann, Shervin Malmasi, Gustavo Paetzold, Luci Specia, Sanja Štajner, Anaïs Tack, and Marcos Zampieri. 2018. A Report on the Complex Word Identification Shared Task 2018. In *Proceedings of BEA*.

Marcos Zampieri, Shervin Malmasi, Gustavo Paetzold, and Lucia Specia. 2017. Complex Word Identification: Challenges in Data Annotation and System Performance. In *Proceedings of NLP-TEA*.

Liu Zhuang, Lin Wayne, Shi Ya, and Zhao Jun. 2021. A Robustly Optimized BERT Pre-training Approach with Post-training. In *Proceedings of CCL*.

A Appendix

		All		Bible		News		Biomed	
#	Model-Prompt	A@1@Top1	Potential	A@1@Top1	Potential	A@1@Top1	Potential	A@1@Top1	Potential
1	Falcon-40B-Context	0.1708	0.5291	0.2086	0.5043	0.1329	0.5606	0.1428	0.5324
2	Falcon-40B-ZeroShot	0.1375	0.4333	0.1826	0.4521	0.0867	0.4219	0.1168	0.4025
3	Mistral-8x7B-Context	0.1375	0.4083	0.1695	0.4173	0.1040	0.3988	0.1168	0.4025
4	Mistral-8x7B-ZeroShot	0.1125	0.3187	0.1260	0.2739	0.0693	0.3294	0.1688	0.4285
5	Llama-2-13B-Context	0.1104	0.3208	0.1260	0.2869	0.0867	0.3526	0.1168	0.3506
6	GPT 3.5-ZeroShot	0.1083	0.3479	0.1217	0.3043	0.0867	0.3930	0.1168	0.3766
7	GPT 3.5-Context	0.1062	0.4250	0.1304	0.3956	0.0693	0.4797	0.1168	0.3896
8	Mistral-7B-Context	0.0937	0.2750	0.1086	0.2652	0.0693	0.2716	0.1038	0.3116
9	BERTimbau	0.0916	0.2645	0.1086	0.2434	0.0751	0.2890	0.0779	0.2727
10	Mistral-7B-ZeroShot	0.0729	0.2062	0.0826	0.1913	0.0578	0.2080	0.0779	0.2467
11	Llama-2-13B-ZeroShot	0.0520	0.1187	0.0739	0.1565	0.0231	0.0809	0.0519	0.0909
12	XLM-R	0.0458	0.1250	0.0478	0.0913	0.0462	0.1618	0.0389	0.1428
13	RoBERTa-PT-BR	0.0333	0.1229	0.0434	0.1000	0.0173	0.1329	0.0389	0.1688
14	mBERT	0.0229	0.1145	0.0217	0.0826	0.0231	0.1445	0.0259	0.1428
15	Llama-2-7B-ZeroShot	0.0229	0.1000	0.026	0.0782	0.0115	0.1213	0.0389	0.1168
16	MPT-7B-Context	0.0229	0.0958	0.0260	0.0826	0.0115	0.1040	0.0389	0.1168
17	BR-BERTo	0.0250	0.0770	0.0304	0.0391	0.0173	0.1098	0.0259	0.1168
18	MPT-7B-ZeroShot	0.0208	0.0750	0.0260	0.0652	0.0057	0.0867	0.0389	0.0779
19	Llama-2-7B-Context	0.0208	0.0541	0.0260	0.0391	0.0057	0.0635	0.0389	0.0779
20	Falcon-7B-Context	0.0166	0.0416	0.0173	0.0478	0.0057	0.0346	0.0389	0.0389
21	Albertina PT-BR	0.0145	0.0541	0.0173	0.0478	0.0115	0.0635	0.0129	0.0519
22	Albertina PT-PT	0.0145	0.0520	0.0173	0.0478	0.0115	0.0578	0.0129	0.0519
	TSAR-2022 Benchmark (PT-BR)								
1	BERTimbau	-	-	-	-	0.2540	0.4812	-	-

Table 8: Shows substitute generation performances on instances separated by genre with at least five gold candidate substitutions in MultiLS-PT. Models are ranked (#) from best to worst A@1@Top1. LLMs are separated by inputted prompt. The winning system from TSAR-2022 (Saggion et al., 2022) provided as a benchmark.

			All			Bible			News			Biomed		
Approach	#	Model	MSE	R	ρ	MSE	R	ρ	MSE	R	ρ	MSE	R	ρ
Transformers	1	BERTimbau	0.0664	0.8423	0.8081	0.0726	0.8260	0.8275	0.0558	0.7244	0.7047	0.0677	0.8959	0.8740
	2	BERTimbau-L	0.0681	0.8324	0.8086	0.0746	0.8144	0.8227	0.0533	0.7450	0.7308	0.0746	0.8720	0.8573
	3	XLM-R-L	0.0698	0.8295	0.8054	0.0777	0.8055	0.8224	0.0550	0.7212	0.7214	0.0724	0.8907	0.8586
	4	XLM-R	0.0706	0.8187	0.7974	0.0773	0.8012	0.8155	0.0595	0.6774	0.6995	0.0716	0.8824	0.8612
	5	mBERT	0.0743	0.7968	0.7724	0.0815	0.7746	0.7808	0.0585	0.6801	0.6941	0.0804	0.8502	0.8332
	6	RoBERTa-PT-BR	0.1469	0.7968	0.7539	0.1506	0.7440	0.7395	0.1169	0.7214	0.6834	0.1811	0.8768	0.8430
	7	BR-BERTo	0.1844	0.7522	0.6791	0.1842	0.6865	0.6500	0.1488	0.6518	0.5906	0.2340	0.8569	0.8111
LLMs	8	Mistral-8X7B	0.1810	0.4603	0.4816	0.1576	0.5608	0.5480	0.1953	0.4663	0.4566	0.2063	0.3762	0.3877
	9	Llama-2-13B	0.2249	0.2737	0.3441	0.2089	0.2226	0.3330	0.2289	0.2569	0.3233	0.2535	0.2687	0.2903
	10	Mistral-7B	0.4156	0.2758	0.3349	0.4117	0.3762	0.3880	0.4428	0.3379	0.3327	0.3739	0.1148	0.2261
	11	GPT 3.5	0.5050	0.0520	0.0895	0.5019	0.0134	0.0481	0.5286	0.0624	0.1197	0.4692	0.1411	0.1504
	12	Llama-2-7B	0.4031	0.0392	0.1535	0.4064	0.0394	0.1343	0.4199	0.1951	0.2084	0.3631	-0.0121	0.1287
	13	Falcon-7B	0.4273	0.0008	0.0353	0.4150	-0.019	-0.0132	0.4722	0.0718	0.0993	0.3703	0.0285	0.0613
		LCP-2021 Benchmark (English)												
Transformers	1	BERT-Ensemble	0.0609	0.7886	0.7369	-	-	-	-	-	-	-	-	-

Table 9: LCP performances on instances separated by genre. Models are ranked (#) from best to worst Pearson Correlation (R) for all instances. Results produced by LLMs were from our highest performing prompt 1. ZeroShot-5-Likert (Table 6). The winning system from LCP-2021 (Shardlow et al., 2021a) provided as a benchmark.

OtoBERT:
Identifying Suffixed Verbal Forms in Modern Hebrew Literature

Avi Shmidman[1,2,†], **Shaltiel Shmidman**[1,‡]
[1]DICTA, Jerusalem, Israel
[2]Bar Ilan University, Ramat Gan, Israel
[†]avi.shmidman@biu.ac.il
[‡]shaltieltzion@gmail.com

Abstract

We provide a solution for a specific morphological obstacle which often makes Hebrew literature difficult to parse for the younger generation. The morphologically-rich nature of the Hebrew language allows pronominal direct objects to be realized as bound morphemes, suffixed to the verb. Although such suffixes are often utilized in Biblical Hebrew, their use has all but disappeared in modern Hebrew. Nevertheless, authors of modern Hebrew literature, in their search for literary flair, do make use of such forms. These unusual forms are notorious for alienating young readers from Hebrew literature, especially because these rare suffixed forms are often *orthographically identical* to common Hebrew words with different meanings. Upon encountering such words, readers naturally select the usual analysis of the word; yet, upon completing the sentence, they find themselves confounded. Young readers end up feeling "tricked", and this in turn contributes to their alienation from the text. In order to address this challenge, we pretrained a new BERT model specifically geared to identify such forms, so that they may be automatically simplified and/or flagged. We release this new BERT model to the public for unrestricted use.

1 Introduction

A primary obstacle for readers of Hebrew literature is the use of pronominal verbal suffixes. Hebrew allows the use of a bound suffix in place of a direct-object pronoun for virtually all object-taking verbs. For instance, the two-word Hebrew sentence ראיתי אותו (*raiti oto*, "I saw him") can be condensed into a single verb with pronominal suffix, with the equivalent meaning: ראיתיהו (*re'itihu*, "I saw him"). Although such suffixes are often utilized in Biblical Hebrew, their use is quite rare in modern Hebrew. Nevertheless, authors of modern Hebrew literature, in their search for literary flair, do select such forms at times. These unusual forms pose substantial difficulty for readers.

Prima facie, an effective solution to this obstacle in Hebrew literature would be to simplify the text (i.e., to convert instances of these rare suffixed verb forms into the equivalent pairs of non-suffixed verb followed by direct-object pronoun), or, alternatively, to add a gloss alerting the reader to the fact that a pronominal suffix is wrapped up inside the word.

Unfortunately, this is not a trivial procedure; because, it is not just that these forms are *rare*, but rather that they are often *ambiguous*; that is, they are often orthographically identical to common Hebrew words with very different morphological properties. To take a few examples:

- הזמינו ("they ordered" and "he ordered it")
- לימדו ("they taught" and "he taught him")
- הגישה ("she offered" and "he offered her")
- ניהלה ("she managed" and "he managed her")

Thus, we cannot automatically simplify or flag such words based on their letters alone; we can only do so if it can be inferred from the context that the suffixed analysis is intended. Nor would it make sense to flag every instance of such words as a cautionary measure; for, even in literary works, the overwhelming majority of these ambiguous forms are not in fact suffixed verbs. Flagging all of them would flood the reader with unnecessary alerts. Furthermore, as we will see below, existing NLP systems for Hebrew are not equipped to make this determination, because there are so few cases of suffixed verbs in their training data. To be sure, the question of how to optimally annotate Hebrew suffixed forms in training corpora for NLP systems has been explored (Tsarfaty and Goldberg, 2008). Nevertheless, at the end of the day, when faced with an ambiguous form that may or may not be a suffixed verb, existing morphological tagging systems for Hebrew too often blindly choose the usual non-suffixed form. Due to the fact the benchmarks used to evaluate these systems barely contain any cases of suffixed verbs, this myopic approach does

Proceedings of the Third Workshop on Text Simplification, Accessibility and Readability (TSAR 2024), pages 12–19
November 15, 2024

not impact accuracy scores, and hence there is little motivation for the developers to address this shortcoming.

These ambiguous forms pose a formidable challenge for would-be readers of Hebrew literature. Upon encountering such words, readers naturally select the usual analysis of the word; indeed, in most cases, the analysis with the pronominal suffix is one that many readers will never before have encountered. Upon completing the sentence, they will find themselves confounded. Because there is no direct indication in the text that anything is special about the word, readers end up feeling "tricked" by the text, and this in turn contributes to the younger generation's alienation from Hebrew literature.

For example, in his novel *A Simple Story*, S. Y. Agnon writes (Agnon, 1953a, p. 76):

צייר גדול צייר את דמות תבניתה של בלומה וקבעה בלבו של הירשל...

"A great artist painted the image of Bluma *and he set it* in the heart of Hershel..."

The italicized phrase is the translation of a suffixed verb in the Hebrew. However, that same word is virtually always used as a non-suffixed verb, meaning "and she set". Upon first encountering the word, the reader will naturally adopt this latter analysis (with Bluma as the subject). Only at the sentence's completion will the reader be perplexed that the expected object of the verb "set" never materialized; this will hopefully trigger a reread, during which the reader will recognize the word as a suffixed verb.

In order to quantify just how big the gap is between standard Hebrew and literay Hebrew with regard to these suffixed verbs, our human annotators analyzed two corpora of daily Hebrew newspapers, as well a corpus of high-register Hebrew literature.[1] The results (table 1) reveal a sharp contrast: the literature corpus has over 35 times as many cases of suffixed verbal forms as do either of the newspaper corpora. Furthermore, within the literature corpus, a substantial number of the forms were ambiguous (64 cases), while each of the news corpora had but a single instance of an ambiguous suffixed verb. Thus, it is conceivable that a person could be completely proficient in reading Hebrew newspapers, yet never have had to cope with parsing an ambiguous suffixed verb.

[1]The literature corpus includes works of Hebrew novelists S. Y. Agnon, Haim Beer, Amoz Oz, and David Grossman. The news corpora are drawn from the daily Hebrew newspapers *Maariv* ("News1") and *Ynet* ("News2").

Corpus	Corpus Size (Words)	Suffixed Verbs	Freq (Per 10K Words)	Ambig Cases	Freq of Ambig (Per 10K)
News1	185K	7	0.38	1	0.05
News2	43K	2	0.47	1	0.23
Lit	135K	222	17.76	64	4.74

Table 1: Hebrew verbs with pronominal suffixes are exceedingly rare in regular newspaper text, but far more likely to appear in literary texts. We note the overall number of such verbs, and also the number of ambiguous cases which can be alternatively read as a more usual Hebrew word.

The present paper presents a new BERT model pretrained from scratch with the goal of providing a solution to this challenge. This new model provides a method to identify most of these troublesome forms with a high degree of confidence, in order to make these treasured literary works accessible to today's readers. We dub our model *OtoBERT* (after the Hebrew direct-object pronoun **אותו** (*oto*, "him").

2 Related Work

The challenge that we address in this paper - the task of identifying ambiguous Hebrew forms which unexpectedly serve as suffixed verbs - is a case of Complex Word Identification (CWI). CWI entails the identification of words which pose a challenge to readers of a given text, due to their unusual or complex usage within the context. CWI is a critical step within Text Simplification tasks, because it identifies the words that need to be simplified in order to make the text more accessible.

For a historical overview of machine-learning methods utilized for CWI, see North et al. (2023, pp. 14-23). Current methods for addressing CWI generally utilize BERT pretrained language models, leveraging the capabilities of the existing BERT models in a variety of different methods. For instance, Kelious et al. (2024) train a classifier for English CWI using embeddings produced by the pretrained model DeBERTa.

Other researchers have proposed emsemble methods which combine output from multiple BERT models. For instance, Bani Yaseen et al. (2021) utilize two different BERT models (standard BERT and RoBERTa) in order to produce four measurements for each word. Each word is evaluated in each model twice - once on its own, and once with its full context. All of these measurements are then combined in a weighted scheme to produce an optimal measure. In a similar vein, Pan et al. (2021) fine-tune a wide series of BERT models (BERT, ALBERT, RoBERTa, and ERNIE) for the CWI task, and they combine the fine-tuned models via a stacking mechanism in order to produce a final prediction.

A novel method of leveraging BERT models is proposed by Kumbhar et al. (2023). They implement a procedure which follows the information flow of a given word through the hidden layers of the BERT model, measuring the complexity of the computation needed to process a given word with its context. This measured complexity is then used as a basis on which to perform CWI.

On the backdrop of these studies, our unique angle is that rather than building upon the foundation of existing pretrained BERT models, we pretrain a new dedicated BERT model from scratch, specifically designed to address our CWI challenge. We add a specialized step to the BERT tokenization training stage - prior to the pretraining of the model - in order to optimize its ability to identify the rare and elusive cases of Hebrew suffixed verbs.

3 Our Approach

In order to address the challenge of identifying verbs with a pronominal suffix, we seek to create a BERT model which is particularly sensitive to contexts which entail a <verb, direct-object pronoun> pair. We thus pretrain a new BERT from scratch, tokenizing it such all such cases of direct-object pronouns are combined together with the preceding word. For instance, the two-word sequence ראיתי אותו ("I saw him") would be stored as a single token in the BERT vocabulary, with an underscore in place of the space. The inclusion of these compound tokens in BERT's vocabulary allows the BERT model to directly learn representations for combined units of <verb, direct-object pronoun>, which correspond precisely to the meaning of the elusive suffixed verbs which we seek to identify. Furthermore, this allows BERT's masked language model (MLM) head to predict multiword tokens which consist of a verb followed by a direct-object suffix. We hypothesize that the prediction of such tokens at the position of an ambiguous Hebrew word will indicate that the word consists of a verb with pronominal suffix. This is because the two-word sequence of the verb followed by the direct-object pronoun is semantically equivalent to the verb with the bound pronominal suffix; they are two alternate ways of expressing the same thing in the Hebrew language.

Essentially, this extra tokenization step provides BERT with a new expressive power. The single-word vocabularies of existing Hebrew BERT models do not provide sufficient expressiveness to disambiguate Hebrew verbs with pronominal suffixes; even if the models properly analyze the word and predict a series of suffixed verbs for that word position, those words themselves will generally be ambiguous, and hence cannot serve to disambiguate the nature of the verb. In contrast, the vocabulary of our new model contains a large set of two-word phrases which each contain a verb together with a direct-object pronoun; thus, our model is equipped with the capacity to express token predictions that directly indicate that a given word position within the sentence can be occupied by a verb with pronominal suffix.

In the section below we provide details regarding the pretraining of this new BERT model; afterward we describe our experiments with it, our results, and our proposal for applying this model in practice to make Hebrew literature more accessible.

4 Model

4.1 Tokenizer

The first stage involves training a new word-piece tokenizer for BERT, optimally suited for encoding Hebrew texts in general, and for solving the issue of suffixed Hebrew verbs in particular. We use the Word-Piece tokenization method proposed by Song et al. (2021), with adjustments to handle the apostrophe and double-quote marks, which mark Hebrew abbreviations, and which otherwise would have been tokenized into separate word pieces.

Further, as discussed at length in the previous section, we add a preprocess procedure to the tokenizer which combines all cases of direct-object pronouns with the preceding word, treating these words pairs as single compound tokens.

Following previous work on Hebrew BERT models, (Gueta et al., 2023; Shmidman et al., 2023), the tokenizer was trained with a vocabulary size of 128,000 tokens.

4.2 Architecture

The model's architecture is based on BERT-base (Devlin et al., 2019a), trained using the same data and objectives as Shmidman et al. (2023), with the adjustment of using the custom tokenizer described in the §4.1. For full details regarding the training details please see Appendix A.

5 Experimental Setup

Corpus: In order to properly evaluate OtoBERT, we assemble a corpus of naturally-occurring Hebrew sentences with ambiguous verbal forms, that is, homographs which can be analyzed either as a verb with pronominal suffix, or as a verb with no suffix at all. The homographs are manually annotated as to their correct analysis. The corpus contains a total of 2,589 instances of non-suffixed verbs, and 264 instances of suffixed verbs.

Classification based on BERT's MLM predictions: We run the MLM head of our new BERT model on each of the aforementioned homographs. For each case, we retrieve K predictions. If at least N of these predictions include compound tokens with direct-object pronouns, then we classify the word as a suffixed verb. We experiment with a range of values for both K and N.

For example, take the following sentence from S. Y. Agnon's *Only Yesterday* (Agnon, 1953b, p. 280): הקיפו וחזר והקיפו ונכנס ("*he encircled him*, and once again *he encircled him*, and entered"). Here, the (doubled) italics phrase "he encircled him" (a suffixed verb) corresponds to an ambiguous Hebrew word that can also mean "they encircled" (the usual analysis). If we take the initial occurrence of this ambiguous word in the sentence and run it through the MLM head of OtoBERT, the top 1000 predictions include numerous tokens with direct-object pronouns, including: ראו_אותו ("they saw him"), מצאו_אותו ("they found him"), and ראה_אותו ("he saw him"). OtoBERT's choice of these tokens among its predictions indicates that the context entails the use of a verb with pronominal suffix.

In contrast, take this sentence from the same novel (Agnon, 1953b, p. 294): אמרה שפרה עייף מר מן החום ("*Said* Shifra, master is tired from the heat"). The italicized word "said" corresponds to an ambiguous Hebrew verb which can also function as a suffixed verb, meaning "he said it". However, OtoBERT's top 1000 predictions for this word position don't include a single instance of a compound token with a direct-object pronoun, indicating that the context entails a regular non-suffixed verb.

Alternate Methods of Classification: In order to evaluate whether it was in fact necessary to train a completely new BERT model for this task, we also attempt to address this challenge using two standard methods of resolving Hebrew ambiguity. First, we use the SOTA morphological tagger available for Hebrew, DictaBERT (Shmidman et al., 2024) to tag the sentences in the corpus, and we measure whether it correctly assigned the "suffix" tag to the relevant verbs.

Second, we train a classifier to distinguish between cases of suffixed verbs and cases of non-suffixed verbs, based on the BERT embedding of the word. In order to avoid possible bias of one specific BERT model, we train classifiers separately for each of three BERT models with Hebrew support: mBERT, the original multilingual BERT, based upon Devlin et al. (2019b); AlephBERT, the impactful dedicated Hebrew BERT model produced by Seker et al. (2021), and finally with DictaBERT (Shmidman et al., 2023), the current SOTA of Hebrew BERT models. With each model, we train an MLP to recognize embeddings for the "suffixed verb" class by providing it with a corpus of sentences which have a verb followed by a direct-object pronoun, and we train it for the "non-suffixed verb" class via cases of unambiguous verbs which can only function as non-suffixed words. We then evaluate its ability to distinguish between suffixed verbs and non-suffixed verbs on the aforementioned test corpus.

6 Results

Results are displayed in Figure 1. We plot our method's performance across a range of values for the K and N thresholds. The performance is measured vis-a-vis the Suffixed Verb class; that is, the precision and recall lines depict the method's ability to pinpoint cases of Suffixed Verbs without falsely flagging non-suffixed verbs. In Table 2, we compare the results of our method (at K=1000, the highest-recall setting) with that of the two alternate methods mentioned above.

Model	Precision	Recall	F1
OtoBERT, K=1000, N=1	15.75	**95.57**	.270
OtoBERT, K=1000, N=5	54.15	73.89	.625
OtoBERT, K=1000, N=10	84.13	52.22	**.644**
OtoBERT, K=1000, N=25	**100**	19.21	.322
mBERT w/ Classifier	28.23	62.12	.388
AlephBERT w/ Classifier	38.92	62.50	.480
DictaBERT w/ Classifier	48.27	73.86	.584
DictaBERT Morph Tagger	88.73	23.86	.376

Table 2: Precision, recall, and F1 vis-a-vis the class of suffixed verbal forms for each of the evaluated methods.

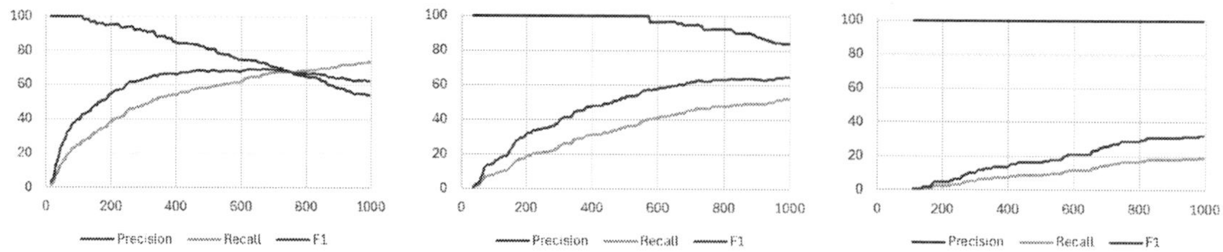

(a) N=5 (b) N=10 (c) N=25

Figure 1: Precision and Recall for three different settings of N (the threshold for the number of compound tokens that must be predicted in order to support the classification of a word as a suffixed verb). The X-axis represents the K value (the number of predictions we retrieve form the MLM), and the Y-axis represents the Precision/Recall score.

7 Applying it to the Texts

Based upon the results in Table 2, we propose that OtoBERT, when run with K=1000, is sufficiently robust to automatically annotate Hebrew literary texts in a helpful and accessible way, as follows:

(1) With N set to 25, we achieve a precision of 100% on the test corpus; we conclude that given 25 or more predictions of compound tokens from the MLM head, we can be confident that a suffixed verb is intended. Given this confidence, we can directly simplify the text, breaking up the single suffixed verb into a non-suffixed verb with a subsequent direct-object pronoun. Alternatively, if we wish to avoid tampering directly with the literary text, we could add the simplified version as an interlinear gloss on top of the suffixed verb. This method provides recall of close to 20% of the cases.

(2) With N set to 10, we achieve a precision of over 84 percent. Although not sufficient to tamper directly with the text, this precision is sufficient to justify adding an interlinear gloss above the word qualified by the word "likely"; for instance, the gloss might read, "alert: likely a verb with bound suffix". Together with the previous step, this provides coverage of over half of the suffixed verbs in the test set.

(3) With N set to 5, we have a wide recall of over 72 percent, and we still have a precision of 54.15%. This might justify a gloss qualified by the word "perhaps".

Thus, OtoBERT can potentially provide a substantial readability boost to a Hebrew literary text. It can confidently identify a substantial set of suffixed verbs within a text, and for many other cases, it can mark the possibility of a suffixed verb while reliably indicating a lower confidence level. This paves the way for an automatic system which insert confident interlinear glosses where relevant, and qualified glosses at other places. In contrast, the other two methods don't provide a similarly versatile platform for simplifying the text. Our attempts to train classifiers on top of BERT models produce results of low precision (62.58%), which would not allow for any high-confidence glosses; and the DictaBERT Morphology Tagging system has very poor recall (22.11%), which would leave most suffixed forms unmarked.

8 Conclusion

In sum, OtoBERT provides a practical and effective method to automatically address a critical obstacle in the accessibility and readability of Hebrew literature. Through the creation of this new and specialized BERT model, we are able to identify suffixed verbs with a high degree of accuracy, enabling the simplification and/or glossing of most instances. Using this method, we can remove a primary stumbling block which alienates the younger generation of readers, ultimately paving the way for the new generation to enjoy the treasures that the Hebrew literary tradition has to offer.

We release OtoBERT to the public on huggingface, for both commercial and educational use, under an Apache license. Additionally, we release our dataset of naturally occurring Hebrew sentences containing ambiguous words which can be analyzed either as a verb without suffix or as a suffixed verb, with human annotations indicating the correct analysis for each.[2] We hope that this dataset will pave the way for additional studies further enhancing our ability to address this accessibility challenge of Hebrew texts.

[2]The model is available here: `https://huggingface.co/dicta-il/otobert`, and the dataset is available here: `https://huggingface.co/datasets/dicta-il/hebrew_suffix_verbal_forms`

9 Limitations

The method presented here relies on the ability to generate Masked Language Model predictions for the token which represents the ambiguous word. This entails the existence of the ambiguous word within the BERT vocabulary. If it is not present in the vocabulary, and the word is broken up into word pieces, then the MLM head cannot be relied upon to produce a reliable prediction for our purpose here, no matter which word piece we submit for the MLM predictions. Thus, the method presented here is limited to cases where the ambiguous word is contained in the BERT vocabulary as a single token.

Fortunately, in practice, this limitation affects only a small minority of cases. First of all, we pretrained the BERT model presented here with a substantially sized vocabulary, of 128K words, which means that from the get-go, most words in a modern Hebrew text need not be split into word pieces. Furthermore, the suffixed verbs that we focus upon here - the ones which are generally analyzed as a common non-suffixed Hebrew word, and which also contain the possibility of analysis as a verb with pronominal suffix - are, by their very nature, frequent words, which are most likely included in the vocabulary.

10 Lay Summary

In this paper, we address a specific obstacle which makes Hebrew literary texts difficult for students and youth: complex Hebrew words which are actually a series of multiple words combined together into one. For instance, instead of using multiple Hebrew words to say "and he threw it", they would all be combined into one complex Hebrew word. The problem is twofold. First of all, such complex words are exceedingly rare in modern Hebrew, outside of literary contexts. This already poses a difficulty for student readers who are not used to encountering such words. However, the real difficulty is that these complex words are often ambiguous: the very same Hebrew letters can be read as a different and non-complex Hebrew word, and that is the usual way that the word is used. Thus, it's not just that the students will be unfamiliar with the possibility of the complex word and not know how to understand it. Rather, it is that the students will recognize the word as a standard Hebrew word that they are used to seeing, and they will continue to read the sentence with that understanding. Yet, when they reach the end of the sentence, they will find themselves perplexed. When they are finally taught that the word in question actually doubles as a complex word, different in meaning from what they are used to, they feel tricked by the text, and this ends up alienating them from the literary treasures of the language.

To bridge this gap for student readers, we wish to design a system that automatically annotates these literary texts, adding little alerts or warnings in between the lines of the text in order to alert the reader to the fact that these words don't function here as they normally do. However, in order to do so, we need an automatic method to identify these complex words; and, because the words are ambiguous, this is not easy to do. As we demonstrate, the regular computational processes for clarifying text don't work well here, due to the extreme rarity of the complex words. We have therefore trained a new dedicated neural network language model, designed from the ground up specifically to identify this type of complex word. We release our new model here to the public.

Acknowledgements

This paper has been funded by the Israel Science Foundation (Grant No. 2617/22) and by the European Union (ERC, MiDRASH, Project No. 101071829), for which we are grateful. Views and opinions expressed are, however, those of the authors only and do not necessarily reflect those of the European Union or the European Research Council Executive Agency. Neither the European Union nor the granting authority can be held responsible for them.

References

S. Y. Agnon. 1953a. *At the Handles of the Lock*. Schocken Publishing House.

S. Y. Agnon. 1953b. *Only Yesterday*. Schocken Publishing House.

Tuqa Bani Yaseen, Qusai Ismail, Sarah Al-Omari, Eslam Al-Sobh, and Malak Abdullah. 2021. JUST-BLUE at SemEval-2021 task 1: Predicting lexical complexity using BERT and RoBERTa pre-trained language models. In *Proceedings of the 15th International Workshop on Semantic Evaluation (SemEval-2021)*, pages 661–666, Online. Association for Computational Linguistics.

Jacob Devlin, Ming-Wei Chang, Kenton Lee, and Kristina Toutanova. 2019a. Bert: Pre-training of deep bidirectional transformers for language understanding. *Preprint*, arXiv:1810.04805.

Jacob Devlin, Ming-Wei Chang, Kenton Lee, and Kristina Toutanova. 2019b. Bert: Pre-training of deep bidirectional transformers for language understanding. *Preprint*, arXiv:1810.04805.

Eylon Gueta, Avi Shmidman, Shaltiel Shmidman, Cheyn Shmuel Shmidman, Joshua Guedalia, Moshe Koppel, Dan Bareket, Amit Seker, and Reut Tsarfaty. 2023. Large pre-trained models with extra-large vocabularies: A contrastive analysis of hebrew bert models and a new one to outperform them all. *Preprint*, arXiv:2211.15199.

Abdelhak Kelious, Mathieu Constant, and Christophe Coeur. 2024. Complex word identification: A comparative study between ChatGPT and a dedicated model for this task. In *Proceedings of the 2024 Joint International Conference on Computational Linguistics, Language Resources and Evaluation (LREC-COLING 2024)*, pages 3645–3653, Torino, Italia. ELRA and ICCL.

Atharva Kumbhar, Sheetal Sonawane, Dipali Kadam, and Prathamesh Mulay. 2023. CASM - context and something more in lexical simplification. In *Proceedings of the 20th International Conference on Natural Language Processing (ICON)*, pages 506–515, Goa University, Goa, India. NLP Association of India (NLPAI).

Yinhan Liu, Myle Ott, Naman Goyal, Jingfei Du, Mandar Joshi, Danqi Chen, Omer Levy, Mike Lewis, Luke Zettlemoyer, and Veselin Stoyanov. 2019. Roberta: A robustly optimized bert pretraining approach. *Preprint*, arXiv:1907.11692.

Kai North, Marcos Zampieri, and Matthew Shardlow. 2023. Lexical complexity prediction: An overview. *ACM Comput. Surv.*, 55(9).

Chunguang Pan, Bingyan Song, Shengguang Wang, and Zhipeng Luo. 2021. DeepBlueAI at SemEval-2021 task 1: Lexical complexity prediction with a deep ensemble approach. In *Proceedings of the 15th International Workshop on Semantic Evaluation (SemEval-2021)*, pages 578–584, Online. Association for Computational Linguistics.

Amit Seker, Elron Bandel, Dan Bareket, Idan Brusilovsky, Refael Shaked Greenfeld, and Reut Tsarfaty. 2021. Alephbert:a hebrew large pre-trained language model to start-off your hebrew nlp application with. *Preprint*, arXiv:2104.04052.

Vitaly Shalumov and Harel Haskey. 2023. Hero: Roberta and longformer hebrew language models. *arXiv:2304.11077*.

Shaltiel Shmidman, Avi Shmidman, and Moshe Koppel. 2023. Dictabert: A state-of-the-art bert suite for modern hebrew. *Preprint*, arXiv:2308.16687.

Shaltiel Shmidman, Avi Shmidman, Moshe Koppel, and Reut Tsarfaty. 2024. MRL parsing without tears: The case of Hebrew. In *Findings of the Association for Computational Linguistics ACL 2024*, pages 4537–4550, Bangkok, Thailand and virtual meeting. Association for Computational Linguistics.

Xinying Song, Alex Salcianu, Yang Song, Dave Dopson, and Denny Zhou. 2021. Fast wordpiece tokenization. *Preprint*, arXiv:2012.15524.

Reut Tsarfaty and Yoav Goldberg. 2008. Word-based or morpheme-based? annotation strategies for Modern Hebrew clitics. In *Proceedings of the Sixth International Conference on Language Resources and Evaluation (LREC'08)*, Marrakech, Morocco. European Language Resources Association (ELRA).

A Appendix: Training Details

The model's architecture is based on the BERT-base architecture (Devlin et al., 2019a), trained on a DGX-A100 with 4xA100 40GB cards. The training was done with the fused lamb optimizer combined with AMP (Automatic Mixed Precision). A polynomial warmup learning rate scheduler was used to warm up for a portion of the training steps and then decay the learning rate over the total steps.

A.1 Training Data & Objectives

We train our model using the same training data & objectives as done for training `DictaBERT` (Shmidman et al., 2023). The training dataset is a mixture of several sources (such as the HeDC4 corpus (Shalumov and Haskey, 2023)), summing to a total of three billion words (3.8B tokens) of naturally occurring texts.

We trained the model using only the MLM (masked language modeling) training objective, as done by Liu et al. (2019). In addition, we adjusted the construction of the training examples for the MLM objective according to the guidelines specified by Shmidman et al. (2023). The main adjustments were:

1. We don't mask tokens that are broken up into multiple word-pieces since the non-masked word-pieces provide valuable information and make the task less challenging.

2. We never truncate part of a sentence, documents are always truncated with sentence units so that a training example is never cut off in the middle.

A.2 Training Details and Hyperparameters

We trained our model with the HuggingFace architecture wrapped with NVIDIA libraries[3] which are highly optimized for training compute-heavy machine learning models on NVIDIA hardware. We pre-trained the model on 4 A100 40GB GPUs for a total of 32,800 iterations, completing a total of 1.85 epochs. The training was done with sequences of up to 256 tokens, with 2 phases. First phase with a learning rate of 6e-3 for 1 epoch, followed by a second phase with a learning rate of 1e-4 for 0.85 epochs.

The total training time was 4.5 days. The training was done with a global batch size of 8,192 and a warmup proportion of 0.2843 for both phases.

[3] https://github.com/NVIDIA/DeepLearningExamples/tree/master/PyTorch/LanguageModeling/BERT

CompLex-ZH: A New Dataset for Lexical Complexity Prediction in Mandarin and Cantonese

Le Qiu[1], Shanyue Guo[1], Tak-sum Wong[1], Emmanuele Chersoni[1], John S. Y. Lee[2], Chu-Ren Huang[1]

[1]The Hong Kong Polytechnic University, [2]City University of Hong Kong

Correspondence: emmanuele.chersoni@polyu.edu.hk

Abstract

The prediction of *lexical complexity* in context is assuming an increasing relevance in Natural Language Processing research, since identifying complex words is often the first step of text simplification pipelines. To the best of our knowledge, though, datasets annotated with complex words are available only for English and for a limited number of Western languages.

In our paper, we introduce *CompLex-ZH*, a dataset including words annotated with complexity scores in sentential contexts for Chinese. Our data include sentences in Mandarin and Cantonese, which were selected from a variety of sources and textual genres. We provide a first evaluation with baselines combining hand-crafted and language models-based features.

1 Introduction

In psycholinguistics and Natural Language Processing (NLP) research, the notion of *complexity* relates to the difficulty faced by a speaker in reading and understanding specific linguistic productions (Blache, 2011; Chersoni et al., 2016, 2017, 2021; Sarti et al., 2021; Iavarone et al., 2021; Xiang et al., 2021), and its assessment has important applications in education technology, such as the simplification of text for second language learners and/or populations with special needs (Štajner, 2021; North et al., 2023). One major source of complexity is depending on word choice, it corresponds to the difficulty that one may encounter in understanding a specific word in context, which could be solved with the help of NLP systems by i) automatically identifying the complexity of the target word (*lexical complexity in context*); ii) proposing simpler and more familiar words as replacements (*lexical simplification*).

Although the problem of lexical complexity received increasing attention in the NLP community in the last few years (Shardlow et al., 2020; Štajner et al., 2022; Ai, 2022; Yang et al., 2023), with the introduction of new benchmark datasets and the organization of several shared tasks (Paetzold and Specia, 2016; Yimam et al., 2018; Shardlow et al., 2021; Saggion et al., 2023; Shardlow et al., 2024), the evaluation in this task has been so far limited to a small number of Western languages.

Our research effort aims at filling this gap, by introducing **CompLex-ZH**, the first evaluation benchmark for lexical complexity prediction in Chinese. CompLex-ZH includes data annotated for word complexity in context by native speakers, and has been built by carefully sampling sentences from different sources and text genres. In addition to Mandarin Chinese, we also provide lexical complexity data for Cantonese: Cantonese is a major variety of Chinese with a large population of speakers worldwide (more than 85 million of speakers, according to recent estimates by Eberhard et al. (2022)) but having a low-resource status in terms of availability of NLP models, corpora and resources, and thus it might prove more challenging to handle for LLMs trained on standard Chinese (Xiang et al., 2024). Our initial evaluation results show that a baseline regressor based on a combination of handcrafted

Proceedings of the Third Workshop on Text Simplification, Accessibility and Readability (TSAR 2024), pages 20–26
November 15, 2024

features and contextualized embeddings only reaches a moderate accuracy in predicting Chinese lexical complexity. [1]

2 Related Work

An early shared task on lexical complexity in English was organized in 2016 by Paetzold and Specia (2016), with complexity defined as a binary variable: raters and automatic systems had to decide whether a word was complex/difficult to understand or not. Of course, this is a simplifying and problematic assumption, as there are many situations in which word complexity cannot be determined in a clear-cut way, and it is better described by a continuous value. Another shared task in 2018 (Yimam et al., 2018) also focused on complexity prediction as a binary decision, but it included an additional regression subtask in which the systems, given a target word in context and a specific annotator, had to predict the likelihood that the annotator would have considered the target as complex.

The Task 1 at SemEval-2021 (Shardlow et al., 2021) was the first one treating lexical complexity prediction as a regression task. As a gold standard, this shared task used the CompLex corpus (Shardlow et al., 2020, 2022), which includes words in sentential contexts from three different genres, i.e. the Bible, the proceedings of the European Parliament and biomedical articles, and the scores are mean complexity ratings between 0 and 1. Moreover, this benchmark features not only single words as targets, but also multiword expressions.

Notice that the identification of complex words is only the first step of pipelines aiming at the lexical simplification of a text (Saggion and Hirst, 2017). Additional steps generally require the generation of simpler substitution words and their ranking. Over the years, several studies have been dedicated to lexical simplification in English (Paetzold and Specia, 2017; Qiang et al., 2020), Chinese (Qiang et al., 2021), Portuguese (North et al., 2022) and Spanish (Ferrés and Saggion, 2022), and a shared task has been organized in co-location with EMNLP 2022 (Saggion et al., 2023). In many of these studies, a target word has already been identified as complex and the systems have to focus on the substitute generation and ranking component: for example, the selection of the target words in the Chinese dataset by Qiang et al. (2021) only includes words classified as "high-level" (meaning, understandable only by advanced speakers) in the Chinese HSK Vocabulary (Zhao et al., 2003). Our current work is focusing instead on the previous step of lexical complexity detection, and aims at providing the first benchmark for the Chinese language with words of varying degrees of complexity.

3 Dataset Creation

In order to create a challenging benchmark, we decided to include not only data for lexical complexity in Mandarin Chinese, which is the standard variety of Chinese, but also for Yue Chinese or Cantonese. Cantonese is commonly used in colloquial scenarios (e.g., daily conversation and social media) and it exhibits different vocabulary, grammar, and pronunciation compared to Mandarin. It is natively spoken by a large number of speakers in Hong Kong, Macao, Guangdong and part of Guangxi, and in many overseas Chinese communities in South-East Asia, North America, and Western Europe (Sachs and Li, 2007; Yu, 2013; Xiang et al., 2024).

We believe its inclusion is an interesting feature of our dataset, as it will allow to test the robustness of Chinese language models to different Chinese varieties. This is useful because, despite being a mainly spoken variety, Cantonese can also be used in some written contexts, such as the Legislative Council of the Hong Kong Special Administrative Region, in medical document transcriptions, or in sections of special interests of local newspapers (Xiang et al., 2024), and thus there might be the need for simplification of Cantonese texts.

3.1 Target Selection and Sentence Sampling

In constructing our dataset, we collected most Mandarin data from the Chinese Wikipedia (*Zh-Wikipedia*), *Weibo* and *People's Daily*, and most Cantonese data from the Cantonese Wikipedia (*Yue-Wikipedia*) and from the *LIHKG* dataset for topic classification. [2]

[1] Code and data will be made available at https://github.com/Laniqiu/CompLex-ZH.

[2] https://github.com/toastynews/lihkg-cat-v2.

People's Daily stands as one of the most authoritative newspapers in China, while Weibo is a popular micro-blogging site in mainland China, and LIHKG is a Reddit-like forum based in Hong Kong. We also sourced supplementary materials (categorized as *Other*) from the BCC corpus (Xun et al., 2016) for Mandarin, from a counseling corpus (Lee et al., 2020) and from the PolyU Corpus of Spoken Chinese (Hong Kong Polytechnic University, 2015) for Cantonese. By incorporating these varied sources, we managed to cover a wide range of topics, including daily life, sports, public health, politics, and so on.

The raw materials have been tokenized, using Jieba[3] for Mandarin and PyCantonese (Lee et al., 2022) for Cantonese. We examined the vocabulary of our corpora and identified target words. We primarily found high-frequency content words that are more colloquial and frequently encountered in everyday conversations from Weibo, People's Daily, LIHKG, etc.. Low-frequency content words were also included from BCC and Wikipedia, offering a broader spectrum of vocabulary beyond colloquial expressions. We then sampled at least 1 sentence for each target. Multiword expressions, following Shardlow et al. (2021), could also be chosen as targets (They constitute 1.97% of Mandarin targets and 2.69% of Cantonese targets.). These targets and the sentences including them made up then for our unrated datasets. Finally, it should be mentioned that the number of target words we could sample is much lower for Cantonese, as our Cantonese corpora were much smaller (i.e. with lower frequencies for the candidate target words) and with less variety of textual genres.

3.2 Rating Collection

For rating collection, we created about 300 questionnaires for both varieties, using the data from section 3.1. Participants are requested to evaluate the difficulty in understanding the given words within the given contexts. The provided options are designed in a 5-point Likert scale, ranging from 1 indicating *Very easy* to 5 *Very difficult*. Each questionnaire consists of about 100 rating questions and 2 validation questions. The validation samples are prepared with *gold* answers. Before the questionnaire distribution, we conducted a small pilot study, and identified some questions where participants highly agreed on the options (i.e., *gold answers*). These are then inserted in the instruction messages, and in the questionnaires. The annotators whose answers significantly deviated from the gold answers for those samples were considered as non-reliable raters and their responses were rejected. Concretely, we had examples where all the pilot study participants gave very low/easy scores, such as the Cantonese 呢份試卷好**簡單**呀! (*This exam is too easy*), or very high/difficult scores, such as the Mandarin 她谈着她婚后的**睽离**和甜蜜的生活 (*She talked about her detached and sweet life after marriage*): an annotator's answer were discarded if easy validation questions were rated higher than 3 (the mid point of the scale), and difficult ones were rated lower than 3.

Our raters (refer to the Appendix for more information) have mostly been recruited in Hong Kong, where Cantonese is the principal vernacular language and Mandarin Chinese is one of the official languages. Each rater was paid 100 HKD (≈ 12.8 USD) for a single questionnaire.

Each sample has been rated by at least 5 raters. The complexity score of a sample is then the average score assigned by all the raters, while the complexity score of a target word is the average of the scores of all its samples. We provided some examples in Table 1. The statistics of the dataset can be found in Table 3 in the Appendix.

Context	Score
... 忽然变得澄清见底，翳障 全无。 ...it turns crystal, without obstacles in sight.	.213
此前有团队 已经在粪便里发现新冠病毒。 The team had found coronavirus in feces.	.893
... 感受到被失蹤、被跟蹤的實在... ...I truly felt disappeared and stalked...	.588
點解講GOOD JOB 佢反而又呆哂... Why he acts so dumb and ... when you said GOOD JOB?	.200

Table 1: Some examples with high/ low complexity scores. The first 2 are in Mandarin and the last 2 in Cantonese. Target words are underlined.

[3] https://github.com/fxsjy/jieba

	Feat.	MAE	R^2	ρ
Mand.	HC	.065	.186	.091
	Stroke	.065	.083	.107
	WLen	.065	.055	.082
	LogF	.065	.201	.061
	Emb	**.059**	**.355**	**.338**
	Comb.	.060	.086	.322
Canto.	HC	**.060**	.051	.191
	Stroke	.063	-.001	.008
	WLen	.063	.0184	.158
	LogF	.061	.022	.149
	Emb	.061	**.056**	.353
	Comb.	.061	.045	**.354**
Joint	HC	.065	.047	.135
	Stroke	.066	-.002	-.015
	WLen	.066	-.002	-.109
	LogF	.066	.040	.116
	Emb	**.062**	.131	**.329**
	Comb.	**.062**	**.136**	.326

Table 2: Summary of evaluation results. We investigated overall and individual HC features, embedding features and the combination of the most influential LogF feature and of the word embeddings (Comb.). The metrics are: mean absolute error (MAE), R-squared value (R^2), and Spearman correlation coefficient (ρ). Notice that the metrics are not directly comparable across language settings, given the different number of items in the test sets.

4 Evaluation Experiments

We ran some preliminary evaluation experiments using a Ridge Regression model with handcrafted features (HC) and contextualized word embeddings (Emb) as predictors and the complexity score for each sentence as the target variable. The data were splitted in training, validation and test set with a 8:1:1 split percentage, and we ran separate evaluations for the two varieties and for the two feature types to assess their impact. Handcrafted features of the target word include its logarithmic frequency (LogF), extracted via the Wordfreq Python package (Speer, 2022); the number of characters (WLen) and the number of strokes[4], which are well-known visual complexity indexes (Tse et al., 2017; Sun et al., 2018). For the contextualized embeddings in the two varieties, we used CINO (Yang et al., 2022), a RoBERTa-based architecture trained on texts both in standard Chinese and in several minority languages of China, in order to obtain vector representations for both Mandarin and Cantonese by means of a single model.

The most common regression metrics have been calculated on the test sets (324 instances for Mandarin, 250 for Cantonese, 574 for a joint dataset of both) and are shown in Table 2. We can notice that, in each corpus partition, contextualized embeddings contribute to improve significantly over the results of the out-of-context HC features, and among those features, it can be seen that logarithmic frequency is predictive of lexical complexity in Mandarin, but it performs much more weakly in the settings including Cantonese data, which might be due to a more limited coverage of frequency norms in this variety. Compared to the original results in Shardlow et al. (2020) on English, it is interesting to observe that on our data HC features are not consistently more informative than embeddings. This could be due to differences in the embeddings type: static embeddings from GloVe (Pennington et al., 2014) and sentence embeddings from InferSent (Conneau et al., 2017) in the previous work, contextualized, token-level embeddings from a more recent RoBERTA-based architecture in our present evaluation.

We can also observe that correlation values and MAE in Mandarin and Cantonese are similar, but explained variance in Cantonese is much lower, confirming that the Cantonese data pose a non-trivial challenge for Chinese NLP. Scores in general are relatively low, suggesting the need for more sophisticated approaches to improve the modeling of lexical complexity in Chinese.

5 Conclusion

In this paper, we have introduced CompLex-ZH, the first dataset for evaluating predictions of lexical complexity in context for two major Chinese varieties, Mandarin and Cantonese. We have sampled target words in context from a variety of text genres and collected ratings from speakers in Hong Kong.

Our preliminary evaluation shows that the contextualized embeddings of a language model trained on multiple Chinese varieties significantly help in improving the prediction over handcrafted, out-of-context features. However, the accuracy is not high - as suggested by the limited amount of explained variance and by the weak-to-moderate correlation scores, leaving space for future improvements.

[4]Source: https://github.com/WuChengqian520/

Lay Summary

The first step that a computer has to take to simplify a text and make it more accessible is to identify difficult words and expressions. So far, datasets to train machine learning systems to recognize the complexity of understanding words in context (lexical complexity) have been available only for English and a few other Western languages.

In our work, we put together a dataset of human complexity judgements for words in context in Chinese, and we included two different Sinitic varieties: Mandarin and Cantonese. We carry out a first test for predicting lexical complexity in Chinese, and obtained our best results with the features extracted from CINO, a language model trained on multiple Chinese dialects. On the other hand general accuracy remains moderate, as the models seem to struggle with the more rare and data scarce Cantonese variety.

Acknowledgements

EC acknowledges the financial support from the start-up fund project "Building and Predicting Neurocognitive-Motivated Lexical-Semantic Norms for Mandarin Chinese" (1-BE8G), sponsored by the Faculty of Humanities of the Hong Kong Polytechnic University. JL acknowledges support from a Strategic Research Grant (7006037) at City University of Hong Kong.

References

Haiyang Ai. 2022. Automating Lexical Complexity Measurement in Chinese with WeCLECA. *International Journal of Asian Language Processing*, 32(01):2250011.

Philippe Blache. 2011. Evaluating Language Complexity in Context: New Parameters for a Constraint-based Model. In *Proceedings of the International Workshop on Constraints and Language Processing*.

Emmanuele Chersoni, Philippe Blache, and Alessandro Lenci. 2016. Towards a Distributional Model of Semantic Complexity. In *Proceedings of the COLING Workshop on Computational Linguistics for Linguistic Complexity*.

Emmanuele Chersoni, Alessandro Lenci, and Philippe Blache. 2017. Logical Metonymy in a Distributional Model of Sentence Comprehension. In *Proceedings of *SEM*.

Emmanuele Chersoni, Enrico Santus, Alessandro Lenci, Philippe Blache, and Chu-Ren Huang. 2021. Not All Arguments Are Processed Equally: A Distributional Model of Argument Complexity. *Language, Resources and Evaluation*, pages 1–28.

Alexis Conneau, Douwe Kiela, Holger Schwenk, Loic Barrault, and Antoine Bordes. 2017. Supervised Learning of Universal Sentence Representations from Natural Language Inference Data. In *Proceedings of EMNLP*.

David M Eberhard, Gary F Simons, and Charles D Fennig. 2022. *Ethnologue: Languages of the World*. Dallas: SIL International.

Daniel Ferrés and Horacio Saggion. 2022. ALEXSIS: A Dataset for Lexical Simplification in Spanish. In *Proceedings of LREC*.

Department of English Hong Kong Polytechnic University. 2015. PolyU Corpus of Spoken Chinese.

Benedetta Iavarone, Dominique Brunato, and Felice Dell'Orletta. 2021. Sentence Complexity in Context. In *Proceedings of the NAACL Workshop on Cognitive Modeling and Computational Linguistics*.

Jackson Lee, Litong Chen, Charles Lam, Chaak Ming Lau, and Tsz-Him Tsui. 2022. PyCantonese: Cantonese Linguistics and NLP in Python. In *Proceedings of LREC*.

John Lee, Tianyuan Cai, Wenxiu Xie, and Lam Xing. 2020. A Counselling Corpus in Cantonese. In *Proceedings of the Joint SLTU and CCURL Workshop (SLTU-CCURL)*.

Kai North, Marcos Zampieri, and Tharindu Ranasinghe. 2022. ALEXSIS-PT: A New Resource for Portuguese Lexical Simplification. *arXiv preprint arXiv:2209.09034*.

Kai North, Marcos Zampieri, and Matthew Shardlow. 2023. Lexical Complexity Prediction: An Overview. *ACM Computing Surveys*, 55(9):1–42.

Gustavo Paetzold and Lucia Specia. 2016. Semeval 2016 Task 11: Complex Word Identification. In *Proceedings of SemEval*.

Gustavo Paetzold and Lucia Specia. 2017. Lexical Simplification with Neural Ranking. In *Proceedings of EACL*.

Jeffrey Pennington, Richard Socher, and Christopher Manning. 2014. Glove: Global Vectors for Word Representation. In *Proceedings of EMNLP*.

Jipeng Qiang, Yun Li, Yi Zhu, Yunhao Yuan, and Xindong Wu. 2020. LSBert: A Simple Framework for Lexical Simplification. *arXiv preprint arXiv:2006.14939*.

Jipeng Qiang, Xinyu Lu, Yun Li, Yunhao Yuan, and Xindong Wu. 2021. Chinese Lexical Simplification. *IEEE/ACM Transactions on Audio, Speech, and Language Processing*, 29:1819–1828.

Gertrude Tinker Sachs and David CS Li. 2007. Cantonese as an Additional Language in Hong Kong. *Multilingua*, 26(95):130.

Horacio Saggion and Graeme Hirst. 2017. *Automatic Text Simplification*, volume 32. Springer.

Horacio Saggion, Sanja Štajner, Daniel Ferrés, Kim Cheng Sheang, Matthew Shardlow, Kai North, and Marcos Zampieri. 2023. Findings of the TSAR-2022 Shared Task on Multilingual Lexical Simplification. *arXiv preprint arXiv:2302.02888*.

Gabriele Sarti, Dominique Brunato, and Felice Dell'Orletta. 2021. That Looks Hard: Characterizing Linguistic Complexity in Humans and Language Models. In *Proceedings of the NAACL Workshop on Cognitive Modeling and Computational Linguistics*.

Matthew Shardlow, Fernando Alva-Manchego, Riza Theresa Batista-Navarro, Stefan Bott, Saul Calderon-Ramirez, Rémi Cardon, Thomas François, Akio Hayakawa, Andrea Horbach, and Anna Huelsing. 2024. The BEA 2024 Shared Task on the Multilingual Lexical Simplification Pipeline. In *Proceedings of the Workshop on Innovative Use of NLP for Building Educational Applications (BEA)*.

Matthew Shardlow, Michael Cooper, and Marcos Zampieri. 2020. CompLex–A New Corpus for Lexical Complexity Predicition from Likert Scale Data. In *Proceedings of the LREC Workshop on Tools and Resources to Empower People with REAding DIfficulties*.

Matthew Shardlow, Richard Evans, Gustavo Paetzold, and Marcos Zampieri. 2021. SemEval-2021 Task 1: Lexical Complexity Prediction. In *Proceedings of SemEval*.

Matthew Shardlow, Richard Evans, and Marcos Zampieri. 2022. Predicting Lexical Complexity in English texts: The Complex 2.0 Dataset. *Language Resources and Evaluation*, 56(4):1153–1194.

Robyn Speer. 2022. rspeer/wordfreq: v3. 0. *Version v3. 0.2. Sept.*

Sanja Štajner. 2021. Automatic Text Simplification for Social Good: Progress and Challenges. *Findings of ACL-IJCNLP*.

Sanja Štajner, Daniel Ferrés, Matthew Shardlow, Kai North, Marcos Zampieri, and Horacio Saggion. 2022. Lexical Simplification Benchmarks for English, Portuguese, and Spanish. *Frontiers in Artificial Intelligence*, 5.

Ching Chu Sun, Peter Hendrix, Jianqiang Ma, and Rolf Harald Baayen. 2018. Chinese Lexical Database (CLD) a Large-Scale Lexical Database for Simplified Mandarin Chinese. *Behavior Research Methods*, 50:2606–2629.

Chi-Shing Tse, Melvin J Yap, Yuen-Lai Chan, Wei Ping Sze, Cyrus Shaoul, and Dan Lin. 2017. The Chinese Lexicon Project: A Megastudy of Lexical Decision Performance for 25,000+ Traditional Chinese Two-character Compound Words. *Behavior Research Methods*, 49:1503–1519.

Rong Xiang, Emmanuele Chersoni, Yixia Li, Jing Li, Chu-Ren Huang, Yushan Pan, and Yushi Li. 2024. Cantonese Natural Language Processing in the Transformers Era: A Survey and Current Challenges. *Language Resources and Evaluation*, pages 1–27.

Rong Xiang, Jinghang Gu, Emmanuele Chersoni, Wenjie Li, Qin Lu, and Chu-Ren Huang. 2021. PolyU CBS-Comp at SemEval-2021 Task 1: Lexical Complexity Prediction (LCP). In *Proceedings of SemEval*.

Endong Xun, Gaoqi Rao, Xiaoyue Xiao, and Jiaojiao Zan. 2016. The Construction of the BCC Corpus in the Age of Big Data. *Corpus Linguistics*.

Cheng-Zen Yang, Jin-Jian Li, and Shu-Chang Lin. 2023. Lexical Complexity Prediction using Word Embeddings. In *Proceedings of ROCLING*.

Ziqing Yang, Zihang Xu, Yiming Cui, Baoxin Wang, Min Lin, Dayong Wu, and Zhigang Chen. 2022. CINO: A Chinese Minority Pre-trained Language Model. In *Proceedings of COLING*.

Seid Muhie Yimam, Chris Biemann, Shervin Malmasi, Gustavo H Paetzold, Lucia Specia, Sanja Štajner, Anaïs Tack, and Marcos Zampieri. 2018. A Report on the Complex Word Identification Shared Task 2018. In *Proceedings of the NAACL Workshop on Innovative Use of NLP for Building Educational Applications*.

Henry Yu. 2013. Mountains of Gold: Canada, North America, and the Cantonese Pacific. In *Routledge Handbook of the Chinese Diaspora*, pages 124–137. Routledge.

J Zhao, B Zhang, and J Cheng. 2003. Some Suggestions on the Revision of the Outline of the Graded Vocabulary for HSK. *Chinese Teaching in the World*.

A Statistics of the dataset

Table 3 presents the statistics of the target words, samples, and ratings of the dataset.

	Source	Sent.	Word	Sent./ Word	R./ Sent.	R./ Word	Complex.	STD
Mand.	Weibo	1600	770	2.08	8.28	17.21	.269	.061
	People's Daily	1228	713	1.72	8.36	14.41	.268	.064
	Other	412	255	1.62	6.61	10.67	.323	.164
	All	3240	1017	3.19	8.10	25.80	.283	.094
Canto.	LIHKG	1043	222	4.70	9.45	6.97	.284	.077
	Wiki	1037	219	4.74	6.97	32.99	.268	.073
	Other	425	129	3.29	9.10	29.98	.274	.067
	All	2505	260	9.63	8.36	80.58	.274	.065

Table 3: Statistics of CompLex-ZH. The original ratings have been normalized to a 0-1 range following Shardlow et al. (2020)'s convention: $1 \rightarrow 0, 2 \rightarrow 0.25, 3 \rightarrow 0.5, 4 \rightarrow 0.75, 5 \rightarrow 1$. Denotation: Mand. = Mandarin, Canto. = Cantonese, Sent. = Sentence, R./ Sent. = Ratings per Sent., R./ Word = Ratings per word, Complex. = average word-wise complexity score, STD = Standard deviation.

B Background information of raters

We recruited 318 raters for the Mandarin dataset, and 299 raters for Cantonese. After rejecting some annotators' answers, following the validation procedure in section 3.2, we eventually have 314 raters for Mandarin and 298 raters for Cantonese. As shown in Figure 1 and Figure 2, most of our raters are aged between 18 to 35, holding a bachelor or a higher level degree.

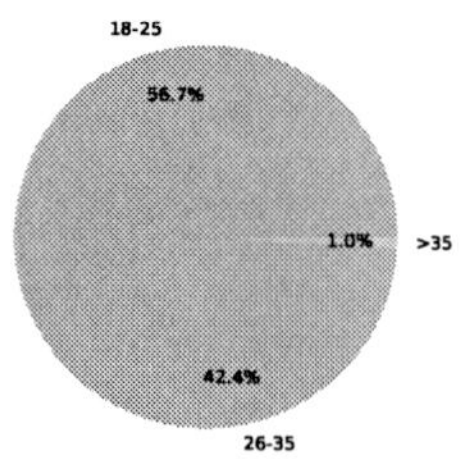

(a) Mandarin

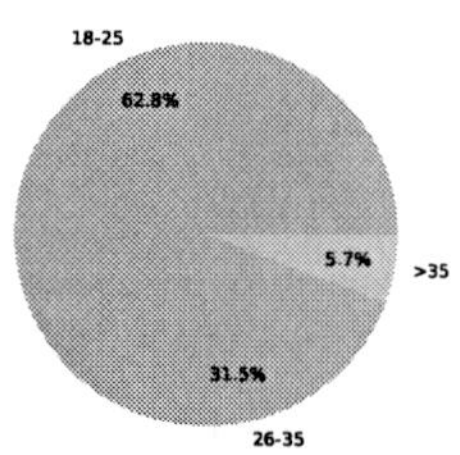

(b) Cantonese

Figure 1: Age Distribution of annotators.

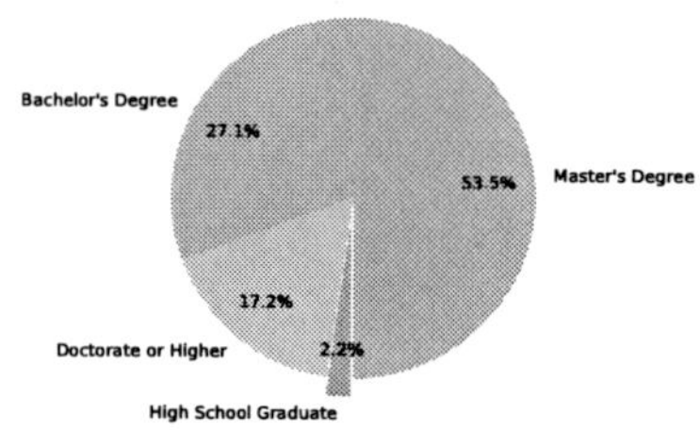

(a) Mandarin

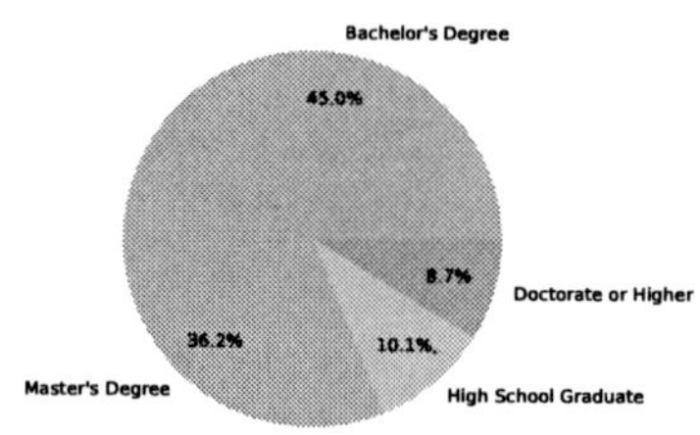

(b) Cantonese

Figure 2: Education levels of annotators.

Images Speak Volumes: User-Centric Assessment of Image Generation for Accessible Communication

Miriam Anschütz and Tringa Sylaj and Georg Groh
School for Computation, Information and Technology
Technical University of Munich, Germany
{miriam.anschuetz, tringa.sylaj}@tum.de, grohg@in.tum.de

Abstract

Explanatory images play a pivotal role in accessible and easy-to-read (E2R) texts. However, the images available in online databases are not tailored toward the respective texts, and the creation of customized images is expensive. In this large-scale study, we investigated whether text-to-image generation models can close this gap by providing customizable images quickly and easily. We benchmarked seven, four open- and three closed-source, image generation models and provide an extensive evaluation of the resulting images. In addition, we performed a user study with people from the E2R target group to examine whether the images met their requirements. We find that some of the models show remarkable performance, but none of the models are ready to be used at a larger scale without human supervision. Our research is an important step toward facilitating the creation of accessible information for E2R creators and tailoring accessible images to the target group's needs.

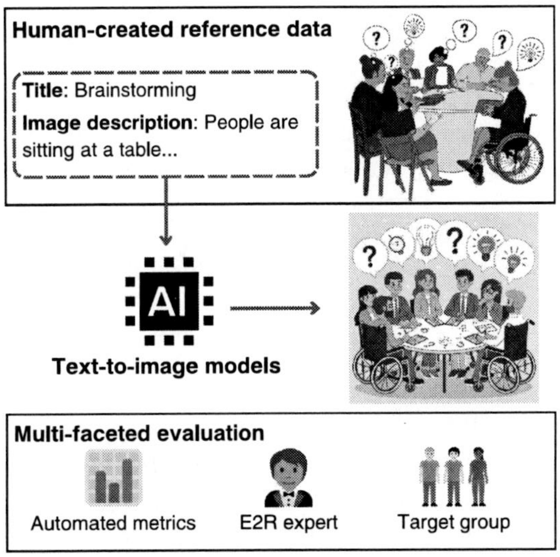

Figure 1: Overview of our approach: We selected a human-created reference dataset that was validated by the target group already. Based on the images' titles and descriptions, we used seven different text-to-image models to recreate the original images. Then, we evaluated the generated images across multiple aspects using automated and human evaluation.
© JSCHKA Kommunikationsdesign I www.jschka.de

1 Introduction

Easy-to-read (E2R) and its German derivative *Leichte Sprache* (Easy Language) are accessibility- and readability-enhanced versions of language. They follow a strict ruleset and are targeted at people with disabilities, learning difficulties, or low literacy (DIN-Normenausschuss Ergonomie, 2023). The creation of a more accessible version of an original text is called text simplification (TS). Since this process is laborsome, previous work explored the applicability of large language models to facilitate or even automatize the creation of E2R texts (Madina et al., 2023). For German Easy language, Schomacker et al. (2023) investigated how well the currently available, text-oriented models and datasets comply with the ruleset of German Easy language and multiple open-source automatic TS models for German exist (Anschütz et al., 2023; Stodden et al., 2023).

However, one important feature of E2R texts is that they are illustrated with images that improve and facilitate the text's understanding even further. The guidelines in the DIN-SPEC 33429 (DIN-Normenausschuss Ergonomie, 2023) recommend that these images should be created specifically for each text and that they should be up-to-date and close to the target group's everyday life. Even though large image databases exist[1] that were reviewed and validated by the target group, these images were created for a general purpose and cannot be altered by the text creators. In addition, while human artists are unchallenged in creating

[1] e.g. https://www.lag-sb-rlp.de/projekte/bildergalerie-leichte-sprache

Proceedings of the Third Workshop on Text Simplification, Accessibility and Readability (TSAR 2024), pages 27–40
November 15, 2024 ©2024 Association for Computational Linguistics

the most targeted and realistic images, their employment is financially infeasible for most E2R translators. Therefore, our work explores whether text-to-image (T2I) models can solve this problem by creating quickly available, flexible, and cheap images. An overview of our approach is presented in Figure 1.

Our contribution can be summarized as follows:

- We benchmark seven text-to-image models (four open-sourced and three closed-source) on their ability to create images for accessible communication.
- The resulting images are published as a dataset consisting of 2,217 images[2]. This dataset is relevant for text creators searching for a large and diverse image database as well as for AI researchers who want to train models or evaluation metrics for this task.
- We manually reviewed 560 images and annotated them by their closeness to the prompt, correctness, bias toward people with disabilities, and suitability for the target group. Our findings indicate that the quality of the generated images is highly dependent on the depicted content and the T2I models used and that even the best models cannot be utilized for a broader scale without further restrictions.
- We conducted a user study with seven people from the target group and report their opinions and preferences about the generated images.

2 Related work

Previous work has utilized images to enhance text accessibility, particularly in fields such as language learning. Geislinger et al. (2023) developed an iPad app for language learners that included an eye-tracking feature. When a reader focused on a word for a longer time, they retrieved a picture illustrating that word and showed it next to the text to improve the text's understanding. Similarly, Singh et al. (2023) and Schneider et al. (2021) focused on retrieving images for textbooks to improve the learning experience and make the books more appealing. To train and benchmark those retrieval models, Wang et al. (2022) published the MOTIF dataset. The dataset consists of sentences with complex words within the sentences and images that represent the context of the sentences. The complex word is highlighted within the images to give an easy-to-grasp explanation of those complex words. However, all of the previous methods only search for images in existing image databases and explore the capabilities of image retrieval methods. In contrast to this, our focus lies on the generation of new images and benchmarking models to create those images. A similar task was proposed by Kiesel et al. (2024), who tried to strengthen argumentation chains by providing images supporting the argument's premise. Nevertheless, to the best of our knowledge, this is the first work to explore image generation to automatically enhance accessible communication.

There exist multiple studies about the characteristics of image generation models, but none of them addresses their applicability to accessible communication. Mack et al. (2024) benchmarked different T2I models like DALL-E 2, Stable Diffusion, and Midjourney about how they depict disabilities. Even though the prompts described different forms of disabilities, the models mostly depicted disabled people as sitting in wheelchairs. The findings were repeated in the study from Tevissen (2024). The author investigated the latest Stable Diffusion checkpoints, SDXL and Stable Diffusion 3, DALL-E 3, and Midjourney. Again, people with disabilities were depicted very stereotypically: as old and sad people sitting in wheelchairs.

In our study, we include people from the target group and also report their perspectives on image generation models for accessible communication. Similar user studies were conducted in previous work. Huh et al. (2023) aim to make image generation as a process more accessible. They created a framework called GenAssist, in which blind and low-vision creators can ask questions about the image to determine whether the image generation models followed their prompts or whether additional content was added. A user study with the target group proved that the tool made visual creations more accessible. Another target group study was conducted by James Edwards et al. (2021), who worked with people with disabilities and asked them how their disability should be depicted in generated images. They especially focused on disability descriptions and the best level of detail for these descriptions. Similarly, Das et al. (2024) worked together with image creators and screen reader users to evaluate images' alt texts from different perspectives. They report that manually created alt texts

[2]https://github.com/MiriUll/Image-Generation-for-Accessible-Communication

are often too subjective and that prompts for T2I models cannot be used as alt text alternatives.

3 Methodology

Our study investigates whether the latest T2I models can create images suitable for E2R texts. For this, we use an open-source database of images for German Easy language and try to recreate the images based on their title and descriptions. Most of the images in E2R image databases are cartoon images since they are often easier than photo-realistic images, and the readers don't get confused by actual people. Therefore, we only focus on the generation of cartoon images as well.

3.1 Reference dataset

Our target dataset is the publicly available Leichte Sprache image gallery[3] from the LAG Selbsthilfe von Menschen mit Behinderungen und chronischen Erkrankungen Rheinland-Pfalz e.V. (State working group for self-help for people with disabilities and chronic illnesses Rhineland-Palatinate, Germany), a state-level organization uniting self-help associations and groups of individuals with disabilities or chronic illnesses and their relatives. It offers 413 images within 16 categories drawn by the artist Juliane Kriegereit[4]. The images were created for E2R texts and reviewed by the target group. An example image is shown in Figure 2. The images' license is very permissive to enable content creators to illustrate their texts. The categories are targeted to people with disabilities and cover areas like assisting technologies, diseases, and body parts. Each picture comes with a topic that is depicted and a description of the image's contents.

For our experiments, we randomly selected five images per category, yielding a dataset of $16 \times 5 = 80$ reference images in total. We translated the image titles and descriptions into English using ChatGPT (OpenAI et al., 2024) since some image generation models only work with English prompts.

3.2 Text2Image models

Our model selection featured a mix of open and closed-source models, SOTA and older models, as well as models of various sizes, culminating in a comprehensive evaluation of seven models in total. An overview of the models can be found in Table 3 in the Appendix.

[3] https://www.lag-sb-rlp.de/projekte/bildergalerie-leichte-sprache

[4] JSCHKA Kommunikationsdesign | www.jschka.de

Figure 2: Example image for the word "Inclusion" from the Leichte Sprache image gallery. The image description is "A group of very different people with and without disabilities is sitting at a table and eating together." © JSCHKA Kommunikationsdesign | www.jschka.de

We constructed the model prompts as "Cartoon picture of {title} - {description}" where we filled the placeholders with the values from the dataset and used the same prompts for all models.

For the open-sourced models, we utilized various versions of Stable Diffusion (Rombach et al., 2022) and Würstchen (Pernias et al., 2024). Stable Diffusion v1.4, v2.1 base, and v3 were employed to generate 512x512 pixel images. For SD3, we used the default parameters optimized for the output quality: *num_inference_steps* was configured to 28, defining the number of denoising steps the model takes during image generation. A higher number of inference steps generally leads to finer details and improved image quality. Additionally, the *guidance_scale* was set to 7.0, indicating the strength of the conditioning on the input text prompt. A higher guidance scale helps produce images that are more closely aligned with the given text descriptions, ensuring the semantic accuracy of the generated images.

Würstchen (Pernias et al., 2024) is another diffusion model where the text-conditional component functions within a significantly compressed latent space of images, attaining a 42x spatial compression. This enables the model to be much more time- and memory-efficient, significantly reducing training and inference time. Würstchen was used to produce higher-resolution images at 1024x1024 pixels, using a *prior_guidance_scale* set to 4.0, which similarly influences the model's adherence to the textual input.

For the closed-sourced model we focused on DALL-E-3 (Ramesh et al., 2021), Midjourney [5], and Artbreeder [6]. We accessed DALL-E-3 through the Bing Image Creator by Microsoft [7], which Microsoft states is powered by an advanced version of the DALL-E model. We used the free version, which allows 15 prompts per day. For Artbreeder, we use the Composer model, which is a GAN architecture (Goodfellow et al., 2020) incorporating elements of BigGAN (Brock et al., 2019) and StyleGAN (Karras et al., 2021).

3.3 Evaluation

We evaluated our generated images on different aspects, which include the closeness to the reference images, how well the models follow the image description in the prompt, and the image correctness.

The most popular automatic evaluation metric to measure the quality of a generated image is the Inception Score (Salimans et al., 2016). However, it compares the generated images against photo-realistic reference images from the CIFAR-10 dataset that are limited in the items they depict. Hence, the inception score is not suitable for our cartoon-style images (Proven-Bessel et al., 2021; Barratt and Sharma, 2018). To automatically assess the quality of our generated images, we used the Fréchet Inception Distance (FID). In contrast to the inception score, FID compares the generated images against a set of user-selected reference images. It estimates the distributions of the reference and generated image sets and reports the distance between the two distributions. Therefore, a lower FID score indicates better matches with the reference images and, thus, a better overall image quality. For our experiments, we used the FID implementation by PyTorch Lightning[8].

The second aspect of our evaluation is how well the generated images follow the image descriptions. For this, we evaluate two different metrics. The first metric is Contrastive Language-Image Pre-training (CLIP), which is trained to determine if an image and a text are paired together (Radford et al., 2021). It encodes the images and texts into a joint embedding space and selects the most probable pairs among them. For our experiments, we use the pre-trained CLIP ViT-L/14@336px model that achieves the highest accuracies according to the authors (Figure 10 in Radford et al. (2021)).

Our third metric, TIFA (Hu et al., 2023), also evaluates the fit between an image and its description, similar to the CLIP score, but chooses a different approach: visual question answering. For this, Hu et al. (2023) created a three-step pipeline: First, an LLM creates single-choice, multiple-choice, and free-form questions and their answers from the image descriptions. Each question is categorized by the elements it is asking for, e.g., color or location, and the number of questions and the element types vary among the different images. Then, a second question-answering model tries to answer the questions based on the image descriptions. Only questions that receive the same answers from both systems are kept for visual evaluation. Finally, a visual question-answering model answers the questions by looking at the images. The image-based accuracy of the answers indicates how faithful the image is to the image description. TIFA incorporates the accuracy metric, and thus, the scores range between 0 and 1. The authors show that TIFA has a much higher correlation with human judgments than previous metrics like CLIP (Hessel et al., 2021).

For our study, we use the pre-trained checkpoints for the different parts of the pipeline. For the question generation, we use the author's fine-tuned Llama2 (Touvron et al., 2023) model. For the question filtering, we use a UnifiedQA (Khashabi et al., 2020) model. The set of questions was only created once per image prompt and then used for all model evaluations. With this, we reduce biases in the scores that could come from non-determinism in the question generation or filtering models. Finally, for the visual question-answering, the authors compared different models. We selected the model with the highest correlation with human judgment, according to the authors, which is mPLUG-large (Li et al., 2022).

4 Results

To obtain a diverse image collection, we created up to four images per model an prompt. We investigate seven different models, and thus, expected to generate $80 \times 4 \times 7 = 2,240$ images. How-

[5]`https://www.midjourney.com/` Last accessed: Jul 2024

[6]`https://www.artbreeder.com/` Last accessed: Jul 2024

[7]`https://www.bing.com/images/create` Last accessed: Jul 2024

[8]`https://lightning.ai/docs/torchmetrics/stable/image/frechet_inception_distance.html`

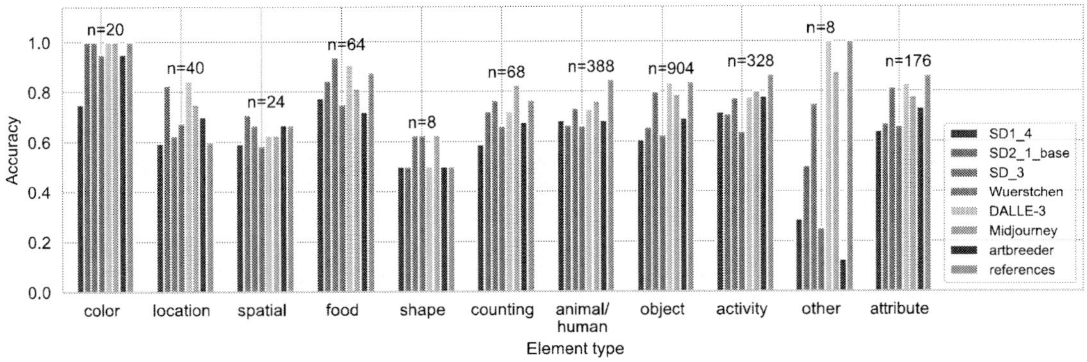

Figure 3: TIFA accuracies for different element types targeted by the TIFA questions. The performance of the models depends on the content that they have to depict. Images with all black content were filtered.

ever, we only obtained 2,217 images in total. For some descriptions, Copilot's DALL-E interface returned less than four images, resulting in only 297 instead of 320 images from DALL-E. In addition, Stable Diffusion 1 and DALL-E marked some of our image descriptions as offensive and blocked the input. For Stable Diffusion, this resulted in images that were all black. We followed this approach and added four black images for each of the five blocked inputs for DALL-E as well. This results in 51 images that are blackened.

4.1 Automatic evaluation

To further assess our generated images, we calculated metric scores as shown in Table 1. The best FID scores are achieved by Stable Diffusion 3 and Midjourney. This indicates that their style of images comes closest to the style of the reference image and that the images have similar features.

Model	FID↓	CLIP↑	TIFA↑
SD1_4	1.49	0.22	0.58
SD2_1_base	1.37	0.24	0.68
SD_3	**0.89**	**0.27**	**0.78**
Würstchen	0.90	0.24	0.65
DALL-E-3	1.26	**0.26**	0.74
Midjourney	**0.90**	**0.26**	**0.78**
Artbreeder	1.52	0.25	0.70
References	-	0.27	0.84

Table 1: Macro-averaged automatic evaluation scores to evaluate the images' distribution compared to the references (FID) and their closeness to the prompts (CLIP and TIFA). Stable Diffusion 3, DALL-E-3, and Midjourney come closest to the human-created reference images.

The CLIP and TIFA metrics evaluate how well the images align with the image descriptions. These metrics don't rely on the reference images, and hence, we calculated the scores on the references as well. We manually set the scores to 0 for all-black images with blocked contents and ignored one image title in the CLIP evaluation whose prompt was too long for the CLIP model. For both metrics, Stable Diffusion 3 has the highest scores, performing on par with the references according to the CLIP score. The other open-source models fall far behind in terms of automatic scores. For the closed-source models, Midjourney performs best, closely followed by DALL-E-3. However, none of the models can match the TIFA accuracies of the reference images. Interestingly, even the human-created images don't achieve perfect accuracy. Yet, this could be due to the shortcomings of the models in the TIFA pipeline.

The TIFA score is based on visual question answering, and the questions are categorized into the different elements that are evaluated. To dig deeper into the strengths and weaknesses of the T2I models, Figure 3 shows the models' TIFA accuracies per element type. Most of the questions are targeted toward animals or humans, activities, and especially the objects depicted. The reference images (grey bars) outperform the image generation models, especially for animals/humans, activities, and attributes. This aligns with our assumption that body parts and movements are the hardest aspects for the models to generate. In contrast, almost all models outperform the reference images in terms of location and shape, and Stable Diffusion, as well as DALL-E, outperforms the references in the food category.

Model	Prompt coherence↑	Correctness↑	Bias↓	Suitability↑
SD1_4	0.48 (± 0.80)	0.19 (± 0.45)	**0.00** (± 0.00)	0.06 (± 0.29)
SD2_1_base	0.50 (± 0.75)	0.16 (± 0.51)	**0.00** (± 0.00)	0.06 (± 0.29)
SD_3	**1.48** (± 0.98)	**0.90** (± 0.94)	0.14 (± 0.61)	**0.51** (± 0.83)
Würstchen	0.76 (± 0.82)	0.46 (± 0.84)	**0.00** (± 0.00)	0.20 (± 0.51)
DALL-E-3	**2.23** (± 0.91)	**2.19** (± 0.96)	0.21 (± 0.74)	**1.85** (± 1.12)
Midjourney	2.06 (± 0.88)	1.99 (± 0.88)	0.09 (± 0.48)	1.20 (± 1.11)
Artbreeder	1.25 (± 0.88)	1.05 (± 0.99)	**0.01** (± 0.11)	0.39 (± 0.68)

Table 2: Results from our human evaluation. The scores range from 0-3 and are averaged across all generated images. SD_3 and DALL-E created the most accurate and most suitable images.

4.2 Human evaluation

While TIFA scores have a high correlation with human judgments (Hu et al., 2023), automatic metrics can't cover all evaluation aspects. Especially for the overall correctness and simplicity of the images, there is currently no metric available. Therefore, we added a human evaluation of our generated images. For this, we asked an expert for German Easy language (one of the authors) to manually review and rate the images. Images are an essential part of German Easy language (DIN-Normenausschuss Ergonomie, 2023), and many Easy language courses also address criteria for selecting appropriate images. To reduce the overall workload, we selected one image per model and title, resulting in a dataset of 560 images. For each combination, we selected the image with the highest TIFA score. If two or more images shared the highest score, we sampled an image from among them. The images were evaluated on four different scales by asking these questions:

- *Does the image follow the prompt?*: This question checks for missing or additional content. We only focused on relevant content and ignored aspects that did not affect the meaning of the image (e.g., the prompt describing a group of nine people, but the model only drew seven).

- *Is the image correct?*: This question evaluates if the depicted content aligns with world knowledge, e.g., that people don't have three arms.

- *Does the image exhibit a bias towards people with disabilities?*: This question is targeted towards the findings of previous work (Mack et al., 2024; Tevissen, 2024) and evaluates whether the models tend to show people with disabilities as old or unhappy, even if the prompt does not define that.

- *Is the image suitable for the target group?*: For the target group, it is important that the images are not overloaded with details, text, or colors and that they align with situations familiar to the target group. These criteria are in line with the DIN SPEC for German Easy language (DIN-Normenausschuss Ergonomie, 2023). In addition, this question checks whether the image is helpful to understand the original concept.

The human annotator could choose between four possible answers to the questions: no/indeterminable, partly, mostly, and yes. We mapped these answers to a numerical scale between 0 (answer no) and 3 (answer yes). The images were blinded, i.e., we only showed the annotator the images and the descriptions but not the name of the model that generated the image.

Table 2 shows the averaged scores from the human evaluation. While Stable Diffusion 3 outperformed the closed-source models in the automatic evaluation, it can not hold up to the expectation in the human evaluation, receiving significantly worse scores across all scales. Still, it is by far the best open-source model. The bad scores for the other open-source models are mostly due to unclear and indeterminable content. Remarkably, these open-source models show the least biases. However, this is an artifact from our evaluation setup: If the image does not show any depictable content, then it also can't show biases toward people with disabilities.

During our manual review, we made additional observations. Examples of them are depicted in Figure 4. The models sometimes hallucinate additional details. For example, one of the prompts is "Cartoon picture of Security - Depicted are a

(a) Cartoon picture of **Security** - Depicted are a woman and a man lovingly embracing a child.
Created by SD3

(b) Cartoon picture of **Security** - Depicted are a woman and a man lovingly embracing a child.
Created by DALL-E-3

(c) Cartoon picture of **Fear** - A woman covers her mouth with both hands. Her eyes and mouth are wide open. Sweat runs down her forehead.
Created by SD3

(d) Cartoon picture of **Refusal of Physical Contact** - A woman tries to hug a girl. The girl looks away and resists.
Created by Midjourney

Figure 4: Example prompts and generated images.

woman and a man lovingly embracing a child.". Many models draw a policeman or officer, even though the prompt does not describe any (see Figure 4a). This indicates that the models have an inherent interpretation of world knowledge and, thus, associate security with police (Fu et al., 2024).

The biggest issues with the generated images arise with body parts and human motions. Examples are presented in Figures 4a, 4c and 4d where body parts such as arms or legs are missing, or too many fingers were added. Another issue is that the models don't pay enough attention to small details, and thus, important aspects are missing. For example, for the prompt "Cartoon picture of Refusal of Eye Contact - A woman stands directly in front of a man and speaks to him. The man has his arms crossed in front of his chest. He does not look at her.", all models created two people standing in front of one another, but no model could depict the refusal of eye contact properly. This could also be an issue with input token limits, i.e., that this important information was truncated. In addition, missing or misinterpreted details can change the meaning of the image. The images in Figures 4c and 4d should show the emotions of fear and the refusal of physical contact. However, in both pictures, the people look rather angry and as if they would fight one another. Especially for people struggling with reading emotion from human expressions, this could evoke wrong associations. Therefore, such images are not suitable for the target group without further restrictions.

As indicated by the low bias scores in Table 2, the models exhibit hardly any bias toward people with disabilities. The biases that we find are mostly related to hearing or vision impairments, where models tend to add an eye fold to visualize that a person is blind or draw incorrect hearing aids that look more like headsets. None of the models depicted people with disabilities as especially unhappy, except if the prompt especially stated it. On the contrary, most of them were smiling and happy.

The model with the best human evaluation scores is by far DALL-E-3. It was able to create correct images even for difficult body positions like in Yoga or hugging. In addition, the images were especially inclusive in terms of diversity: Pictures with multiple people often depicted people of color or people with glasses as parts of the groups. An example is Figure 4b, where the woman wears a head scarf, a garment only seen in minority groups in Western countries. These features were not described in the image prompts but added by the model and its world knowledge.

4.3 Feedback from the target group

In line with the UN inclusion slogan "Nothing about us without us!" (Harpur and Stein, 2017) and in accordance with the DIN SPEC recommendation that the target group should review all content, we wanted to hear the opinion about the images from the target group. Therefore, we invited seven people with different disabilities (physical, mental, and combinations of both) between the ages of 21 and 42 for a workshop at the university. They were accompanied by their living assistants and two German Easy language experts. The study participants received a compensation of 32,50€ for their effort. We conducted two types of studies: comparative voting and a free-form discussion. Direct quotes

(a) Cafeteria Created by SD1 | (b) Brainstorming Created by DALL-E-3 | (c) Empathy Created by DALL-E-3 | (d) Self-love Created by DALL-E-3

Figure 5: Term-guessing images. The images were shown to the target group participants, and they had to guess the title or describe what the word could mean if they didn't know it.

from the participants are formatted in italic.

For the first part, we filtered the titles from the image dataset, where at least three models created suitable or mostly suitable images. Then, we selected seven titles from them. We presented all images with the same title at the same time but in a randomized order. The participants were asked to vote for all images they liked. We allowed multiple selections to account for equally good images. We used the voting platform Mentimeter[9] where every participant can participate on their smartphones and submit their votes anonymously. With this, we could collect their opinions independently without being influenced by other participants. Some participants were supported by their living assistants when interacting with the smartphones. The images and the participants' votes are presented in Table 4 in the Appendix.

For most of the images, DALL-E received the most votes, often even more than the reference images. In general, colorful images with few additional or decorative content were preferred. Some images seemed a bit abstract, e.g., the fruit depicted for the bowl of vitamins had a few mistakes or weird coloring. Nevertheless, the participants showed great creativity when naming the fruits. Therefore, if the context is clear, small mistakes don't bother too much. This also came clear when participants explained why they chose certain images for the bedroom: they chose the ones that looked the most "*cozy*". In contrast, some toothbrushes in the hygiene product images looked unrealistic, not suitable for the teeth, or were simply wrong. Multiple participants were distracted by these mistakes and started a discussion about what was wrong with the toothbrushes and how it would hurt to actually use them.

[9] https://www.mentimeter.com/

The second part of the workshop was more open to direct feedback. We presented four different images, one from Stable Diffusion 1 and three from DALL-E-3, and the participants should guess the depicted content. The images and their titles are shown in Figure 5. We chose some complex terms on purpose to assess whether the images could help with understanding them. For example, the word "Brainstorming" was unfamiliar to half of the participants. Nevertheless, they could describe and explain the word as "*people are sitting together and collect ideas*" only based on the image. This shows that the selected images are not only suitable for illustrating texts, but they also fulfill their purpose of explaining complex terms with ease.

In addition to the term guessing of the second part, the participants were also invited to express their thoughts and opinions about the presented images. We try to summarize them in the following:

- Participants did not like black&white-only images because "*it makes you depressed*".
- Different illustrations of the same objects (e.g., the light bulbs in the brainstorming image) were confusing, and participants tried to find a reason for the differences, even if there was no reason for that.
- The images should show accessible situations, i.e., suitable for people using wheelchairs or hearing aids. We had a discussion about whether the counter in SD1's cafeteria was accessible for wheelchairs and whether people would need help to reach all the offers. For this discussion, the blurry and abstract style of the image was of minor relevance.
- In the DALL-E-3 image for yoga (Table 4 in Appendix), the person using the wheelchair is very old. When the two participants who

used a wheelchair were asked whether they felt discriminated by this, they answered "*No, why should I? Even old people can do yoga!*"

5 Conclusion

In this paper, we have explored whether text-to-image models can be utilized to create illustrations for easy-to-read texts. For this, we evaluated the generated images in large-scale human studies, including seven participants from the target group. Closed-source models like DALL-E-3 and Midjourney and the open-source Stable Diffusion 3 have shown impressive performance in creating these images, sometimes creating even more favorable images than the gold-standard references. However, their performance highly depends on the depicted content, and the models struggle with difficult postures and specific body parts especially. Therefore, they cannot be used without human oversight or multiple iterations of image description optimization. In addition, the best-performing models are closed-source or very large in parameter size, meaning that text creators will still have to pay for their images. Since text creators will use the models, they have human expert oversight, and thus, every generated image will be reviewed, and erroneous images can be filtered before being shown to the target group. Finally, we believe that T2I models are especially suited for accessible communication due to their fast availability and options for tailored, customizable, and copyright-free content.

In future research, we would like to get rid of the intermediate step of explicit image descriptions and hope to see models that can create the images directly from the text paragraph. In addition, we would like to investigate their compliance with prompts in German and other non-English languages and investigate conditioning the images on the reference images during generation.

Limitations and ethical considerations

Our work presents a quite extensive comparison of different T2I images. While we did our best to include as many models with different architectures, sizes, and availabilities, we can only test the models published by the time of writing this paper. The current developments and improvements in AI are rapid, and thus, there may be newer and better models soon that we couldn't include in our study.

We tried to design this study as participatory as possible and included seven people from the target group in our human evaluation. They received 32,50€ to compensate for their effort. Nevertheless, the feedback session was moderated, and the authors pre-selected the images. A target group evaluation of all images would be infeasible and not of any help to the target group. Still, our image selection and moderation introduced a bias from the authors on them that we can not neglect. In addition, the disabilities and needs of the target group are very diverse and cannot be represented by only seven people. Nevertheless, we try to make their opinions be heard and invite all researchers in the area of accessible communication to work together with the target group.

Finally, we are aware that generative AI, whether it generates text, images, or any other modality, is being criticized for threatening jobs and content quality. The goal of our work is in no way to replace humans in the process of creating accessible content. However, we believe that the benefits of the short-time availability of simplified texts and images are important to overcome information barriers, especially on the internet. Studies such as ours can be of great help to further improve the quality of those models and to align their objectives with what is actually needed by the target group. In the end, our investigations show that the T2I models are far from being perfect and still need careful human oversight. Especially in terms of image evaluation, we could not find an automatic metric that was satisfactory in alignment with our judgment.

Lay Summary

Creating texts that are easy to read and understand is important for people with disabilities, learning difficulties, or those who have trouble with reading. These easy-to-read (E2R) texts often include pictures to help explain the information. However, it can be hard to find images that fit the specific needs of each text. Hiring artists to make customized images can be expensive, and existing image databases don't allow for easy changes to match the content of the text.

Our study looks at whether we can use artificial intelligence (AI) to generate these images quickly and cheaply. We tested seven different AI tools, called text-to-image models, which create pictures based on written descriptions. Some of these tools are open to the public, while others are not. We wanted to see if these AI-generated images could be a good solution for E2R creators.

We evaluated over 2,000 images created by these models and manually reviewed 560 of them. During the review, we looked at how well the images matched the description, if they were accurate, if they had any bias against people with disabilities, and if they were useful for the target group. Our results show that while some models produced high-quality images, none of them are ready to be used on a large scale without human oversight.

We also conducted a user study with seven people from the E2R target group to gather feedback on how well the images met their needs. It is important to include the target group and their opinions and preferences when doing research. The feedback was helpful in identifying areas where the AI models worked well and where they fell short.

Our research is an important first step toward making it easier and more affordable to create images that help make information more accessible. However, more improvements are needed before these AI tools can fully replace human involvement in creating custom images for E2R texts.

Acknowledgments

The images were provided by the Landesarbeitsgemeinschaft Selbsthilfe von Menschen mit Behinderungen und chronischen Erkrankungen Rheinland-Pfalz e.V. with the kind support of AOK Rheinland-Pfalz/Saarland. We thank them for their assistance that made our research possible in the first place!
In addition, we thank the *FÜP - FortSchritt Übersetzungs- & Prüfbüro für Leichte Sprache* (office for German Easy language translation and evaluation) by the FortSchritt Verein zur Verbreitung der Konduktiven Förderung e.V.[10] and especially their review group for the insightful feedback.
This research has been funded by the German Federal Ministry of Education and Research (BMBF) through grant 01IS23069 Software Campus 3.0 (Technical University of Munich) as part of the Software Campus project "LIANA".
This paper is based on a joined work in the context of Tringa Sylaj's master's thesis (Tringa Sylaj, 2024).

[10]`https://www.fortschritt-bayern.de/angebote/leichte-sprache`

References

Miriam Anschütz, Joshua Oehms, Thomas Wimmer, Bartłomiej Jezierski, and Georg Groh. 2023. Language models for German text simplification: Overcoming parallel data scarcity through style-specific pre-training. In *Findings of the Association for Computational Linguistics: ACL 2023*, pages 1147–1158, Toronto, Canada. Association for Computational Linguistics.

Shane Barratt and Rishi Sharma. 2018. A note on the inception score. *Preprint*, arXiv:1801.01973.

Andrew Brock, Jeff Donahue, and Karen Simonyan. 2019. Large scale GAN training for high fidelity natural image synthesis. In *International Conference on Learning Representations*.

Maitraye Das, Alexander J. Fiannaca, Meredith Ringel Morris, Shaun K. Kane, and Cynthia L. Bennett. 2024. From provenance to aberrations: Image creator and screen reader user perspectives on alt text for ai-generated images. In *Proceedings of the CHI Conference on Human Factors in Computing Systems*, CHI '24, New York, NY, USA. Association for Computing Machinery.

DIN-Normenausschuss Ergonomie. 2023. Empfehlungen für Deutsche Leichte Sprache (DIN SPEC 33429).

Xingyu Fu, Muyu He, Yujie Lu, William Yang Wang, and Dan Roth. 2024. Commonsense-t2i challenge: Can text-to-image generation models understand commonsense? In *First Conference on Language Modeling*.

Robert Geislinger, Ali Ebrahimi Pourasad, Deniz Gül, Daniel Djahangir, Seid Muhie Yimam, Steffen Remus, and Chris Biemann. 2023. Multi-modal learning application – support language learners with NLP techniques and eye-tracking. In *Proceedings of the 1st Workshop on Linguistic Insights from and for Multimodal Language Processing*, pages 6–11, Ingolstadt, Germany. Association for Computational Linguistics.

Ian Goodfellow, Jean Pouget-Abadie, Mehdi Mirza, Bing Xu, David Warde-Farley, Sherjil Ozair, Aaron Courville, and Yoshua Bengio. 2020. Generative adversarial networks. *Commun. ACM*, 63(11):139–144.

Paul Harpur and Michael Ashley Stein. 2017. The convention on the rights of persons with disabilities as a global tipping point for the participation of persons with disabilities. In *Oxford Research Encyclopedia of Politics*.

Jack Hessel, Ari Holtzman, Maxwell Forbes, Ronan Le Bras, and Yejin Choi. 2021. CLIPScore: A reference-free evaluation metric for image captioning. In *Proceedings of the 2021 Conference on Empirical Methods in Natural Language Processing*, pages 7514–7528, Online and Punta Cana, Dominican Republic. Association for Computational Linguistics.

Y. Hu, B. Liu, J. Kasai, Y. Wang, M. Ostendorf, R. Krishna, and N. A. Smith. 2023. Tifa: Accurate and interpretable text-to-image faithfulness evaluation with question answering. In *2023 IEEE/CVF International Conference on Computer Vision (ICCV)*, pages 20349–20360, Los Alamitos, CA, USA. IEEE Computer Society.

Mina Huh, Yi-Hao Peng, and Amy Pavel. 2023. Genassist: Making image generation accessible. In *Proceedings of the 36th Annual ACM Symposium on User Interface Software and Technology*, UIST '23, New York, NY, USA. Association for Computing Machinery.

Emory James Edwards, Kyle Lewis Polster, Isabel Tuason, Emily Blank, Michael Gilbert, and Stacy Branham. 2021. "that's in the eye of the beholder": Layers of interpretation in image descriptions for fictional representations of people with disabilities. In *Proceedings of the 23rd International ACM SIGACCESS Conference on Computers and Accessibility*, ASSETS '21, New York, NY, USA. Association for Computing Machinery.

Tero Karras, Samuli Laine, and Timo Aila. 2021. A style-based generator architecture for generative adversarial networks. *IEEE Trans. Pattern Anal. Mach. Intell.*, 43(12):4217–4228.

Daniel Khashabi, Sewon Min, Tushar Khot, Ashish Sabharwal, Oyvind Tafjord, Peter Clark, and Hannaneh Hajishirzi. 2020. UNIFIEDQA: Crossing format boundaries with a single QA system. In *Findings of the Association for Computational Linguistics: EMNLP 2020*, pages 1896–1907, Online. Association for Computational Linguistics.

Johannes Kiesel, Çağrı Çöltekin, Maximilian Heinrich, Maik Fröbe, Milad Alshomary, Bertrand De Longueville, Tomaž Erjavec, Nicolas Handke, Matyáš Kopp, Nikola Ljubešić, Katja Meden, Nailia Mirzakhmedova, Vaidas Morkevičius, Theresa Reitis-Münstermann, Mario Scharfbillig, Nicolas Stefanovitch, Henning Wachsmuth, Martin Potthast, and Benno Stein. 2024. Overview of Touché 2024: Argumentation Systems. In *Experimental IR Meets Multilinguality, Multimodality, and Interaction. 15th International Conference of the CLEF Association (CLEF 2024)*, volume 14959 of *Lecture Notes in Computer Science*, pages 308–332, Berlin Heidelberg New York. Springer.

Chenliang Li, Haiyang Xu, Junfeng Tian, Wei Wang, Ming Yan, Bin Bi, Jiabo Ye, He Chen, Guohai Xu, Zheng Cao, Ji Zhang, Songfang Huang, Fei Huang, Jingren Zhou, and Luo Si. 2022. mPLUG: Effective and efficient vision-language learning by cross-modal skip-connections. In *Proceedings of the 2022 Conference on Empirical Methods in Natural Language Processing*, pages 7241–7259, Abu Dhabi, United Arab Emirates. Association for Computational Linguistics.

Kelly Avery Mack, Rida Qadri, Remi Denton, Shaun K. Kane, and Cynthia L. Bennett. 2024. "they only care to show us the wheelchair": disability representation in text-to-image ai models. In *Proceedings of the CHI Conference on Human Factors in Computing Systems*, CHI '24, New York, NY, USA. Association for Computing Machinery.

Margot Madina, Itziar Gonzalez-Dios, and Melanie Siegel. 2023. Easy-to-read language resources and tools for three european languages. In *Proceedings of the 16th International Conference on PErvasive Technologies Related to Assistive Environments*, PETRA '23, page 693–699, New York, NY, USA. Association for Computing Machinery.

OpenAI, Josh Achiam, Steven Adler, Sandhini Agarwal, Lama Ahmad, Ilge Akkaya, Florencia Leoni Aleman, Diogo Almeida, Janko Altenschmidt, Sam Altman, Shyamal Anadkat, Red Avila, Igor Babuschkin, Suchir Balaji, Valerie Balcom, Paul Baltescu, Haiming Bao, Mohammad Bavarian, Jeff Belgum, Irwan Bello, Jake Berdine, Gabriel Bernadett-Shapiro, Christopher Berner, Lenny Bogdonoff, and et al. 2024. Gpt-4 technical report. *Preprint*, arXiv:2303.08774.

Pablo Pernias, Dominic Rampas, Mats Leon Richter, Christopher Pal, and Marc Aubreville. 2024. Würstchen: An efficient architecture for large-scale text-to-image diffusion models. In *The Twelfth International Conference on Learning Representations*.

Ben Proven-Bessel, Zilong Zhao, and Lydia Chen. 2021. Comicgan: Text-to-comic generative adversarial network. *Preprint*, arXiv:2109.09120.

Alec Radford, Jong Wook Kim, Chris Hallacy, Aditya Ramesh, Gabriel Goh, Sandhini Agarwal, Girish Sastry, Amanda Askell, Pamela Mishkin, Jack Clark, Gretchen Krueger, and Ilya Sutskever. 2021. Learning transferable visual models from natural language supervision. In *Proceedings of the 38th International Conference on Machine Learning*, volume 139 of *Proceedings of Machine Learning Research*, pages 8748–8763. PMLR.

Aditya Ramesh, Mikhail Pavlov, Gabriel Goh, Scott Gray, Chelsea Voss, Alec Radford, Mark Chen, and Ilya Sutskever. 2021. Zero-shot text-to-image generation. In *Proceedings of the 38th International Conference on Machine Learning*, volume 139 of *Proceedings of Machine Learning Research*, pages 8821–8831. PMLR.

Robin Rombach, Andreas Blattmann, Dominik Lorenz, Patrick Esser, and Björn Ommer. 2022. High-resolution image synthesis with latent diffusion models. In *Proceedings of the IEEE/CVF Conference on Computer Vision and Pattern Recognition (CVPR)*, pages 10684–10695.

Tim Salimans, Ian Goodfellow, Wojciech Zaremba, Vicki Cheung, Alec Radford, Xi Chen, and Xi Chen. 2016. Improved techniques for training gans. In *Advances in Neural Information Processing Systems*, volume 29. Curran Associates, Inc.

Florian Schneider, Özge Alaçam, Xintong Wang, and Chris Biemann. 2021. Towards multi-modal text-image retrieval to improve human reading. In *Proceedings of the 2021 Conference of the North American Chapter of the Association for Computational Linguistics: Student Research Workshop*, Online. Association for Computational Linguistics.

Thorben Schomacker, Michael Gille, Marina Tropmann-Frick, and Jörg von der Hülls. 2023. Data and approaches for German text simplification – towards an accessibility-enhanced communication. In *Proceedings of the 19th Conference on Natural Language Processing (KONVENS 2023)*, pages 63–68, Ingolstadt, Germany. Association for Computational Lingustics.

Janvijay Singh, Vilém Zouhar, and Mrinmaya Sachan. 2023. Enhancing textbooks with visuals from the web for improved learning. In *Proceedings of the 2023 Conference on Empirical Methods in Natural Language Processing*, pages 11931–11944, Singapore. Association for Computational Linguistics.

Regina Stodden, Omar Momen, and Laura Kallmeyer. 2023. DEplain: A German parallel corpus with intralingual translations into plain language for sentence and document simplification. In *Proceedings of the 61st Annual Meeting of the Association for Computational Linguistics (Volume 1: Long Papers)*, pages 16441–16463, Toronto, Canada. Association for Computational Linguistics.

Yannis Tevissen. 2024. Disability representations: Finding biases in automatic image generation. *Preprint*, arXiv:2406.14993.

Hugo Touvron, Louis Martin, Kevin Stone, Peter Albert, Amjad Almahairi, Yasmine Babaei, Nikolay Bashlykov, Soumya Batra, Prajjwal Bhargava, Shruti Bhosale, Dan Bikel, Lukas Blecher, Cristian Canton Ferrer, Moya Chen, Guillem Cucurull, David Esiobu, Jude Fernandes, Jeremy Fu, Wenyin Fu, Brian Fuller, Cynthia Gao, Vedanuj Goswami, Naman Goyal, Anthony Hartshorn, Saghar Hosseini, Rui Hou, Hakan Inan, Marcin Kardas, Viktor Kerkez, Madian Khabsa, Isabel Kloumann, Artem Korenev, Punit Singh Koura, Marie-Anne Lachaux, Thibaut Lavril, Jenya Lee, Diana Liskovich, Yinghai Lu, Yuning Mao, Xavier Martinet, Todor Mihaylov, Pushkar Mishra, Igor Molybog, Yixin Nie, Andrew Poulton, Jeremy Reizenstein, Rashi Rungta, Kalyan Saladi, Alan Schelten, Ruan Silva, Eric Michael Smith, Ranjan Subramanian, Xiaoqing Ellen Tan, Binh Tang, Ross Taylor, Adina Williams, Jian Xiang Kuan, Puxin Xu, Zheng Yan, Iliyan Zarov, Yuchen Zhang, Angela Fan, Melanie Kambadur, Sharan Narang, Aurelien Rodriguez, Robert Stojnic, Sergey Edunov, and Thomas Scialom. 2023. Llama 2: Open foundation and fine-tuned chat models. *Preprint*, arXiv:2307.09288.

Tringa Sylaj. 2024. Image generation for accessible communication. Master's thesis, Technical University of Munich. Advised and supervised by Miriam Anschütz and Georg Groh.

Xintong Wang, Florian Schneider, Özge Alacam, Prateek Chaudhury, and Chris Biemann. 2022. MOTIF: Contextualized images for complex words to improve human reading. In *Proceedings of the Thirteenth Language Resources and Evaluation Conference*, pages 2468–2477, Marseille, France. European Language Resources Association.

A Appendix

Model	Prompt Limitation	Flagging Content	Resources Used
SD1_4	77 tokens	Black image	T4 GPU, 15GB RAM
SD2_1_base	77 tokens	Black image	T4 GPU, 15GB RAM
SD_3	77 tokens	Black image	L4 GPU, 24GB RAM
Würstchen	77 tokens	Black image	T4 GPU, 15GB RAM
DALL-E-3	380 characters	Not processed + warning	Free via Microsoft
Midjourney	None	N/A	\$10/month for $\approx$ 200 images
Artbreeder	$\sim$ 129 tokens	N/A	Free with multiple accounts

Table 3: Comparison of the different models we investigated: Limitations, content flagging, and resource usage

Model	Multi-family House	Bedroom	Vitamins	Poor Memory Performance	Hygiene Products	Yoga	Cafeteria
SD_3	3 	4 	4 	**6** 	-	1 	-
Wuerstchen	2 	-	3 	-	-	-	-
DALLE-3	**6** 	**6** 	4 	**6** 	4 	**2** 	**4** 
Midjourney	4 	5 	6 	**6** 	**5** 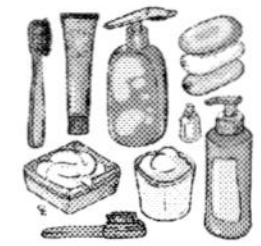	**2** 	**4** 
artbreeder	5 	1 	3 	-	4 	-	-
References	4 	3 	**7** 	5 	4 	**2** 	2 

Table 4: Number of votes from the target group during their review session. We only included images that the German Easy language expert deemed suitable for the target group. Thus, no images from Stable Diffusion 1 and 2 were shown.

Cochrane-auto: An Aligned Dataset for the Simplification of Biomedical Abstracts

Jan Bakker
University of Amsterdam
Amsterdam, The Netherlands
j.bakker@uva.nl

Jaap Kamps
University of Amsterdam
Amsterdam, The Netherlands
kamps@uva.nl

Abstract

The most reliable and up-to-date information on health questions is in the biomedical literature, but inaccessible due to the complex language full of jargon. Domain specific scientific text simplification holds the promise to make this literature accessible to a lay audience. Therefore, we create Cochrane-auto: a large corpus of pairs of aligned sentences, paragraphs, and abstracts from biomedical abstracts and lay summaries. Experiments demonstrate that a plan-guided simplification system trained on Cochrane-auto is able to outperform a strong baseline trained on unaligned abstracts and lay summaries. More generally, our freely available corpus complementing Newsela-auto and Wiki-auto facilitates text simplification research beyond the sentence-level and direct lexical and grammatical revisions.

1 Introduction

Biomedical research has the potential to directly impact people's decision-making with regards to health. However, most reliable and up-to-date sources in biomedicine contain complex language and assume a high degree of background knowledge, making them difficult to understand for the general public. Automatic text simplification approaches can be applied in an effort to make these sources more accessible. Yet, training neural models to simplify biomedical documents is a complex task which requires high quality training data.

To this end, Devaraj et al. (2021) introduced a corpus of paired (complex, simple) texts in English, derived from the Cochrane Database of Systematic Reviews. The CDSR comprises systematic reviews which are internationally recognized as the highest standard in evidence-based health care and which are accompanied by both technical abstracts and plain language summaries. Plain language summaries are written directly from the full reviews; they are not simplified versions of the abstracts.

Complex paragraph

Fifteen heterogeneous trials, involving 1022 adults with dorsally displaced and potentially or evidently unstable distal radial fractures, were included. While all trials compared external fixation versus plaster cast immobilisation, there was considerable variation especially in terms of patient characteristics and interventions. Methodological weaknesses among these trials included lack of allocation concealment and inadequate outcome assessment.

Simple paragraph

Fifteen trials, involving 1022 adults with potentially or evidently unstable fractures, were included. While all trials compared external fixation versus plaster cast immobilisation, there was considerable variation in their characteristics especially in terms of patient characteristics and the method of external fixation.

Figure 1: A complex-simple paragraph pair from Cochrane-auto.

Even so, the authors argued that portions of the lay summaries could be considered simplifications of analogous sections in the abstracts. Their corpus therefore consists of parallel technical abstracts and plain language summaries, both starting at the section describing studies and results. Nevertheless, the authors did not align the corpus at the sentence-level, and upon manual inspection, we find that roughly 29% of the simple sentences in their corpus cannot be aligned to one or more corresponding complex sentences based on its meaning. This of course limits the extent to which a large language model can benefit from training on the corpus.

In this paper, we leverage the neural alignment model proposed by Jiang et al. (2020) in order to automatically align the simple and complex sentences in the corpus. We then improve the quality of the corpus by deleting all simple sentences that are not aligned from the references. We filter out instances in which the resulting reference resembles a summarization rather than a simplification. Furthermore, we leverage the generated alignments in order to provide references not only for each complex document, but also for each sentence and

Proceedings of the Third Workshop on Text Simplification, Accessibility and Readability (TSAR 2024), pages 41–51
November 15, 2024 ©2024 Association for Computational Linguistics

paragraph within the document. Hence, we present Cochrane-auto: a large, high quality dataset for the simplification of biomedical abstracts at the document-, paragraph- and sentence-level. An example is shown in Figure 1.

We validate that Cochrane-auto is a valuable resource by training simplification systems on this dataset and evaluating them against a baseline trained on the original corpus. Our results demonstrate that the plan-guided simplification system from Cripwell et al. (2023b) is indeed able to outperform the baseline after training on our dataset.

The rest of this paper continues with related work (§2), the CDSR (§3), the Cochrane corpus (§4), our new Cochrane-auto corpus (§5), our experiments (§6), and ends with the conclusion (§7) and limitations (§8).

2 Related Work

This section describes the related work on biomedical text simplification and lay summarization.

Biomedical text simplification Our approach closely follows Devaraj et al. (2021), who introduced a dataset of parallel plain language summaries and technical abstracts from the Cochrane Database of Systematic Reviews. We describe their dataset in Section 4 below. Grabar and Cardon (2018) created the CLEAR corpus, which includes 13 manually aligned Cochrane abstracts and plain language summaries in French. Ermakova et al. (2022) introduced a pilot scientific text simplification corpus of aligned sentence pairs with manual simplifications by non-experts. This pilot data set contains 147 abstracts with 648 sentences, of which 25 abstracts and 179 sentences are from the biomedical domain. Attal et al. (2023) created a set of 750 medline abstracts containing 7,643 sentences paired with expert-created sentence-level plain language adaptations. This data set is used at the TREC 2024 Plain Language Adaptation of Biomedical Abstracts (PLABA) track.[1] These earlier biomedical text simplification data sets are immensely valuable, but limited in size and restricted to sentence-level simplifications, with less freedom than observed in real-world paragraph or document level plain English summaries.

Plain English summaries Several journals, in particular in the biomedical domain, have collected plain English summaries. These plain English summaries are provided by the original authors of the paper, with varying degrees of instruction. In particular for systematic reviews very detailed instructions exist. Whiting and Davenport (2023) in the Cochrane Handbook for Systematic Reviews of Diagnostic Test Accuracy, provide detailed instructions on plain language summaries. Systematic reviews follow very strict evidence based medicine rules, such as PRISMA 2020 (Page et al., 2021). The specific guidelines for writing Cochrane Plain Language Summaries were published in 2020.[2] Our Cochrane-auto dataset contains both lay summaries from before and after the introduction of detailed template and guidelines in 2020.

Lay summarization The lay summarization task was introduced at SDProc in 2020. Chandrasekaran et al. (2020) discuss the LaySumm task of the Scholarly Document Processing Workshop at EMNLP2020.[3] LaySumm provided 572 author-generated lay summaries from a multidisciplinary collection of journals together with their corresponding full text content and abstracts. Goldsack et al. (2022) create a PLOS and e-Life corpora containing full scientific articles paired with manually created lay summaries. There was a BioLaySumm Task 1 shared task, held at the BioNLP 2023 Workshop (Demner-Fushman et al., 2023).[4] This task uses similar PLOS/e-Life corpora for a lay summarization task. Recently, Pu et al. (2024) created another SciNews corpus for plain English summarization, based on crawling scientific articles discussed in popular science news web site Science X.[5]

Prior work focused on the summarization aspects of lay summarization, whereas our paper focuses on realligning the abstracts and lay summaries, to create matching documents, paragraphs, and sentence-pairs, in a way that replicates earlier text simplification corpora.

3 The CDSR

The Cochrane Database of Systematic Reviews[6] (CDSR) comprises systematic reviews of research in health care and health policy. A *systematic review* attempts to identify, appraise and synthesize

[1] https://bionlp.nlm.nih.gov/plaba2024/

[2] https://training.cochrane.org/handbook/current/chapter-iii-s2-supplementary-material

[3] https://sdproc.org/

[4] https://biolaysumm.org/

[5] https://sciencex.com/

[6] https://www.cochranelibrary.com/cdsr/reviews

all empirical evidence that is relevant to a specific research question. Cochrane reviews are internationally recognized as the highest standard in evidence-based health care. They are written according to a comprehensive set of guidelines.[7] Each review includes a technical abstract, which is targeted at healthcare decision makers, and a plain language summary, which should be understandable for a wide range of non-expert readers.

4 The Cochrane corpus

In this section, we first give a short description of the Cochrane corpus. Second, we present a limited analysis on a selection of its contents. Third, we introduce an updated version of the corpus.

Description Devaraj et al. (2021) observed that portions of the plain language summaries in the CDSR contain roughly the same content as analogous sections in the technical abstracts. This motivated them to compile a corpus of paired (complex, simple) texts in English, comprising parallel subsets of abstracts and lay summaries from the CDSR. Each subset contains the full text from the description of studies and results onward. Abstracts adhere to a standard format, and so each complex text in the corpus covers the *Main Results* and *Authors' Conclusions* sections of the technical abstract. Plain language summaries are structured heterogeneously. Therefore, the authors made use of substring matching to determine the approximate location of the first section, paragraph or sentence (depending on the structure) describing the studies and results. They defined everything in the lay summary from that point onward as the simple text.

Analysis We randomly select ten paired (complex, simple) texts from the corpus. Next, we manually align sentences between these pairs that are equivalent or partially equivalent in meaning. As a result, we obtain 79 alignments. Of the total of 98 simple sentences in the selected texts, 68 are aligned to at least one of the 139 complex sentences. Thus, 30 out of 98 simple sentences are not aligned. While 2 of them are elaborations, the remaining 28 contain information that is present in the full review but not in the complex text. This is largely because the plain language summaries are written directly from the full review, instead of being simplified versions of the technical abstracts, and partially because the complex texts are only subsets of these abstracts. Consequently, around 29% of the sentences in the simple reference texts cannot be generated from the complex source text. This of course limits the suitability of the corpus for directly training and evaluating simplification models.

Update We run the authors' code[8] to obtain an updated version of their corpus. This corpus is based on systematic reviews that were published in the CDSR up until March 14, 2024. We apply the same preprocessing, except for the filtering of texts with more than 1,024 tokens. The resulting corpus consists of 4,468 train, 558 validation and 559 test pairs. On average, the complex and simple texts consist of 17.1 and 12.5 sentences, respectively.

5 Cochrane-auto

In this section we describe i) our alignment model, ii) our alignment procedure, iii) our alignment results, iv) the preprocessing of the resulting dataset, and v) the labeling.

5.1 Alignment model

We make use of the neural CRF alignment model proposed by Jiang et al. (2020). When provided with a (complex, simple) text pair as input, this model automatically aligns each sentence in the simple text to either one or zero corresponding sentences in the complex text. In doing so, it leverages the similar order of sentences in parallel texts and utilizes a fine-tuned BERT model to capture the semantic similarity between sentence pairs. Aligned sentences should be equivalent or partially equivalent in meaning, and multiple simple sentences may be aligned to the same complex sentence.

The authors applied their model to two simplification corpora: Newsela (Xu et al., 2015), which comprises news articles that were manually rewritten at different levels of simplification, and an updated version of the Wikipedia corpus (Zhang and Lapata, 2017), which consists of paired articles from English Wikipedia and Simple English Wikipedia. More specifically, the authors first created Newsela-manual and Wiki-manual by manually aligning 50 article groups from Newsela and 500 article pairs from Wikipedia. Then they fine-tuned BERT (Devlin et al., 2019) and trained their alignment models on train splits of these datasets. Finally, they applied their trained models to the

[7] https://training.cochrane.org/handbook

[8] https://github.com/AshOlogn/Paragraph-level-Simplification-of-Medical-Texts

	TP	FP	FN	**F1**
$\text{BERT}_{finetune}$	52	32	27	63.8
CRF Aligner	53	6	26	76.8
+ merge	56	8	23	78.3

Table 1: Performance of sentence alignment methods on 10 annotated text pairs from the Cochrane corpus.

	Cochrane-auto	Newsela-auto	Wiki-auto
Domain	Biomedical	News	General
# Doc Pairs	5,585	18,820	138,095
# Sent Pairs	35,800	813,972	685,769

Table 2: Statistics for the automatically aligned Cochrane-auto, Newsela-auto and Wiki-auto datasets.

remaining data to create the automatically aligned Newsela-auto and Wiki-auto datasets.

5.2 Alignment procedure

We create Cochrane-auto by applying the sentence alignment model that was pretrained on Wiki-manual to the updated Cochrane corpus. More precisely, we utilize the neural CRF model that we trained on Wiki-manual ourselves by running the authors' code.[9] It employs the BERT model[10] which the authors fine-tuned on the same train set to capture semantic similarity. According to Jiang et al. (2020), their fine-tuned BERT models should be able to achieve competitive performance on other monolingual parallel data, and the performance boost of adding the neural CRF model is related to the structure of the articles. Our motivation for pretraining the alignment model on Wiki-manual, and not Newsela-manual, is that the Cochrane and Wikipedia corpora both contain (complex, simple) text pairs in which the simple text is no direct simplification of the complex text.

Wiki-auto and Newsela-auto were created by first aligning paragraphs and then aligning the sentences within those paragraphs. We can also divide the texts in the updated Cochrane corpus into paragraphs based on sections and newlines. However, the sentence-level alignments between these texts generally do not reside within paragraph pairs, since these texts can be structured in a different way. We therefore apply our alignment model to the full text pairs to create Cochrane-auto.

As a result of our alignment strategy, similar sentences from different paragraphs in a simple text may be automatically aligned to the same sentence in the parallel text. For example, two simple paragraphs describing the results and conclusion may feature equivalent sentences that are both aligned to the same complex sentence; yet only one of them should be used as a reference simplification.

[9] https://github.com/chaojiang06/wiki-auto

[10] https://huggingface.co/chaojiang06/wiki-sentence-alignment

In those cases, we leverage the fine-tuned BERT model to find the simple paragraph in which the aligned sentences have the highest similarity with the complex sentence. Then we delete all alignments between the complex sentence and the simple sentences in other paragraphs.

5.3 Alignment results

Given the paragraph alignments that were generated by Jiang et al. (2020), our trained sentence alignment model achieves an F1-score of 81.5 on the Wiki-manual test set. This is lower than the F1-score of 85.3 reported in their paper, but we do not have access to the original model weights. We also evaluate the performance of the fine-tuned BERT model alone, and find its F1-score to be 83.4. This value is obtained by computing the semantic similarity of each sentence pair within the aligned paragraphs, and aligning the pairs with a similarity higher than a threshold tuned on the dev set.

On our manually annotated subset of the Cochrane corpus, the neural CRF aligner significantly outperforms the fine-tuned BERT model. This is shown in Table 1. The higher F1-score indicates that our pretrained model is effectively able to capitalize on the structure of parallel texts in the Cochrane corpus. Since the neural CRF model normally cannot align multiple complex sentences to one simple sentence, its upper bound for the number of true positives is 68 out of 79. Nevertheless, in Section 5.5 we introduce merge operations, which can be translated into such n-to-1 alignments. Table 1 shows that adding these alignments leads to a small improvement in F1-score on our manually annotated subset.

Finally, we apply the neural CRF model to all 5,585 text pairs in the updated Cochrane corpus. This yields 39,497 automatic sentence alignments, some of which we delete as described in Section 5.2. The remaining 35,800 sentence pairs together with the corresponding document pairs

	Cochrane-auto	Newsela-auto	Wiki-auto
# Doc Pairs	1,085	18,319	85,123
# Para Pairs	4,171	361,964	178,982
# Sent Pairs	14,719	707,776	461,852
Avg. $\|c_i\|$	35.61	22.49	28.64
Avg. $\|s_i\|$	27.75	15.84	21.57
Avg. n	13.57	38.64	5.43
Avg. k	9.01	42.60	4.53
Avg. p	3.53	1.96	2.58

Table 3: Statistics of the datasets after preprocessing, where n is # sentences in C, and k is # sentences in S and p is # sentences per paragraph in C.

constitute Cochrane-auto. In Table 2, we compare this dataset to other automatically aligned simplification datasets. We make Cochrane-auto publicly available to foster research on the simplification of biomedical documents.

5.4 Preprocessing

For the training and evaluation of simplification systems on Cochrane-auto, we preprocess our data similarly to how Cripwell et al. (2023b) preprocessed Newsela-auto and Wiki-auto. That is, for each sentence c_i in a complex document, we use the simple sentence s_j to which it is aligned as a reference. If it is aligned to multiple s_js, we concatenate them; if it is not aligned, we use an empty string. Next, we create paragraph- and document-level references by concatenating the references for each sentence in a complex paragraph or document. Note that this may change the order of the simple sentences. Even so, we find that the resulting references are relatively coherent, as the simple sentences mostly stand on their own. Importantly, also note that simple sentences which are not aligned to any c_i are not included in any reference. Henceforth, when we refer to the simple sentences, paragraphs and documents in Cochrane-auto, we mean these references.

Let us define an instance of Cochrane-auto to be the collection of all (source, reference) pairs derived from a single text pair. We filter out instances where less than 50% of the sentences in the corresponding complex document C are aligned to any s_j. Therewith, we ensure that the remaining instances are derived from text pairs that are sufficiently similar in meaning. We also remove

Copy	Rephrase	Split	Merge	Delete
8.4	45.3	4.5	6.5	35.3

Table 4: Operation class distribution for Cochrane-auto in percentages.

instances where the length of a document exceeds 1,024 tokens, or would exceed 1,024 tokens after adding the special tokens needed for the plan-guided simplification approach of Cripwell et al. (2023a). As a result, the preprocessed Cochrane-auto dataset consists of 894 train, 125 validation and 121 test instances. In Table 3, we compare the statistics of our dataset to those of the preprocessed Newsela-auto and Wiki-auto datasets, as reported by Cripwell et al. (2023b).

Figure 2 displays a short example of a complex-simple document pair from the preprocessed Cochrane-auto dataset, along with the corresponding original reference from the Cochrane corpus. In this example, the first sentence from the original reference cannot be generated based on the complex document, and as such it should not be used as a reference. Indeed, it is excluded from the new reference, because it could not be aligned to any complex sentence. Moreover, the four sentence pairs that were aligned, are correctly aligned. However, this example also shows that correctly aligned sentences may still contain information that is not present in the source sentence (*with PAD*), that the deletion and reordering of sentences may impact the discourse structure of the reference document (*None of the other*), and that it is often debatable whether the meaning of source and target sentences is similar enough to align them (the last sentence in the original reference).

5.5 Labelling

Using the same approach that Cripwell et al. (2023b) applied to Newsela- and Wiki-auto, we label each complex sentence c_i in Cochrane-auto with a simplification operation as follows:

Delete: c_i is not aligned to any s_j.

Copy: c_i is aligned to a single s_j with a Levenshtein similarity above 0.92.

Rephrase: c_i is aligned to a single s_j with a Levenshtein similarity below 0.92.

Split: c_i is aligned to multiple s_js.

Additionaly, we introduce a new simplification operation, namely ***merge***. This is motivated by the observation that one sentence in a plain lan-

Complex document

Two randomised trials with a total of 161 participants were included in this review. The studies did not report on mortality and rate of limb loss. One randomised trial with a total of 133 participants showed that there was a significant improvement in ankle brachial index (ABI) in participants who received folic acid compared with placebo (mean difference (MD) 0.07, 95% confidence interval (CI) 0.04 to 0.11, P < 0.001) and in participants who received 5-methyltetrahydrofolate (5-MTHF) versus placebo (MD 0.05, 95% CI 0.01 to 0.10, P = 0.009).A second trial with a total of 18 participants showed that there was no difference (P non-significant) in ABI in participants who received a multivitamin B supplement (mean ± SEM: 0.7 ± 01) compared with placebo (mean ± SEM: 0.8 ± 0.1). No major events were reported.

Currently, no recommendation can be made regarding the value of treatment of hyperhomocysteinaemia in peripheral arterial disease. Further, well constructed trials are urgently required.

Simple document

Two trials with 161 participants with PAD were included in this review. None of the other predefined primary outcomes (mortality and rate of limb loss) were assessed in these studies. One trial showed a significant improvement in the ankle brachial index (ABI) in participants treated daily with 400 μg folic acid or 5-methyltetrahydrofolate (5-MTHF). A second trial showed that there was no difference in ABI in participants who received a multivitamin B supplement compared with placebo.

Original reference

We looked at studies where treatments to lower homocysteine were used in people with PAD and hyperhomocysteinaemia. Two trials with 161 participants with PAD were included in this review. One trial showed a significant improvement in the ankle brachial index (ABI) in participants treated daily with 400 μg folic acid or 5-methyltetrahydrofolate (5-MTHF). A second trial showed that there was no difference in ABI in participants who received a multivitamin B supplement compared with placebo. None of the other predefined primary outcomes (mortality and rate of limb loss) were assessed in these studies. More research about the effect of homocysteine lowering therapy on the clinical progression of disease in people with PAD and hyperhomocysteinaemia is needed.

Figure 2: A complex-simple document pair from the preprocessed Cochrane-auto dataset, along with the corresponding original reference from the Cochrane corpus.

guage summary can have the same meaning as multiple complex sentences in the parallel abstract. By swapping the (complex, simple) inputs of our alignment model, we automatically align each complex sentence to one or zero simple sentences, instead of the reverse. Then we assign consecutive sentences c_i within the same paragraph the *merge* operation label if (1) they are aligned to the same simple sentence s_j, (2) one of them was already aligned to s_j and labelled *rephrase*, and (3) the other complex sentences were labelled *delete*. Because of the latter two conditions, we only add alignments from previously unaligned complex sentences to simple sentences that were already included in our references. Table 1 showed that adding these alignments can indeed lead to an improvement in alignment quality.

Table 4 shows the distribution of simplification operations for Cochrane-auto. In comparison with Newsela-auto and Wiki-auto, the classes are more imbalanced, as Cochrane-auto contains more rephrase and delete operations, and less copy and split operations. This is clearly a result of the plain language summaries being written largely independently from the technical abstracts.

6 Experiments

In this section, we train document simplification systems on Cochrane-auto and evaluate them against a baseline on the updated Cochrane corpus. We describe our planning and simplification models, our experimental setup and evaluation metrics, and our results.

6.1 Simplification models

We finetune BART (Lewis et al., 2020) to perform simplification on the documents (BART_{doc}), paragraphs ($\text{BART}_{\text{para}}$), and sentences ($\text{BART}_{\text{sent}}$) in Cochrane-auto. In doing so, we exclude sentences which are labelled *merge* from the training data for $\text{BART}_{\text{sent}}$. As a baseline, we use BART finetuned on the updated Cochrane corpus.

Furthermore, using same approach that Cripwell et al. (2023b) applied to Newsela-auto, we train a plan-guided simplification model ($\hat{O} \rightarrow \text{BART}_{\text{sent}}$) on Cochrane-auto. This is a modified version of $\text{BART}_{\text{sent}}$ that takes a control-token at the beginning of each input, representing the simplification operation (Section 5.5) that should be applied to it. Sentences which should be merged are concatenated and provided to the model together. During training, the ground-truth simplification operation labels are used as control-tokens. At inference time, the operations are predicted by a planning model.

6.2 Planning model

The task of a planning model is to predict a simplification operation for each sentence in a complex document. For example, the RoBERTa-based (Liu et al., 2019) classifier from Cripwell et al. (2023b) takes a tokenized sentence as input and outputs a

System	BARTScore ↑			BLEU ↑	FKGL ↓	SARI ↑	Length	
	P ($r \rightarrow h$)	R ($h \rightarrow r$)	F1				Tok.	Sent.
Input	-3.44	-3.01	-3.22	13.7	13.4	9.3	534.0	15.0
Reference	-0.62	-0.62	-0.62	100.0	12.6	99.6	286.8	10.8
Baseline	-3.57	-3.32	-3.44	11.4	12.6	34.1	250.5	9.1
BART_{doc}	-3.70	-3.36	-3.53	10.7	**12.3**	31.6	251.4	8.8
$\text{BART}_{\text{para}}$	-3.43	-3.25	-3.34	12.9	12.7	32.9	263.0	9.7
$\text{BART}_{\text{sent}}$	-3.26	**-3.15**	**-3.20**	**14.9**	12.5	32.0	298.8	12.1
$\hat{O} \rightarrow \text{BART}_{\text{sent}}$	**-3.21**	-3.41	-3.31	11.1	12.5	**35.5**	211.6	8.1

Table 5: **Results of document simplification systems trained on Cochrane-auto**, when evaluated on the updated Cochrane corpus. The baseline is BART trained on the updated Cochrane corpus. For BARTScore, h is the hypothesis and r is the reference.

prediction score for each operation class. We train a similar classifier to predict the label of each complex sentence in Cochrane-auto. Since our planning model must be able to predict merge operations, we also provide the subsequent sentence as input to the classifier. If the model predicts that these sentences should be merged, we label both of them with the merge operation. Otherwise, we let the classifier predict the label of the first sentence. We provide the classifier with a single sentence if that sentence appears at the end of a paragraph.

6.3 Experimental setup

We build upon the code[11] of Cripwell et al. (2023b) to train and evaluate our planning and simplification models. Moreover, we apply length-based filtering to the updated Cochrane corpus, so that it contains 3,967 train, 500 validation and 502 test pairs of $\leq$ 1,024 tokens each. We leverage this corpus to evaluate our document simplification systems and to train the baseline, while we train our other models on Cochrane-auto. After training the planning model for 10 epochs, we select the model checkpoint with the highest macro F1-score on the validation set. With regards to the simplification models, we implement early stopping based on the validation loss with a patience of 3 epochs. All other training details are the same as to those originally used by the authors of the code.

6.4 Evaluation metrics

In order to evaluate the simplifications generated by our systems, we leverage BARTScore (Yuan et al., 2021) and BLEU (Papineni et al., 2002) as analogs for meaning preservation and fluency. Furthermore, we assess readability using the Flesch-Kincaid grade level (FKGL) (Kincaid et al., 1975), and simplicity using SARI (Xu et al., 2016).

6.5 Results and Discussion

Table 5 summarizes the results of evaluating our document simplification systems on the updated Cochrane corpus. Along the dimension of readability, all of our systems obtain mean FKGL scores that are comparable to the mean reference score. However, this score is relatively high, underlining the difficulty of writing easy-to-read biomedical lay summaries. Besides, FKGL is computed based on syllable counts and sentence length, so that it does not directly capture the amount of background knowledge needed to read a text. In fact, adding statistics such as confidence intervals to a text may reduce the FKGL score, because it decreases the average amount of syllables per word. This explains why the mean readability score of the inputs is only 0.8 above that of the references.

Taking a look at the other metrics, the scores obtained by our systems appear to be relatively low. This is because, despite being written according to a comprehensive set of guidelines, there is much variety in the Cochrane references compared to the Newsela and Wikipedia references. Not only does this influence evaluation, but also does the resulting unpredictability make our trained systems relatively conservative. In addition, as discussed in Section 4, our scores are negatively impacted by the fact that parts of the references cannot be generated based on the source document. Nevertheless,

[11] `https://github.com/liamcripwell/plan_simp`

Simplification generated by the baseline

Two randomised trials with a total of 161 participants were included in this review. The studies did not report on mortality and rate of limb loss. One randomised trial showed that there was a significant improvement in ankle brachial index (ABI) in participants who received folic acid compared with placebo (mean difference (MD) 0.07, 95% confidence interval (CI) 1.04 to 0.11, P < 0.001). No major events were reported. Currently, no recommendation can be made regarding the value of treatment of hyperhomocysteinaemia in peripheral arterial disease. Further, well constructed trials are urgently required.

Simplification generated by $\hat{O} \rightarrow \text{BART}_{\text{sent}}$

Two randomised controlled trials with a total of 161 participants were included in this review. The studies did not report on mortality and rate of limb loss. One trial with a total of 133 participants showed that there was a significant improvement in ankle brachial index (ABI) in participants who received folic acid compared with placebo. A second trial with a total of 18 participants showed that there was no difference (P non-significant) in ABI in participants who received a multivitamin B supplement compared with placebo. No major events were reported.

Figure 3: The outputs of two document simplification systems for the complex input document in Figure 2.

we find that these evaluation scores are useful for comparing performances between systems.

To begin with, it can be seen that BART_{doc} underperforms compared to the baseline in terms of both meaning preservation and fluency, and simplicity. One reason could be that the baseline was trained on a larger dataset, as Cochrane-auto comprises only those document pairs in which at least 50% of the complex sentences were automatically aligned. Another reason is that the exclusion of unaligned sentences from the references in Cochrane-auto will to some extent have led to a loss of relevant information. This includes elaborations, sentences that were left unaligned due to alignment errors, and information that could only be aligned at the word-level rather than the sentence-level.

Furthermore, it can be observed that $\text{BART}_{\text{para}}$ and – to a larger extent – $\text{BART}_{\text{sent}}$ outperform the baseline along the dimension of fluency and meaning preservation, although they underperform along the dimension of simplicity. $\hat{O} \rightarrow \text{BART}_{\text{sent}}$ even outperforms the baseline in terms of both SARI (simplicity) and BARTScore F1, while its BLEU score is only slightly lower than that of the baseline. These findings demonstrate that training simplification systems on Cochrane-auto, rather than the updated Cochrane corpus, can be beneficial despite all limitations mentioned above. Thus, we conclude that the creation of Cochrane-auto has indeed been a valuable contribution.

Lastly, Figure 3 displays the outputs of our baseline and $\hat{O} \rightarrow \text{BART}_{\text{sent}}$ when they attempt to simplify the complex input document from Figure 2. It can be seen that both systems are indeed relatively conservative. Moreover, in this example, our plan-guided system is better able to determine which sentences should be kept and which ones should be deleted. Because it was trained using oracle labels, the simplification model has learned to actually delete any sentence whose predicted label is *delete*. This explains why our plan-guided simplification system generates the shortest outputs on average, especially when compared to $\text{BART}_{\text{sent}}$, which rarely deletes sentences due to its risk-avoiding nature. We conclude that having a seperate planning and simplification component has helped the system to be less conservative and thereby outperform the baseline.

7 Conclusion

In this paper, we presented Cochrane-auto: a large aligned dataset for the simplification of biomedical abstracts at the document-, paragraph- and sentence-level. Our freely available corpus complementing Newsela-auto and Wiki-auto facilitates text simplification research beyond direct lexical and grammatical revisions. Experiments demonstrated that a plan-guided simplification system trained on this corpus can outperform a strong baseline trained on unaligned abstracts and lay summaries. Future work will investigate the performance of more modern simplification systems when trained on this corpus.

8 Limitations

Our experiments are restricted to English data in the biomedical domain. There is obvious interest in looking at a more diverse set of languages, and several researchers and projects are currently working on this. This is witnessed by, for example, a recent Coling/LREC workshop devoted to this (Nunzio et al., 2024).

For those looking for very strict lexical and grammatical simplifications at the sentence-level, the plain English summaries have greater variation and incorporate the discourse structure of the entire paragraph and document. Although we filter and realign exactly as done in Wiki-auto and Newsela-auto (Jiang et al., 2020; Cripwell et al., 2023a; Bakker and Kamps, 2024), and hence have similar safeguards between aligned sentences, we observe greater variation in Cochrane-auto. As in the other collections, our automatic alignments are imperfect, and the simple sentences that are correctly aligned may still contain information that is not present in the source sentence(s). More generally, the main limitation of our approach is that the real alignments between the complex and simple texts may not reside at the sentence-level. There are also obvious advantages to incorporating the variation and the discourse structure of the entire paragraph and document, and to further extend the scope of text simplification approaches to address all the interesting NLP challenges this presents.

As all generative models, our simplification models may suffer from creative generation (or "hallucination"), and so their outputs should not be used without manual inspection. In our text simplification setting, we can further analyse and ground the output of the model with the original source text. Hence, text simplification present an excellent setting to further study and quantify the degree of revision and additions generated by the model. This also inspired our introduction of a "merge" operator, aligning source content previously considered as delete combined with a creative insertion. As is well-known, existing evaluation measures are almost blind to detect such issues. The importance of studying and addressing these aspects is of paramount importance in future research, as they present one of the greatest challenges of generative models in NLP today.

9 Lay Summary

Many people have questions about health or medical topics. The most accurate and reliable information to answer such questions is in the biomedical literature written and used by medical experts. However, this scientific literature is very difficult to understand for non-experts. Fortunately, sometimes a special lay summary (like this one) is added to a paper to convey the main points. This is really helpful, but only few scientific articles have this, and not all the content of the articles has been "translated" for lay readers. This paper uses pairs of lay summaries and expert abstracts to create the training data for new AI models. We show that our corpus helps to build text simplification models that can automatically "translate" expert biomedical text for lay persons. This can lead to novel tools that make authoritative information from the biomedical literature directly available to non-experts.

Acknowledgments

Experiments in this paper were carried out on the National Supercomputer Snellius, supported by SURF and the HPC Board of the University of Amsterdam. Jan Bakker is funded by the Netherlands Organization for Scientific Research (NWO NWA # 1518.22.105). Jaap Kamps is partly funded by the Netherlands Organization for Scientific Research (NWO CI # CISC.CC.016, NWO NWA # 1518.22.105), the University of Amsterdam (AI4FinTech program), and ICAI (AI for Open Government Lab). Views expressed in this paper are not necessarily shared or endorsed by those funding the research.

References

Kush Attal, Brian Ondov, and Dina Demner-Fushman. 2023. A dataset for plain language adaptation of biomedical abstracts. *Scientific Data*, 10(1):8.

Jan Bakker and Jaap Kamps. 2024. Beyond sentence-level text simplification: Reproducibility study of context-aware document simplification. In *Proceedings of the Workshop on DeTermIt! Evaluating Text Difficulty in a Multilingual Context @ LREC-COLING 2024*, pages 27–38, Torino, Italia. ELRA and ICCL.

Muthu Kumar Chandrasekaran, Guy Feigenblat, Eduard Hovy, Abhilasha Ravichander, Michal Shmueli-Scheuer, and Anita de Waard. 2020. Overview and insights from the shared tasks at scholarly document processing 2020: CL-SciSumm, LaySumm and LongSumm. In *Proceedings of the First Workshop on Scholarly Document Processing*, pages 214–224, Online. Association for Computational Linguistics.

Liam Cripwell, Joël Legrand, and Claire Gardent. 2023a. Context-aware document simplification. In *Findings of the Association for Computational Linguistics: ACL 2023*, pages 13190–13206, Toronto, Canada. Association for Computational Linguistics.

Liam Cripwell, Joël Legrand, and Claire Gardent. 2023b. Document-level planning for text simplification. In *Proceedings of the 17th Conference of the European Chapter of the Association for Computational Linguistics*, pages 993–1006, Dubrovnik, Croatia. Association for Computational Linguistics.

Dina Demner-Fushman, Sophia Ananiadou, and Kevin Cohen, editors. 2023. *The 22nd Workshop on Biomedical Natural Language Processing and BioNLP Shared Tasks*. Association for Computational Linguistics, Toronto, Canada.

Ashwin Devaraj, Iain Marshall, Byron Wallace, and Junyi Jessy Li. 2021. Paragraph-level simplification of medical texts. In *Proceedings of the 2021 Conference of the North American Chapter of the Association for Computational Linguistics: Human Language Technologies*, pages 4972–4984, Online. Association for Computational Linguistics.

Jacob Devlin, Ming-Wei Chang, Kenton Lee, and Kristina Toutanova. 2019. BERT: Pre-training of deep bidirectional transformers for language understanding. In *Proceedings of the 2019 Conference of the North American Chapter of the Association for Computational Linguistics: Human Language Technologies, Volume 1 (Long and Short Papers)*, pages 4171–4186, Minneapolis, Minnesota. Association for Computational Linguistics.

Liana Ermakova, Eric SanJuan, Jaap Kamps, Stéphane Huet, Irina Ovchinnikova, Diana Nurbakova, Sílvia Araújo, Radia Hannachi, Élise Mathurin, and Patrice Bellot. 2022. Overview of the CLEF 2022 simpletext lab: Automatic simplification of scientific texts. In *Experimental IR Meets Multilinguality, Multimodality, and Interaction - 13th International Conference of the CLEF Association, CLEF 2022, Bologna, Italy, September 5-8, 2022, Proceedings*, volume 13390 of *Lecture Notes in Computer Science*, pages 470–494. Springer.

Tomas Goldsack, Zhihao Zhang, Chenghua Lin, and Carolina Scarton. 2022. Making science simple: Corpora for the lay summarisation of scientific literature. In *Proceedings of the 2022 Conference on Empirical Methods in Natural Language Processing*, pages 10589–10604, Abu Dhabi, United Arab Emirates. Association for Computational Linguistics.

Natalia Grabar and Rémi Cardon. 2018. CLEAR – simple corpus for medical French. In *Proceedings of the 1st Workshop on Automatic Text Adaptation (ATA)*, pages 3–9, Tilburg, the Netherlands. Association for Computational Linguistics.

Chao Jiang, Mounica Maddela, Wuwei Lan, Yang Zhong, and Wei Xu. 2020. Neural CRF model for sentence alignment in text simplification. In *Proceedings of the 58th Annual Meeting of the Association for Computational Linguistics*, pages 7943–7960, Online. Association for Computational Linguistics.

Peter Kincaid, Robert P. Fishburne, Richard L. Rogers, and Brad S. Chissom. 1975. Derivation of new readability formulas (automated readability index, fog count and flesch reading ease formula) for navy enlisted personnel.

Mike Lewis, Yinhan Liu, Naman Goyal, Marjan Ghazvininejad, Abdelrahman Mohamed, Omer Levy, Veselin Stoyanov, and Luke Zettlemoyer. 2020. BART: Denoising sequence-to-sequence pre-training for natural language generation, translation, and comprehension. In *Proceedings of the 58th Annual Meeting of the Association for Computational Linguistics*, pages 7871–7880, Online. Association for Computational Linguistics.

Yinhan Liu, Myle Ott, Naman Goyal, Jingfei Du, Mandar Joshi, Danqi Chen, Omer Levy, Mike Lewis, Luke Zettlemoyer, and Veselin Stoyanov. 2019. Roberta: A robustly optimized bert pretraining approach. *ArXiv*, abs/1907.11692.

Giorgio Maria Di Nunzio, Federica Vezzani, Liana Ermakova, Hosein Azarbonyad, and Jaap Kamps, editors. 2024. *Proceedings of the Workshop on DeTermIt! Evaluating Text Difficulty in a Multilingual Context @ LREC-COLING 2024*. ELRA and ICCL, Torino, Italia.

Matthew J Page, David Moher, Patrick M Bossuyt, Isabelle Boutron, Tammy C Hoffmann, Cynthia D Mulrow, Larissa Shamseer, Jennifer M Tetzlaff, Elie A Akl, Sue E Brennan, Roger Chou, Julie Glanville, Jeremy M Grimshaw, Asbjørn Hróbjartsson, Manoj M Lalu, Tianjing Li, Elizabeth W Loder, Evan Mayo-Wilson, Steve McDonald, Luke A McGuinness, Lesley A Stewart, James Thomas, Andrea C Tricco, Vivian A Welch, Penny Whiting, and Joanne E McKenzie. 2021. Prisma 2020 explanation and elaboration: updated guidance and exemplars for reporting systematic reviews. *BMJ*, 372.

Kishore Papineni, Salim Roukos, Todd Ward, and Wei-Jing Zhu. 2002. Bleu: a method for automatic evaluation of machine translation. In *Proceedings of the 40th Annual Meeting of the Association for Computational Linguistics*, pages 311–318, Philadelphia, Pennsylvania, USA. Association for Computational Linguistics.

Dongqi Pu, Yifan Wang, Jia Loy, and Vera Demberg. 2024. SciNews: From scholarly complexities to public narratives – a dataset for scientific news report generation. In *Proceedings of the 2024 Joint International Conference on Computational Linguistics, Language Resources and Evaluation (LREC-COLING 2024)*, pages 14429–14444, Torino, Italia. ELRA and ICCL.

Penny Whiting and Clare Davenport. 2023. *Writing a plain language summary*, chapter 13. John Wiley & Sons, Ltd.

Wei Xu, Chris Callison-Burch, and Courtney Napoles. 2015. Problems in current text simplification research: New data can help. *Transactions of the Association for Computational Linguistics*, 3:283–297.

Wei Xu, Courtney Napoles, Ellie Pavlick, Quanze Chen, and Chris Callison-Burch. 2016. Optimizing statistical machine translation for text simplification. *Transactions of the Association for Computational Linguistics*, 4:401–415.

Weizhe Yuan, Graham Neubig, and Pengfei Liu. 2021. Bartscore: Evaluating generated text as text generation. In *Advances in Neural Information Processing Systems*, volume 34, pages 27263–27277. Curran Associates, Inc.

Xingxing Zhang and Mirella Lapata. 2017. Sentence simplification with deep reinforcement learning. In

Proceedings of the 2017 Conference on Empirical Methods in Natural Language Processing, pages 584–594, Copenhagen, Denmark. Association for Computational Linguistics.

A Data, code, and trained models

We share all our data and the code used to create our new dataset (`https://github.com/JanB100/cochrane-auto`), as well as the code used to train and evaluate our simplification systems (`https://github.com/JanB100/doc_simp`), on GitHub. In addition, we share our pretrained planning and simplification models on HuggingFace (`https://huggingface.co/janbakker`).

Cochrane-auto is freely available for research, and avoids the (almost) impossible to obtain license issues of the Newsela-auto collection. It also complements earlier direct biomedical sentence to sentence level simplification corpora with the great variation observed in human paragraph- and document-level plain English versions broadly conveying the same information.

These resources offer an easy starting point for NLP research in sentence-level, paragraph-level or document-level biomedical text simplification.

B Planning results

Copy	Rephrase	Split	Merge	Delete
3.3	51.2	0.0	0.0	45.5

Table 6: Distribution of operation classes predicted by our classifier on the updated Cochrane corpus in percentages.

Table 6 shows the distribution of operation classes predicted by our planning model on the updated Cochrane corpus. Unfortunately, the classifier never predicts *merge* and *split* operations and rarely predicts *copy* operations. This is largely a result of the infrequency of these labels in the training data.

C Cochrane-auto example

Figure 4 displays another example of a complex-simple document pair from the preprocessed Cochrane-auto dataset, along with the corresponding original reference from the Cochrane corpus.

Complex document

Fifteen heterogeneous trials, involving 1022 adults with dorsally displaced and potentially or evidently unstable distal radial fractures, were included. While all trials compared external fixation versus plaster cast immobilisation, there was considerable variation especially in terms of patient characteristics and interventions. Methodological weaknesses among these trials included lack of allocation concealment and inadequate outcome assessment.

External fixation maintained reduced fracture positions (redisplacement requiring secondary treatment: 7/356 versus 51/338 (data from 9 trials); relative risk 0.17, 95% confidence interval 0.09 to 0.32) and prevented late collapse and malunion compared with plaster cast immobilisation. There was insufficient evidence to confirm a superior overall functional or clinical result for the external fixation group. External fixation was associated with a high number of complications, such as pin-track infection, but many of these were minor. Probably, some complications could have been avoided using a different surgical technique for pin insertion. There was insufficient evidence to establish a difference between the two groups in serious complications such as reflex sympathetic dystropy: 25/384 versus 17/347 (data from 11 trials); relative risk 1.31, 95% confidence interval 0.74 to 2.32.

There is some evidence to support the use of external fixation for dorsally displaced fractures of the distal radius in adults. Though there is insufficient evidence to confirm a better functional outcome, external fixation reduces redisplacement, gives improved anatomical results and most of the excess surgically-related complications are minor.

Simple document

Fifteen trials, involving 1022 adults with potentially or evidently unstable fractures, were included. While all trials compared external fixation versus plaster cast immobilisation, there was considerable variation in their characteristics especially in terms of patient characteristics and the method of external fixation.

The complications, such a pin tract infection, associated with external fixation were many but were generally minor. Serious complications occurred in both groups.

The review concludes that there is some evidence to support the use of external fixation for these fractures. The review found that external fixation reduced fracture redisplacement that prompted further treatment and generally improved final anatomical outcome.

Original reference

Fifteen trials, involving 1022 adults with potentially or evidently unstable fractures, were included. While all trials compared external fixation versus plaster cast immobilisation, there was considerable variation in their characteristics especially in terms of patient characteristics and the method of external fixation. Weak methodology, such as using inadequate methods of randomisation and outcome assessment, means that the possibility of serious bias can not be excluded.

The review found that external fixation reduced fracture redisplacement that prompted further treatment and generally improved final anatomical outcome. It appears to improve function too but this needs to be confirmed. The complications, such a pin tract infection, associated with external fixation were many but were generally minor. Serious complications occurred in both groups. The review concludes that there is some evidence to support the use of external fixation for these fractures.

Figure 4: Another complex-simple document pair from the preprocessed Cochrane-auto dataset, along with the corresponding original reference from the Cochrane corpus.

Considering Human Interaction and Variability in Automatic Text Simplification

Jenia Kim[1], Stefan Leijnen[1], Lisa Beinborn[2]

[1]HU University of Applied Sciences Utrecht, Netherlands
[2]University of Göttingen, Germany
Correspondence: jenia.kim@hu.nl

Abstract

Research into automatic text simplification aims to promote access to information for all members of society. To facilitate generalizability, simplification research often abstracts away from specific use cases, and targets a prototypical reader and an underspecified content creator. In this paper, we consider a real-world use case – simplification technology for use in Dutch municipalities – and identify the needs of the content creators and the target audiences in this scenario. The stakeholders envision a system that (a) assists the human writer without taking over the task; (b) provides diverse outputs, tailored for specific target audiences; and (c) explains the suggestions that it outputs. These requirements call for technology that is characterized by *modularity*, *explainability*, and *variability*. We argue that these are important research directions that require further exploration.

1 Introduction

Full participation in modern society requires reading and understanding a wide variety of written information. For example, drawing the right conclusion from a letter from the tax authority, or from instructions about how to apply for unemployment benefits, is crucial for active citizenship. Unfortunately, not everybody is equally skilled at reading. In the Netherlands, for example, about 2.5 million adults (one in six adults) have limited literacy, i.e., difficulty with reading and/or writing (Netherlands Court of Audit, 2016). To ensure fair access to crucial information for everyone, text simplification research aims to develop technology that can automatically identify sources of complexity in text and generate simplifications.

Simplification research often abstracts from specific use cases to facilitate the generalizability of the developed methods. Curated datasets and evaluation setups tend to target a prototypical reader and an underspecified content creator. In practice, however, technology does not exist in a vacuum; it is always interconnected with people. As users engage with technology, they gradually develop a mental model of its functioning, which subsequently shapes their further interaction and engagement (e.g., Baxter and Sommerville, 2011; Lee et al., 2024). Therefore, technology that does not meet the needs of its intended users and their preferences regarding the outputs and the interaction might result in unsuccessful deployment.

Text simplification is at its core a human-centered problem; it operates on a text generated by human writers and reduces its complexity for the sake of human readers. In this paper, we discuss how the preferences of the intended writers and the characteristics of the intended readers shape the properties of the required simplification technology. We do so by exploring a real-world use case: a simplification system that is meant to assist content creators in Dutch municipalities with writing accessible text.

2 Use Case Description

The public sector in the Netherlands is committed to promoting inclusive and accessible communication. For example, the City of Amsterdam published writing guidelines that instruct the employees to use "clear language" in all their written communication, and "simple language" in communication that targets audiences with limited literacy. Unfortunately, these efforts have proven to be insufficient. A recent study (Corsius et al., 2022) that evaluated 240 texts from 70 Dutch government organizations found that the texts – which discussed crucial information about payments and healthcare – were not understandable enough, due to lexical complexity, vague or indirect style, and the length of the text, among other factors.

The civil servants themselves indicate that implementing the guidelines in practice is difficult.

Proceedings of the Third Workshop on Text Simplification, Accessibility and Readability (TSAR 2024), pages 52–60
November 15, 2024 ©2024 Association for Computational Linguistics

The target levels in the guidelines are described in terms of the Common European Framework of Reference for Languages (CEFR); B1-level is considered "clear language", and A2-level is considered "simple language". However, in a workshop conducted by the City of Amsterdam in 2022 (Pinhão and Gornishka, 2022), the participants indicated that it is not straightforward to understand what the A2/B1-level requirements mean in practice, and that they lack this expertise in the organization.

Furthermore, they indicated that it is challenging to write to a broad audience (the residents of Amsterdam) that consists of diverse groups with different linguistic needs. Among the discussed possible solutions, the participants mentioned that they would benefit from a tool that could review what they wrote, highlight potential difficulties, and provide suggestions on how to solve them.

In interviews conducted with representatives of other municipalities in the Netherlands, the interest in automated solutions surfaced as well.[1] When asked about their needs and concerns regarding the introduction of such technologies, the interviewees emphasized the need of the writers to remain in control of the text, mainly because of the concern that automated simplification might result in changes in meaning and loss of nuance.

To summarize, there are three main points raised by the stakeholders. First, the target audience consists of diverse groups with different linguistic needs, so there is no "one-fits-all" solution. Second, the technology is viewed as a source of knowledge about these diverse linguistic needs and how to accommodate them; by using the technology, writers expect to improve their own expertise on the subject. Third, the writers wish to remain in control of the task and to take responsibility for the final output. In other words, they envision a system that (a) assists the human writer without taking over the task; (b) provides diverse outputs, tailored for specific target audiences; and (c) explains the suggestions that it outputs.

3 Automated Text Generation vs. Human-AI Co-Creation

Automated generation of simplified text is not the type of technology that is envisioned by the stakeholders in our use case. The content creators do not want the technology to take over the simplification task; rather, they want to collaborate with the AI, while remaining in control of the writing task and its outputs. This type of assemblage, where a human and an AI algorithm work together on a creative task, is called a *co-creation system* (Allen et al., 1999; Lubart, 2005; Zhu et al., 2018; Guzdial and Riedl, 2019).

Co-creation systems aim to support the endeavor of writing accessible text, while maintaining human agency, control, and ownership. Writing is a creative activity, which people find meaningful and satisfying; this holds not only for creative, but also for professional writing (Brand and Leckie, 1988). Moreover, writers often have a strong personal connection and a feeling of ownership towards the work they produce (e.g., Nicholes, 2017). A successful human-AI collaboration should, therefore, aim to preserve the meaningfulness of the task for the human writers, and their sense of ownership, agency, and control (e.g., Zhou and Sterman, 2023; Biermann et al., 2022).

In addition to preserving the sense of meaningfulness and satisfaction for individual writers, co-creation systems may have benefits on the organizational and societal levels as well. Within organizations, over-reliance on fully automatically generated simplifications might result in the loss of knowledge and expertise among human employees (Gibbs et al., 2021); co-creation systems, on the other hand, have the potential to increase human expertise, as writers gradually learn from the system's feedback.

On a societal level, use of co-creation systems ensures a clearer allocation of responsibility between the authorities and the citizen. For example, an existing application endorsed by the Dutch government (Rijksoverheid, 2023) allows people to scan formal letters (e.g., from the tax authority) with their phone camera and instantly receive a simplified version of them. This type of technology places the responsibility for understanding the letter on the citizen, rather than on the tax authority. It has been shown that this expectation for self-reliance is detrimental for the ability of many citizens, especially from marginalized groups, to realize their basic human rights (Netherlands Institute for Human Rights, 2020). Use of co-creation systems, on the other hand, leaves the responsibility for accessibility and social inclusion with the institutions who create the content, instead of passing it on to the citizen.

[1]The interviews were conducted as part of the preliminary phase of the project *Duidelijke TAAL* (Clear Language), funded by the Dutch National Organisation for Practice-Oriented Research SIA; file number RAAK.PUB13.022.

4 One-Fits-All vs. Heterogeneous Audiences

The simplification technology in our use case targets all (adult) residents of the city, which corresponds to an extremely diverse audience, including people with various education backgrounds, people with cognitive disabilities or learning disorders, non-native speakers, etc.

One possible approach to the heterogeneity of the audience is to write the simplest possible version, which can be understood by (almost) everybody. This has been the dominant approach in the public sector in the Netherlands in the last decade; the guideline was to write on CEFR B1-level, with the assumption that this level is understandable to 95% of the Dutch population (Jansen, 2013). However, this approach has two main limitations.

First, simplifying to the lowest level possible necessarily involves some loss of meaning, or at least loss of nuance. This is not suitable for all contexts, since some communication requires a high degree of semantic precision. For example, Garimella et al. (2022) study simplification of legal text and find significant disagreement between legal experts on the required level of detail.

Second, using CEFR levels as a target is controversial (e.g., Jansen, 2013). CEFR is not a readability metric that is meant to evaluate text complexity; rather, it is meant to evaluate the skills of the learner.[2] These skills are not directly transferable to specific linguistic features of the text; in fact, to assign a CEFR level to a given sentence requires high level of expertise and experience in foreign language teaching (Arase et al., 2022). Furthermore, as this framework was created specifically for foreign language learners, it is unclear whether it is appropriate for other target groups, like low literate native speakers. It has been shown that readability needs to be measured differently for L1 and L2 readers (Beinborn et al., 2014).

As an alternative to the "one-fits-all" approach, one could aim at accommodating the diverse needs of the audience by customizing the outputs to different groups. This was the preferred direction mentioned by the participants of the workshop in our use case, who envisioned creating multiple versions of the same document or webpage,

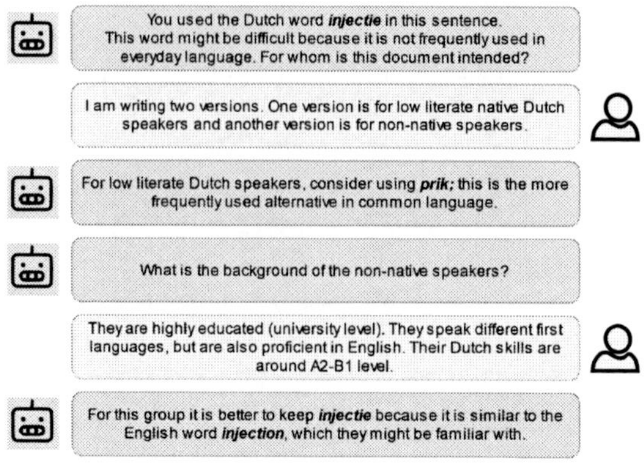

Figure 1: An imaginary co-creation assistant for accessible text, based on the requirements of our use case. It provides modular suggestions, accompanied by explanations, and tailored for various audiences.

from which the readers can choose (Pinhão and Gornishka, 2022). To accomplish this, the particular linguistic requirements of different groups need to be identified. Furthermore, novel technical solutions need to be developed that would allow a more personalized government communication, in which the right type of content reaches each citizen. These challenges are discussed further in Section 6.

5 Explainability, Modularity, Variability

The stakeholders in our use case envision a co-creation system that (a) assists the human writer without taking over the task; (b) provides diverse outputs, tailored for specific target audiences; and (c) explains the suggestions that it outputs. Figure 1 shows an imaginary example of an interaction that fulfills these requirements.

This entails certain characteristics of the underlying technology. First, simplification in this use case cannot be formulated as an end-to-end operation, i.e., rephrasing of a sentence to a simpler version. Rather, the output of the system has to be **modular**; it should suggest specific simplification operations (e.g., lexical substitution in Figure 1), leaving the decision which ones to accept and how to combine them in the hands of the human writer.

Second, the model needs to be able to generate **variable** simplified outputs for the same complexity. This is necessary for two purposes. First, it allows adaptability to different target audiences; e.g., in Figure 1, the system outputs two different synonyms, each of which is tailored to a different target group. Second, it allows adaptability to different writers as well. Simplification is not a well-

[2]For example, B1-level reading skills mean that the learner *"can understand texts that consist mainly of high frequency everyday or job-related language [...and..] can understand the description of events, feelings and wishes in personal letters"* (Council of Europe).

defined, closed-ended operation; it can be achieved through various strategies. Simplification strategies differ both on the inter- and intra-expert level: the proposed editing operations might vary across experts but also for an individual expert over different points in time, while the result may be equally acceptable (Xu et al., 2015; Alva-Manchego et al., 2021). A co-creation assistant should therefore be able to suggest various possible operations for the same complexity (e.g., splitting a complex sentence or reordering its parts); the human writer can choose the most suitable operation, according to their own style and preferences.

Third, the model's outputs and suggestions need to be **explainable**; i.e., they need to be motivated by expert knowledge (e.g., in Figure 1, the importance of cognates for foreign language readability). Our definition of explainability goes beyond visualizing which elements contributed to a model' complexity prediction based on post-hoc attribution methods (Garbacea et al., 2021; Hobo et al., 2023). While this can be an important first step, we envision explanations that one would expect to receive from a human expert. They should provide insights on why certain phenomena cause comprehension difficulties (for certain audiences), and how the suggestion reduces the complexity.

6 Discussion

In this section, we discuss how the requirements described above fit into existing research, and sketch promising directions for future work.

Human-Computer Interaction

Co-creation systems, like the one envisioned in our use case, are extensively researched by the Human-Computer Interaction (HCI) community. This field focuses on interfaces between people and technologies, putting in the center the experience of the users during the interaction, which is explored through user studies.

In the context of simplification, human-computer interaction was explored in reading-assistance systems, i.e., with readers as the intended users. For example, Rello et al. (2013) conducted user studies with people with dyslexia, and Alonzo et al. (2022) studied the preferences of deaf and hard-of-hearing individuals, who use simplification technology in the context of their work.

In our use case, on the other hand, the intended users of the technology are not the readers, but the writers. We therefore build on human-centered research on *interactive writing assistants*: a co-creation tool that assists people with improving the quality and effectiveness of their writing (e.g., Du et al., 2022). In a recent study, Lee et al. (2024) systematically review 115 articles about interactive writing assistants, and create a comprehensive taxonomy of the aspects that play a role in their design. This taxonomy can be a good starting point for a structured exploration of co-creation systems for text simplification. It is important that different use cases are described in a methodical way, and that design decisions for specific scenarios are grounded in user studies.

Personalized Simplification

The civil servants in our use case perceive their heterogeneous audience as a collection of different groups, with diverse linguistic needs. Indeed, research has shown that different target groups have different readability and simplification requirements; for example, people with dyslexia benefit more from seeing a number of synonyms for a complex word, rather than one simple synonym (Rello et al., 2013).

However, recent studies indicate that the perception of complexity varies on individual level, rather than group level. For example, Gooding and Tragut (2022) show that the judgments of non-native English speakers regarding lexical complexity depend not only on their proficiency in English, but also on (a combination of) idiosyncratic characteristics, like the reader's first language and reading experience. To address this, adaptive and personalized models can be created, which obtain individual data from users and learn user-specific simplifications (e.g., Bingel et al., 2018; Gooding and Tragut, 2022).

In the context of our use case, there are a few potential issues with individual-level personalization that need to be considered. First, from an ethical viewpoint, collecting individual data and training personalized models in the municipality context can be viewed as an infringement on the citizen's privacy. Second, such solutions would necessarily involve digital interfaces (e.g., websites, apps), which are not easily accessible for some groups in the Dutch population; in fact, the same vulnerable populations (e.g., people with lower education levels) often have difficulties both with complex texts and with digital literacy (Netherlands Institute for Human Rights, 2020). Lastly, this approach involves less human oversight and control over the simplified content, compared to the co-creation setup. Therefore, we focus on personalization on a group level, which can be performed by the writers and does not require interactive input from the readers. On digital interfaces, readers could choose the desired version of the text themselves (similarly to the choice of language on websites). However, ensuring that the right content reaches every citizen in offline communication remains an open challenge.

Towards Explainability, Modularity, and Variability in Dutch Text Simplification

To the best of our knowledge, no current simplification technology for Dutch fully incorporates explainability, modularity, and variability, as we described them. Commercial writing assistants for text simplification offer a certain degree of modularity and explainability, but remain limited in terms of variability (see Appendix A).

To further advance the research towards explainability, modularity, and variability, a few promising directions can be explored. First, it is crucial to better understand the underlying (psycho-)linguistic and cognitive phenomena that affect text complexity for different target groups. Based on this knowledge, modular and audience-specific simplification operations that address these phenomena can be defined. Work on Dutch readability for specific target groups is limited; for example, Kleijn (2018) explores readability in adolescents (high-school students), Maat and Gravekamp (2022) analyze differences between people with different education levels, and Reichrath and Moonen (2022) study an heterogeneous sample of the residents of Amsterdam, which they divide into two categories of literacy based on the CEFR. We believe that further work in this line is needed, which specifically focuses on identifying differences in the linguistic needs of different groups.

For explainability and variability of outputs, the identified modular and audience-specific operations need to be incorporated into simplification models. It remains an open question how to implement such fine-grained control over the process. For example, for transformer language models, control tokens have been introduced that can modulate specific attributes of the model outputs (Martin et al., 2020). The approach can be applied to achieve audience-specific simplifications; e.g., simplification of English text for people with cognitive disabilities (Chamovitz and Abend, 2022) or simplification of Russian text for foreign language learners with diverse proficiency levels (Dmitrieva, 2023). Seidl and Vandeghinste (2024) apply control tokens to manipulate various lexical and syntactic attributes of Dutch output but do not explicitly connect their approach to specific target audiences.

For the application of control tokens, a parallel corpus of complex-simple sentence pairs in the target language is required to train the model. As no large manually annotated parallel corpora exist for Dutch, Seidl and Vandeghinste (2024) train their model on automatically translated data, and Vlantis et al. (2024) use an English simplification model as an intermediary and automatically translate the input and output sequences. Both approaches suffer from the limited quality of the translation engine.[3]

Large generative language models, like GPT-3.5 and Llama2, can generate simplifications in a few-shot or zero-shot setting. However, it is unclear whether the output can be controlled towards specific operations or target audiences; for example, Farajidizaji et al. (2024) try to steer model outputs towards different readability levels by using different prompts, but with limited success. To achieve explainability in this setup, methods such as chain-of-thought prompting can be explored (Wei et al., 2022; Cohen and Cohen, 2024).

Another promising research direction explores how to align language models outputs with human production variability. Giulianelli et al. (2023) show that text generation models produce lower variability than humans on a text simplification task. Further research into this problem can contribute to more human-like variability in simplification outputs.

7 Conclusion

We argued that considering human-centered aspects is a crucial step in technology development. We discussed a real-world use case, and showed how the type of human-machine interaction envisioned by the content creators, and the variability in the needs of the target readers shape the requirements from the simplification technology. Specifically, they call for technology that is characterized by *modularity*, *explainability*, and *variability*. How this can be achieved, for Dutch as well as other languages, remains an open question which we intend to explore in our future work.

[3]As an alternative to the use of machine translation, a large parallel corpus of synthetic simplification data has been recently generated by prompting ChatGPT (see Appendix B); however, no evaluation of this dataset is publicly available.

8 Lay Summary

In this article, we discuss technology that makes difficult text simpler; it is called "text simplification technology" or "text simplification tools". The goal of this technology is to make written information, like letters and websites, easy to understand for everyone. For example, if somebody is writing an email and uses a difficult word that not many people know, a simplification tool can recognize the difficult word and replace it with an easier word that has the same meaning.

When researchers design simplification tools, they usually try to create a general solution that can be used in many different cases. The problem is that general solutions are not always the best ones. For example, different groups of people need simple text: children, people with dyslexia, immigrants who learn a new language, and others. For each group, different things can be difficult, so there is no general solution that fits everybody.

In our research, we look at a specific case: a simplification tool for municipalities in the Netherlands. The people who work in the municipalities write a lot of important information, like letters about payments and healthcare, or websites about municipal services. These people want to have a tool that can help them write in a way that everybody can understand. It is important to them to stay in control of the writing; this means that the tool should make suggestions about how to improve the text but the final decision is done by the writer. They also want the tool to explain the suggestions that it gives, for example why something is difficult. In addition, they want the tool to provide different suggestions for different groups of readers, according to what each group needs.

The wishes of the writers in the municipalities require a certain type of simplification technology, which does not exist yet. We plan to work on solving this problem in our future research.

References

James E Allen, Curry I Guinn, and Eric Horvtz. 1999. Mixed-initiative interaction. *IEEE Intelligent Systems and their Applications*, 14(5):14–23.

Oliver Alonzo, Lisa Elliot, Becca Dingman, Sooyeon Lee, Akhter Al Amin, and Matt Huenerfauth. 2022. Reading-assistance tools among deaf and hard-of-hearing computing professionals in the us: Their reading experiences, interests and perceptions of social accessibility. *ACM Transactions on Accessible Computing (TACCESS)*, 15(2):1–31.

Fernando Alva-Manchego, Carolina Scarton, and Lucia Specia. 2021. The (un)suitability of automatic evaluation metrics for text simplification. *Computational Linguistics*, 47(4):861–889.

Yuki Arase, Satoru Uchida, and Tomoyuki Kajiwara. 2022. CEFR-based sentence difficulty annotation and assessment. *arXiv preprint arXiv:2210.11766.*

Gordon Baxter and Ian Sommerville. 2011. Socio-technical systems: From design methods to systems engineering. *Interacting with computers*, 23(1):4–17.

Lisa Beinborn, Torsten Zesch, and Iryna Gurevych. 2014. Readability for foreign language learning: The importance of cognates. *ITL-International Journal of Applied Linguistics*, 165(2):136–162.

Oloff C Biermann, Ning F Ma, and Dongwook Yoon. 2022. From tool to companion: Storywriters want AI writers to respect their personal values and writing strategies. In *Proceedings of the 2022 ACM Designing Interactive Systems Conference*, pages 1209–1227.

Joachim Bingel, Gustavo Paetzold, and Anders Søgaard. 2018. Lexi: A tool for adaptive, personalized text simplification. In *Proceedings of the 27th International Conference on Computational Linguistics*, pages 245–258.

Alice G Brand and Phoebe A Leckie. 1988. The emotions of professional writers. *The Journal of psychology*, 122(5):421–439.

Mark Breuker. 2022. Cefr labelling and assessment services. In *European Language Grid: A Language Technology Platform for Multilingual Europe*, pages 277–282. Springer International Publishing Cham.

Eytan Chamovitz and Omri Abend. 2022. Cognitive simplification operations improve text simplification. In *Proceedings of the 26th Conference on Computational Natural Language Learning (CoNLL)*, pages 241–265, Abu Dhabi, United Arab Emirates (Hybrid). Association for Computational Linguistics.

Cassandra A Cohen and William W Cohen. 2024. Watch your steps: Observable and modular chains of thought. *arXiv preprint arXiv:2409.15359*.

Mischa Corsius, Vera Lange, Yvette Linders, Henk Pander Maat, Els van der Pool, Nina Sangers, Keun Sliedrecht, Wouter Sluis-Thiescheffer, and Charlotte Swart. 2022. Monitor Begrijpelijkheid Overheidsteksten (Monitor Understandability of Government Texts). Accessed: 09-July-2024.

Council of Europe. Self-assessment Grids (CEFR). Accessed: 05-September-2024.

Anna Dmitrieva. 2023. Automatic text simplification of Russian texts using control tokens. In *Proceedings of the 9th Workshop on Slavic Natural Language Processing 2023 (SlavicNLP 2023)*, pages 70–77, Dubrovnik, Croatia. Association for Computational Linguistics.

Wanyu Du, Zae Myung Kim, Vipul Raheja, Dhruv Kumar, and Dongyeop Kang. 2022. Read, revise, repeat: A system demonstration for human-in-the-loop iterative text revision. *arXiv preprint arXiv:2204.03685*.

Asma Farajidizaji, Vatsal Raina, and Mark Gales. 2024. Is it possible to modify text to a target readability level? an initial investigation using zero-shot large language models. In *Proceedings of the 2024 Joint International Conference on Computational Linguistics, Language Resources and Evaluation (LREC-COLING 2024)*, pages 9325–9339, Torino, Italia. ELRA and ICCL.

Cristina Garbacea, Mengtian Guo, Samuel Carton, and Qiaozhu Mei. 2021. Explainable prediction of text complexity: The missing preliminaries for text simplification. In *Proceedings of the 59th Annual Meeting of the Association for Computational Linguistics and the 11th International Joint Conference on Natural Language Processing (Volume 1: Long Papers)*, pages 1086–1097, Online. Association for Computational Linguistics.

Aparna Garimella, Abhilasha Sancheti, Vinay Aggarwal, Ananya Ganesh, Niyati Chhaya, and Nandakishore Kambhatla. 2022. Text simplification for legal domain: Insights and challenges. In *Proceedings of the Natural Legal Language Processing Workshop 2022*, pages 296–304, Abu Dhabi, United Arab Emirates (Hybrid). Association for Computational Linguistics.

Jennifer L Gibbs, Gavin L Kirkwood, Chengyu Fang, and J Nan Wilkenfeld. 2021. Negotiating agency and control: Theorizing human-machine communication from a structurational perspective. *Human-Machine Communication*, 2:153–171.

Mario Giulianelli, Joris Baan, Wilker Aziz, Raquel Fernández, and Barbara Plank. 2023. What comes next? evaluating uncertainty in neural text generators against human production variability. *arXiv preprint arXiv:2305.11707*.

Sian Gooding and Manuel Tragut. 2022. One size does not fit all: The case for personalised word complexity models. *arXiv preprint arXiv:2205.02564*.

Matthew Guzdial and Mark Riedl. 2019. An interaction framework for studying co-creative AI. *arXiv preprint arXiv:1903.09709*.

Eliza Hobo, Charlotte Pouw, and Lisa Beinborn. 2023. "geen makkie": Interpretable classification and simplification of Dutch text complexity. In *Proceedings of the 18th Workshop on Innovative Use of NLP for Building Educational Applications (BEA 2023)*, pages 503–517, Toronto, Canada. Association for Computational Linguistics.

Carel Jansen. 2013. Taalniveau B1: de nieuwste kleren van de keizer (Language level B1: the emperor's newest clothes). *Onze Taal*, 82(2):56–57.

Suzanne Kleijn. 2018. *Clozing in on readability: How linguistic features affect and predict text comprehension and on-line processing*. Ph.D. thesis, Utrecht University.

Mina Lee, Katy Ilonka Gero, John Joon Young Chung, Simon Buckingham Shum, Vipul Raheja, Hua Shen, Subhashini Venugopalan, Thiemo Wambsganss, David Zhou, Emad A Alghamdi, et al. 2024. A design space for intelligent and interactive writing assistants. In *Proceedings of the CHI Conference on Human Factors in Computing Systems*, pages 1–35.

Todd Lubart. 2005. How can computers be partners in the creative process: Classification and commentary on the special issue. *International journal of human-computer studies*, 63(4-5):365–369.

Henk Pander Maat and Jet Gravekamp. 2022. Kan een tekst te simpel zijn? hoe lager en hoger opgeleiden oordelen over eenvoudige taal. *Tijdschrift voor Taalbeheersing*, 44(2):62–90.

Louis Martin, Éric de la Clergerie, Benoît Sagot, and Antoine Bordes. 2020. Controllable sentence simplification. In *Proceedings of the Twelfth Language Resources and Evaluation Conference*, pages 4689–4698, Marseille, France. European Language Resources Association.

Netherlands Court of Audit. 2016. Aanpak van laaggeletterdheid (Tackling low literacy). Accessed: 09-July-2024.

Netherlands Institute for Human Rights. 2020. Iedereen op eigen kracht? Nederlanders over zelfredzaamheid en mensenrechten (Every person for themselves? Dutch people on self-reliance and human rights). Accessed: 09-July-2024.

Justin Nicholes. 2017. Measuring ownership of creative versus academic writing: Implications for interdisciplinary praxis. *Writing in Practice*, 3(1).

Cláudia Pinhão and Iva Gornishka. 2022. Workshop Results: Improving readability of city communications. Accessed: 09-July-2024.

Eva D Poort and Jennifer M Rodd. 2019. A database of dutch–english cognates, interlingual homographs and translation equivalents. *Journal of cognition*, 2(1).

Enid Reichrath and Xavier Moonen. 2022. Assessing the effects of language for all. *Nordic Journal of Linguistics*, 45(2):232–248.

Luz Rello, Ricardo Baeza-Yates, Stefan Bott, and Horacio Saggion. 2013. Simplify or help? text simplification strategies for people with dyslexia. In *Proceedings of the 10th international cross-disciplinary conference on web accessibility*, pages 1–10.

Rijksoverheid. 2023. Terugblik Demo Donderdag: Lees Simpel app versimpelt overheidsinformatie. Accessed: 05-September-2024.

Theresa Seidl and Vincent Vandeghinste. 2024. Controllable sentence simplification in dutch. *Computational Linguistics in the Netherlands Journal*, 13:31–61.

Anaïs Tack, Thomas François, Piet Desmet, and Cédrick Fairon. 2018. NT2Lex: A CEFR-graded lexical resource for Dutch as a foreign language linked to open Dutch WordNet. In *Proceedings of the Thirteenth Workshop on Innovative Use of NLP for Building Educational Applications*, pages 137–146, New Orleans, Louisiana. Association for Computational Linguistics.

Charlotte van de Velde. 2023. Automatic sentence-level simplification for dutch. Master's thesis, KU Leuven.

Daniel Vlantis, Iva Gornishka, and Shuai Wang. 2024. Benchmarking the simplification of Dutch municipal text. In *Proceedings of the 2024 Joint International Conference on Computational Linguistics, Language Resources and Evaluation (LREC-COLING 2024)*, pages 2217–2226, Torino, Italia. ELRA and ICCL.

Jason Wei, Xuezhi Wang, Dale Schuurmans, Maarten Bosma, Fei Xia, Ed Chi, Quoc V Le, Denny Zhou, et al. 2022. Chain-of-thought prompting elicits reasoning in large language models. *Advances in neural information processing systems*, 35:24824–24837.

Wei Xu, Chris Callison-Burch, and Courtney Napoles. 2015. Problems in current text simplification research: New data can help. *Transactions of the Association for Computational Linguistics*, 3:283–297.

David Zhou and Sarah Sterman. 2023. Creative struggle: Arguing for the value of difficulty in supporting ownership and self-expression in creative writing. In *The Second Workshop on Intelligent and Interactive Writing Assistants (In2Writing)*.

Jichen Zhu, Antonios Liapis, Sebastian Risi, Rafael Bidarra, and G Michael Youngblood. 2018. Explainable ai for designers: A human-centered perspective on mixed-initiative co-creation. In *2018 IEEE conference on computational intelligence and games (CIG)*, pages 1–8. IEEE.

A Commercial Writing Assistants for Dutch Text Simplification

There are a couple of existing commercial writing assistants for text simplification in Dutch, such as *Klinkende Taal* and *Tolkie Schrijfhulp*. These tools offer a convenient co-creation interface by integrating into widely used software like Microsoft Word and Outlook; the control over the writing process remains mainly with the human writer, who gets feedback from the system and decides whether to incorporate it. The tools provide some degree of modularity and explainability by identifying specific problems in the text, including difficult words and complicated structures (e.g., passive sentences, long sentences); they provide general explanations about the complexity (e.g., *"passive sentences make it unclear who does what, and give the text a distant tone"*), and in some cases suggests alternatives (e.g., synonyms). The incorporation of variability is limited in these tools. Both perform their evaluation based on CEFR levels; while *Tolkie Schrijfhulp* focuses exclusively on the B1-level target, *Klinkende Taal* offers some variability by letting the user choose the target CEFR level herself. In addition, *Tolkie Schrijfhulp* offers one group-specific check: words that are difficult for people with dyslexia.

B Resources for Dutch Text Simplification

Description	Size	Source simplifications / annotations	Domain	Link	Reference
Parallel corpus	1,311 sentence pairs	Manual	Government	Link to GitHub	Vlantis et al. (2024)
Parallel corpus	1,267 sentence pairs	Automatic (LLM)	*unknown*	Link to HuggingFace	van de Velde (2023)
Parallel corpus	2.87M paragraph pairs	Automatic (LLM)	Wikipedia	Link to HuggingFace	*n/a*
Contextualized lexical simplifications	96 sentences	Manual	Government	Link to GitHub	Hobo et al. (2023)
Complex words and simpler alternatives	~800 words / expressions	Manual	Government	link to City of Amsterdam	*n/a*
Complex words and simpler alternatives	~130 words / expressions	Manual	Legal	Link to City of Amsterdam	*n/a*
Words and frequency distributions graded on CEFR levels	17,743 words / expressions	Automatic	*n/a*	Link to NT2Lex	Tack et al. (2018)
Texts graded on CEFR levels	1,200 texts	Manual	Various	Link to Edia	Breuker (2022)
Dutch-English cognates and homographs	~200 words	Manual	*n/a*	Link to OSF	Poort and Rodd (2019)

Table 1: Overview of resources for Dutch text simplification

Society of Medical Simplifiers

Chen Lyu
University of Warwick
chen.lyu@warwick.ac.uk

Gabriele Pergola
University of Warwick
gabriele.pergola.1@warwick.ac.uk

Abstract

Medical text simplification is crucial for making complex biomedical literature more comprehensible to non-experts. Traditional methods struggle with the specialized terms and jargon of medical texts, lacking the flexibility to adapt the simplification process dynamically. In contrast, recent advancements in large language models (LLMs) present unique opportunities by offering enhanced control over text simplification through iterative refinement and collaboration between specialized agents. In this work, we introduce the *Society of Medical Simplifiers*, a novel LLM-based framework inspired by the "Society of Mind" (SOM) philosophy. Our approach leverages the strengths of LLMs by assigning five distinct roles, i.e., Layperson, Simplifier, Medical Expert, Language Clarifier, and Redundancy Checker, organized into interaction loops. This structure allows the agents to progressively improve text simplification while maintaining the complexity and accuracy of the original content. Evaluations on the Cochrane text simplification dataset demonstrate that our framework is on par with or outperforms state-of-the-art methods, achieving superior readability and content preservation through controlled simplification processes.

1 Introduction

Medical text simplification is critical for improving public understanding of biomedical literature, which is often written in highly specialized language laden with domain-specific terminology that can be difficult for non-experts to understand (Osborne et al., 2022; Devaraj et al., 2021a; Štajner et al., 2022; Lu et al., 2023b). Automatic text simplification (ATS) offers a potential solution by transforming complex biomedical language into simpler, more comprehensible text while preserving essential details. However, traditional approaches to medical text simplification often struggle to effectively handle the specialized terminology and syntactic complexity in medical literature, and lack effective mechanisms to granularly control the simplification process (Lu et al., 2023a; Sun et al., 2022).

The recent advancements in large language models (LLMs) have revolutionized the ability to tackle complex tasks (Pergola et al., 2021; Sun et al., 2022, 2024), opening new possibilities for refining ATS. What sets LLMs apart is their flexibility via prompt-engineering, which allows for fine-tuned control over the simplification process—an unprecedented capability in ATS. For the first time, LLMs can be specialized into distinct agents that collaborate and interact with each other in an iterative manner, dynamically refining the text simplification. This flexibility enables the simplification process to become more adaptive and progressive through multiple iterations, ensuring that both clarity and accuracy are maintained.

Inspired by Marvin Minsky's "society of mind" (SOM) philosophy (Minsky, 1988), where intelligence emerges through the interaction of specialized modules, we see LLMs as ideal models for an agent-based system to tackle the complex task of medical text simplification. SOM encourages the cooperative interaction of specialized agents in tasks requiring debate and collaboration. Prior work has shown that hierarchical agent frameworks and iterative, multi-agent discussions (Zhu et al., 2021; Wu et al., 2023; Chen et al., 2023; Du et al., 2023) significantly improve the performance of natural language tasks. However, applying this multi-agent LLM-based SOM approach to medical text simplification remains largely unexplored.

To address this research gap, we introduce a novel framework for medical text simplification, grounded in SOM principles: the *Society of Medical Simplifiers*. To the best of our knowledge, this is the first multi-agent LLM system designed for medical text simplification, as well as the first to

Proceedings of the Third Workshop on Text Simplification, Accessibility and Readability (TSAR 2024), pages 61–68
November 15, 2024 ©2024 Association for Computational Linguistics

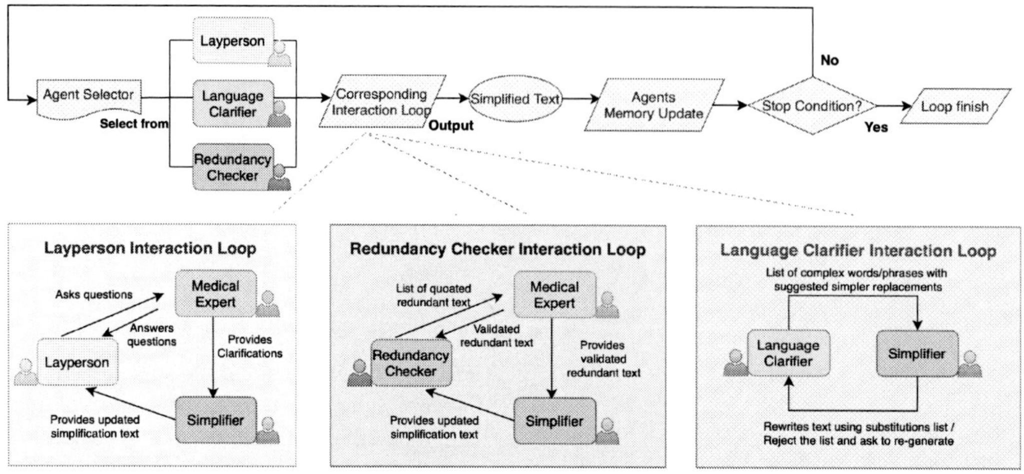

Figure 1: Society of Medical Simplifiers framework. Details of the interaction loops are presented at the bottom.

introduce the concept of interaction loops within the LLM-based SOM framework. Our five-agent framework decomposes the task into five specialized roles, i.e., *Layperson, Simplifier, Medical Expert, Language Clarifier*, and *Redundancy Checker*, and through iterative interaction loops, the system incrementally simplifies complex medical texts. These interaction loops enable the agents to collaborate dynamically, progressively improving the text over multiple iterations, while maintaining the integrity and accuracy of the original content. Experiments on the Cochrane dataset show that our framework outperforms current state-of-the-art methods at readability, even with a fixed number of iterations, demonstrating the potential of multi-agent LLM-based systems in simplifying complex medical texts.

The contribution of this paper can be summarized as follows:

- We introduce the first LLM-based five-agent framework for medical text simplification, decomposing the task into five specialized agent roles: Layperson, Simplifier, Medical Expert, Language Clarifier, and Redundancy Checker.
- We propose the novel concept of organizing LLM agents into three interaction loops, enabling progressive simplification while maintaining content accuracy and integrity.
- Experimental assessments on the Cochrane dataset demonstrate that our framework, even with a fixed number of iterations, surpasses state-of-the-art methods in readability.

2 Methodology

2.1 Agent Roles

Figure 1 provides an overview of the *Society of Medical Simplifiers* framework. Five agents are assigned distinct roles that together complement the medical text simplification process. The agent roles are defined as follows:

- **Layperson**: Acts as a non-expert reader, identifying complex medical jargon and posing questions to highlight areas that need simplification. This agent focuses on domain-specific content, prompting other agents to rewrite difficult medical text.
- **Medical Expert**: Provides detailed answers to the Layperson Agent's questions, offering clarifications that help maintain the original text's core ideas while making it more comprehensible.
- **Simplifier**: Uses feedback from the Medical Expert and other agents to edit and simplify the text, ensuring it remains clear and aligned to the original meaning.
- **Language Clarifier**: Focuses on reducing lexical complexity by identifying and suggesting simpler alternatives for non-medical terms. The suggestions are provided as a list passed to the Simplifier Agent to react on.
- **Redundancy Checker**: This agent identifies and recommends the removal of non-essential content. It is prompted to produce a list of

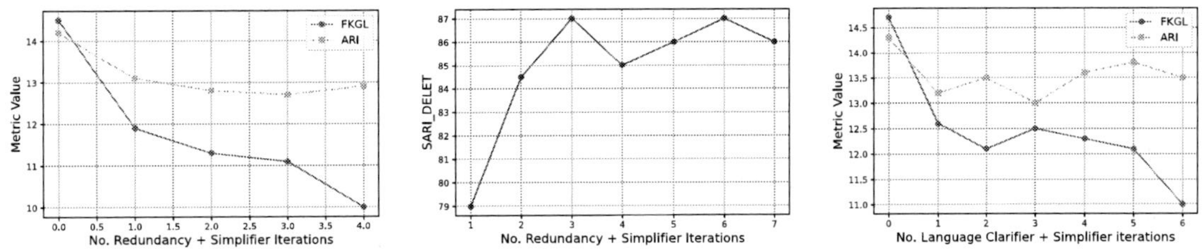

(a) Readability metrics for Layperson and Redundancy Checker

(b) SARI DELET Metric for the Layperson and Redundancy Checker

(c) Readability metrics for the Layperson and Language Clarifier

Figure 2: Relationship between performance on metrics and the number of evaluation iterations.

redundant phrases or sentences with justifications for their exclusion.

We name Layperson, Redundancy Checker and Language Clarifier as ***lead agents***, since they are the agents driving the simplification processes. On the other hand, we refer to Medical Expert and Simplifier as ***function agents*** as they act passively on leader agents' actions and perform the basic functions in this framework. Prompts used to define the agent roles are listed in A.

2.2 Interaction Loops

As illustrated at the bottom part in Figure 1, we define three distinct combinations of agents, referred to as *interaction loops*. Each interaction loop consists of one lead agent and one or more function agents. These interaction groups form the core structure of the simplification process. When a function agent is selected, it enters the corresponding loop, engaging in iterative conversations with other agents until a condition is met and a simplified text is outputted. The loop is then completed.

Layperson loop: In the Layperson interaction loop, the Layperson first identifies difficult medical content by generating questions, to which the Medical Expert provides clarifying responses. The Simplifier agent then processes these clarifications by executing a Chain-of-Thought (CoT) prompt (Wei et al., 2022) to modify and incorporate the clarifications into the simplified text. This involves reasoning about how each clarification can be coherently integrated and rewriting it into a simpler form. The loop then ends, yielding the updated text with the clarifications. This loop performs similar function to the ATS task Complex Word Identification and Substitution as defined in previous works (Finnimore et al., 2019; Saggion et al., 2022).

Language Clarifier Loop: When the Language Clarifier acts as the lead agent, it starts with generating a list of complex words/phrases and their simpler replacements. The Simplifier then reviews these substitutions, deciding whether to accept or reject them. If accepted, the text is updated accordingly. If not, the Language Clarifier will revise the substitutions until they are accepted and incorporated into the text. This loop performs a function similar to the ATS task of Complex Word Identification and Substitution (Nisioi et al., 2017), as outlined in prior studies.

Redundancy Loop: Similarly, in its loop, the Redundancy Checker generates a list of redundant text by quoting sections of the simplified text. The Medical Expert reviews each entry to ensure no essential medical information is removed, justifying whether the text is truly redundant. Once validated, the Simplifier removes the redundant text from the document, ensuring key medical details remain intact. This loop functions similarly to a Sentence Compression module, as described in previous studies (Boudin and Morin, 2013; Shang et al., 2018), where non-essential content is removed to reduce the length of the text while maintaining key facts and grammatical correctness.

2.3 Pipeline of the Framework

To maintain state preservation across simplification iterations, agent memories are stored as natural language. Since the Layperson's role is limited to identifying and querying complex domain-specific language, retaining previous states is unnecessary for this agent. Therefore, only the remaining four agents are equipped with memory.

At the beginning of the framework pipeline, a planning component that we refer to as the Agent Selector determines the most appropriate lead agent to act next based on the entire conversation history. The LLM-powered Agent Selector is prompted with the predefined roles of each agent and past conversations. Once a lead agent is selected, it engages with the function agents in the corresponding interaction loop until all agents agree to conclude the conversation. Each interaction loop outputs a new version of the simplified text, which is passed to the lead agents as a memory update. The *logger* then updates the conversation history, and the Agent Selector chooses the next lead agent for the subsequent loop. This process continues until the predefined stop condition is reached, discussed in detail in the following.

3 Experiment

We deployed multiple instances of GPT-3.5-Turbo-1106[1] to serve as the agents in our framework. Evaluations were conducted using the Cochrane Medical Text Simplification Dataset (Devaraj et al., 2021b) sourced from the Cochrane library, which is a benchmark for medical text simplification tasks providing human-generated pairs of biomedical abstracts and their simplified version.

It is worth noting that the focus of this experimental assessment is not on using the latest LLM, but rather on exploring and validating the effectiveness of the proposed multi-agent framework. As such, our experiments are designed to test the system's ability to improve medical text simplification through interaction loops between specialized agents, rather than to benchmark specific model performances.

3.1 Preliminary Analyses on the Fixed Number of Iterations

To optimize the performance of our framework while managing computational costs, we set a fixed number of iterations as the stop condition for the entire pipeline. This means the framework halts once a predefined iteration count is reached.

To determine the optimal setting for the iteration number, we initially experimented using only the basic interaction loop led by the Layperson agent, without involving the other loops. This approach allowed us to control the hyperparameter more effectively to later observe the performance of the Redundancy Checker and Language Clarifier in isolation. We tested iteration counts between 1 and 3 for the Layperson-led loop, as shown in Table 2. The experiment with 2 iterations yielded the best overall results, leading on three out of six metrics. While 3 iterations achieved the highest readability scores, it performed significantly worse on SARI scores. Therefore, we fixed the iteration count to two for the Layperson-led loop.

For the Redundancy Checker and Language Clarifier loops, our focus shifts to readability metrics only because these agents are primarily responsible for improving text readability. We ran additional experiments with varying iteration counts for combinations of Layperson and Redundancy Checker, and Layperson and Language Clarifier. We additionally recorded the SARI DELETE component of the SARI metric for the Redundancy Checker to evaluate the text removal accuracy for the redundant parts. Results shown in Figure 2 indicate a negative correlation between iteration count and readability for the Redundancy Checker, with its highest SARI DELETE score occurring at three iterations. However, for both agents, the most significant gains were observed by the second iteration, after which improvements level out. Thus, we also selected two iterations as the fixed setting for the Redundancy Checker and Language Clarifier.

3.2 Result and Discussion

To evaluate the effectiveness of our proposed framework, we ran the experiments on the Cochrane simplification dataset and presented the results along with the recent literature in Table 1. Following the conclusion of the previous optimal iteration number investigation, we adopted 2 as the fixed number of loops. This means that each interaction loop will be entered twice by the corresponding lead agent. The whole framework will stop running once all interaction loops have been selected two times and the Agent Selector is out of options.

As shown in Table 1, the designed framework outperforms state-of-the-art methods on the ARI readability metric and also demonstrates superior performance on SARI and FKGL compared to most existing approaches. However, the framework shows a noticeable decrease in ROUGE scores. This issue could stem from excessive content added by the Medical Expert or the removal of relevant information by the Redundancy Checker. Overall, while further improvements are necessary to balance content preservation and simplification, the experiments demonstrate the current framework as a competitive and state-of-the-art approach.

[1] https://platform.openai.com/docs/models/gpt-3-5-turbo

Method	SARI ↑	FKGL ↓	ARI ↓	BLEU ↑	ROUGE1 ↑	ROUGE2 ↑
BART-UL (Devaraj et al., 2022)	40.00	11.97	13.73	7.90	38.00	14.00
TESLEA (Phatak et al., 2022)	40.00	11.84	13.82	-	39.00	11.00
NapSS (Lu et al., 2023b)	**40.37**	**10.97**	14.27	**12.30**	**48.05**	**19.94**
Society of Medical Simplifiers (Our)	40.04	11.40	**12.81**	8.40	28.03	9.61

Table 1: Performance metrics across various text simplification methods

Iteration	SARI ↑	KEEP ↑	DEL ↑	ADD ↑	FKGL ↓	ARI ↓
1	40.00	**28.12**	86.92	4.97	12.14	13.87
2	**40.32**	27.64	**87.73**	**5.59**	12.08	13.22
3	38.28	24.13	86.44	4.26	**11.93**	**12.85**

Table 2: Performance metrics across different numbers of iterations for Layperson Loop

4 Conclusion

In this paper, we introduced the Society of Medical Simplifiers, a novel multi-agent LLM-based framework for medical text simplification. Inspired by the SOM philosophy, our framework designs and organizes five specialized agents into iterative interaction loops, enabling collaborative simplification of complex medical texts. Our experiments on the Cochrane dataset show that the Society of Medical Simplifiers outperforms existing methods in terms of readability and simplification.

5 Limitations

Future improvements to our framework include evaluating its performance on a wider family of LLMs, such as the Llama 3 models (AI@Meta, 2024), the GPT-4 models (OpenAI, 2023), and Mi(x)tral (Jiang et al., 2024). Additionally, experimenting with a larger number of iterations, and potentially automating the selection of optimal iteration counts through LLM inference, could further boost performance. We also aim to explore more complex interactions between agents, introducing new roles that emphasize preserving the original context while simplifying the text.

Acknowledgements

This work was supported by Sulis, the Tier-2 high-performance computing facility at the University of Warwick, funded by the EPSRC through the HPC Midlands+ Consortium (EPSRC grant no. EP/T022108/1).

Lay Summary

Medical research papers often use complicated language that can be hard for non-experts to understand. To make this information more comprehensible, researchers are working on tools that automatically simplify these texts. However, traditional methods struggle to simplify medical jargon and still keep the meaning clear. This paper introduces a new approach called the *Society of Medical Simplifiers*, which uses a system of multiple artificial intelligence (AI) agents, each with a different role. Inspired by the idea that many minds working together can solve complex problems, these AI agents cooperate to simplify medical texts. The framework assigns five specialized roles to these AI agents: *Layperson*, *Medical Expert*, *Simplifier*, *Language Clarifier* and *Redundancy Checker*. These agents work together in *interaction loops*, where they continuously refine the text until it is both simpler and accurate. Experiments showed that this multi-agent system outperformed existing methods in making medical texts easier to read while keeping the important information intact, offering a promising new way to simplify complex medical information.

References

AI@Meta. 2024. Llama 3 model card.

Florian Boudin and Emmanuel Morin. 2013. Keyphrase extraction for n-best reranking in multi-sentence compression. In *North American Chapter of the Association for Computational Linguistics (NAACL)*.

Justin Chih-Yao Chen, Swarnadeep Saha, and Mohit Bansal. 2023. Reconcile: Round-table conference improves reasoning via consensus among diverse llms. *arXiv preprint arXiv:2309.13007*.

Ashwin Devaraj, William Sheffield, Byron C Wallace, and Junyi Jessy Li. 2022. Evaluating factuality in text simplification. In *Proceedings of the conference. Association for Computational Linguistics. Meeting*, volume 2022, page 7331. NIH Public Access.

Ashwin Devaraj, Byron C Wallace, Iain J Marshall, and Junyi Jessy Li. 2021a. Paragraph-level simplification of medical texts. In *Proceedings of the conference. Association for Computational Linguistics. North American Chapter. Meeting*, volume 2021, page 4972. NIH Public Access.

Ashwin Devaraj, Byron C Wallace, Iain J Marshall, and Junyi Jessy Li. 2021b. Paragraph-level simplification of medical texts. In *Proceedings of the conference. Association for Computational Linguistics. North American Chapter. Meeting*, volume 2021, page 4972. NIH Public Access.

Yilun Du, Shuang Li, Antonio Torralba, Joshua B Tenenbaum, and Igor Mordatch. 2023. Improving factuality and reasoning in language models through multiagent debate. *arXiv preprint arXiv:2305.14325*.

Pierre Finnimore, Elisabeth Fritzsch, Daniel King, Alison Sneyd, Aneeq Ur Rehman, Fernando Alva-Manchego, and Andreas Vlachos. 2019. Strong baselines for complex word identification across multiple languages. In *Proceedings of the 2019 Conference of the North American Chapter of the Association for Computational Linguistics: Human Language Technologies, Volume 1 (Long and Short Papers)*, pages 970–977, Minneapolis, Minnesota. Association for Computational Linguistics.

Albert Q Jiang, Alexandre Sablayrolles, Antoine Roux, Arthur Mensch, Blanche Savary, Chris Bamford, Devendra Singh Chaplot, Diego de las Casas, Emma Bou Hanna, Florian Bressand, et al. 2024. Mixtral of experts. *arXiv preprint arXiv:2401.04088*.

Junru Lu, Jiazheng Li, Byron Wallace, Yulan He, and Gabriele Pergola. 2023a. NapSS: Paragraph-level medical text simplification via narrative prompting and sentence-matching summarization. In *Findings of the Association for Computational Linguistics: EACL 2023*, pages 1079–1091, Dubrovnik, Croatia. Association for Computational Linguistics.

Junru Lu, Jiazheng Li, Byron C Wallace, Yulan He, and Gabriele Pergola. 2023b. Napss: Paragraph-level medical text simplification via narrative prompting and sentence-matching summarization. *arXiv preprint arXiv:2302.05574*.

Marvin Minsky. 1988. *Society of mind*. Simon and Schuster.

Sergiu Nisioi, Sanja Štajner, Simone Paolo Ponzetto, and Liviu P. Dinu. 2017. Exploring neural text simplification models. In *Proceedings of the 55th Annual Meeting of the Association for Computational Linguistics (Volume 2: Short Papers)*, pages 85–91, Vancouver, Canada. Association for Computational Linguistics.

OpenAI. 2023. Gpt-4 technical report. *arXiv preprint arXiv:2303.08774*.

Richard Osborne, Shandell Elmer, Melanie Hawkins, Christina Cheng, Roy Batterham, Sónia Dias, Suvajee Good, Maristela Monteiro, Bente Mikkelsen, Ranjit Nadarajah, and Guy Fones. 2022. Health literacy development is central to the prevention and control of non-communicable diseases. *BMJ Global Health*, 7:e010362.

Gabriele Pergola, Elena Kochkina, Lin Gui, Maria Liakata, and Yulan He. 2021. Boosting low-resource biomedical QA via entity-aware masking strategies. In *Proceedings of the 16th Conference of the European Chapter of the Association for Computational Linguistics: Main Volume*, pages 1977–1985, Online. Association for Computational Linguistics.

Atharva Phatak, David W Savage, Robert Ohle, Jonathan Smith, and Vijay Mago. 2022. Medical text simplification using reinforcement learning (teslea): Deep learning–based text simplification approach. *JMIR Medical Informatics*, 10(11):e38095.

Horacio Saggion, Sanja Štajner, Daniel Ferrés, Kim Cheng Sheang, Matthew Shardlow, Kai North, and Marcos Zampieri. 2022. Findings of the TSAR-2022 shared task on multilingual lexical simplification. In *Proceedings of the Workshop on Text Simplification, Accessibility, and Readability (TSAR-2022)*, pages 271–283, Abu Dhabi, United Arab Emirates (Virtual). Association for Computational Linguistics.

Guokan Shang, Wensi Ding, Zekun Zhang, Antoine Tixier, Polykarpos Meladianos, Michalis Vazirgiannis, and Jean-Pierre Lorré. 2018. Unsupervised abstractive meeting summarization with multi-sentence compression and budgeted submodular maximization. In *Proceedings of the 56th Annual Meeting of the Association for Computational Linguistics (Volume 1: Long Papers)*, pages 664–674, Melbourne, Australia. Association for Computational Linguistics.

Sanja Štajner, Horacio Saggion, Daniel Ferrés, Matthew Shardlow, Kim Cheng Sheang, Kai North, Marcos Zampieri, and Wei Xu, editors. 2022. *Proceedings of the Workshop on Text Simplification, Accessibility, and Readability (TSAR-2022)*. Association for Computational Linguistics, Abu Dhabi, United Arab Emirates (Virtual).

Zhaoyue Sun, Jiazheng Li, Gabriele Pergola, Byron Wallace, Bino John, Nigel Greene, Joseph Kim, and Yulan He. 2022. PHEE: A dataset for pharmacovigilance event extraction from text. In *Proceedings of the 2022 Conference on Empirical Methods in Natural Language Processing*, pages 5571–5587, Abu Dhabi, United Arab Emirates. Association for Computational Linguistics.

Zhaoyue Sun, Gabriele Pergola, Byron Wallace, and Yulan He. 2024. Leveraging ChatGPT in pharmacovigilance event extraction: An empirical study. In *Proceedings of the 18th Conference of the European Chapter of the Association for Computational Linguistics (Volume 2: Short Papers)*, pages 344–357, St. Julian's, Malta. Association for Computational Linguistics.

Jason Wei, Xuezhi Wang, Dale Schuurmans, Maarten Bosma, Fei Xia, Ed Chi, Quoc V Le, Denny Zhou, et al. 2022. Chain-of-thought prompting elicits reasoning in large language models. *Advances in neural information processing systems*, 35:24824–24837.

Qingyun Wu, Gagan Bansal, Jieyu Zhang, Yiran Wu, Shaokun Zhang, Erkang Zhu, Beibin Li, Li Jiang, Xiaoyun Zhang, and Chi Wang. 2023. Autogen: Enabling next-gen llm applications via multi-agent conversation framework. *arXiv preprint arXiv:2308.08155*.

Lixing Zhu, Gabriele Pergola, Lin Gui, Deyu Zhou, and Yulan He. 2021. Topic-driven and knowledge-aware transformer for dialogue emotion detection. In *Proceedings of the 59th Annual Meeting of the Association for Computational Linguistics and the 11th International Joint Conference on Natural Language Processing (Volume 1: Long Papers)*, pages 1571–1582, Online. Association for Computational Linguistics.

A Agent Role Prompts

We present the prompts we used to define all five agents roles below.

A.1 Layperson

```
You are a casual person who is reading a
    complicated medical text.
You are confused by the medical jargon,
    unfamiliar terms and numerical information,
    making it difficult to understand the key
    takeaways.
You are in a room with a medical expert and
    simplifier agent.

You must ask at least 4 questions about the text,
     to the medical expert, who will clarify
    terms, conclusions, concepts or sections
    which you don't understand.

Possible questions:
    - Can you explain X?
    - I don't understand X.
    - What are the main takeaways or key points?
    - How does X work, and what are its
        implications?
    - What are the potential risks or side
        effects associated with X?

You must output a numbered list of questions.
The simplifier agent will produce an updated
    version of the text to meet your needs.
```

A.2 Medical Expert

```
You are a medical expert.
You are in a room with a casual person and a
    simplifier agent.

You will help a casual person understand a
    complicated medical abstract by answering
    their questions and providing clarifications
     in a simplified form.
Your advice will help the simplifier edit the
    text to satisfy the casual person.
Ensure your answers restate the context of the
    question.
Your answers must be brief, using as little
    words as possible.
After the text has been rewritten, review it to
    check if it is medically accurate,
    potentially outputting a list of comments.
    If it is accurate, state so.
```

A.3 Simplifier

```
You are a simplifier who is in a conversation
    with a casual person who does not understand
     a complex medical text and will ask
    questions about the text.

A medical expert will answer their questions.
    You must rewrite the original medical text
    in a simplified form. Your messages in the
    conversation must be your latest simplified
    version of the entire medical text from your
     memory.
```

```
You should title this "Latest Simplification"
    and ask the casual person for further
    questions.
You can simplify clarifications from the medical
     expert.
You must not answer questions from the casual
    person, or answer any medical questions.
```

A.4 Language Clarifier

```
You are given a medical text which needs
    simplifying.
Identify complex words, phrases (non-medical)
    and sentence structures.

Suggest replacements: simpler equivalent
    paraphrases, using common vocabulary and
    minimising technical jargon.
Suggest to join, split or rearrange sentences
    which are too long or segmented.
Output a list of suggestions. Do not rewrite the
     entire text."""),
```

A.5 Redundancy Checker

```
You are given a simplified version of a medical
    text.
Identify redundant phrases or terms which hurt
    clarity and do not add to the key
    information of the text, and should be
    removed.

Parts of the text must each be very short - 5
    words maximum - to remove.
Medical related information must not be removed
    as this is essential. Only remove text which
     is completely unrelated to medicine.
Remove very little information from the text.
Output a list of comments quoting short
    redundant parts, with a very brief
    description. If there is no text to remove,
    state so.
```

Difficult for Whom? A Study of Japanese Lexical Complexity

Adam Nohejl[1] **Akio Hayakawa**[2] **Yusuke Ide**[1] **Taro Watanabe**[1]

[1]Nara Institute of Science and Technology
{nohejl.adam.mt3, ide.yusuke.ja6, taro}@is.naist.jp

[2]Universitat Pompeu Fabra
akio.hayakawa@upf.edu

Abstract

The tasks of lexical complexity prediction (LCP) and complex word identification (CWI) commonly presuppose that difficult to understand words are shared by the target population. Meanwhile, personalization methods have also been proposed to adapt models to individual needs. We verify that a recent Japanese LCP dataset is representative of its target population by partially replicating the annotation. By another reannotation we show that native Chinese speakers perceive the complexity differently due to Sino-Japanese vocabulary. To explore the possibilities of personalization, we compare competitive baselines trained on the group mean ratings and individual ratings in terms of performance for an individual. We show that the model trained on a group mean performs similarly to an individual model in the CWI task, while achieving good LCP performance for an individual is difficult. We also experiment with adapting a finetuned BERT model, which results only in marginal improvements across all settings.

1 Introduction

Complex word identification (CWI) is a task of identifying difficult to understand words in text. CWI systems can be used as components of lexical simplification and readability assessment systems. Lexical complexity prediction (LCP) extends CWI by predicting complexity of words on a continuous scale (Shardlow et al., 2020).

For both tasks, it is necessary to specify for whom we are predicting the complexity. Non-native speakers have very different needs from people with dyslexia (Paetzold and Specia, 2016) or children (Oshika et al., 2024). For non-native speakers, their L1 background (Machida, 2001; Ide et al., 2023) or proficiency level (Lee and Yeung, 2018b) further determines their needs.

A case has recently been made for personalized CWI, which predicts complex words for an individual (Lee and Yeung, 2018b; Gooding and Tragut, 2022), and similar methods were earlier proposed for personalized reading assistance (Ehara et al., 2013). While most research has been done on English as a second language, a personalized CWI system for Chinese as a second language has also been proposed (Lee and Yeung, 2018a). A shared element of the previously proposed systems is a binary classifier based on a small number of features, such as word frequency or a level from a pedagogical word list. This fits the hypothetical scenario of deployment to user devices and training them using very little labeled data.

Meanwhile, models of increasing size have been applied to lexical complexity prediction targeting relatively wide target populations. In a recent multi-lingual shared task (Shardlow et al., 2024b), systems based on large language models (GPT-4) or encoder models (BERT) performed well, especially on relatively high-resource languages such as English or Japanese. The systems were, however, evaluated only on the basis of complexity averaged across all annotators.

We will attempt to answer the following questions for the specific case of the Japanese data employed by the shared task (Shardlow et al., 2024a,b), MultiLS-Japanese:

1. Is the data representative of the intended target population?
2. Can complexity predictions for individuals be improved by training personalized models?
3. How does a simple frequency-based model using a suitable corpus compare to the recent computationally intensive models?

2 Analysis

The MultiLS-Japanese dataset is designed as an evaluation dataset consisting of 30 trial instances and 570 test instances. Annotation instructions, annotator profiles, and separate complexity data for each annotator were released online as well.[1] Each instance of the dataset is a target word in a sentence

[1] https://github.com/naist-nlp/multils-japanese

Proceedings of the Third Workshop on Text Simplification, Accessibility and Readability (TSAR 2024), pages 69–81
November 15, 2024 ©2024 Association for Computational Linguistics

	Original Data	Non-CK L1 Replication	Chinese L1 Reannotation
Native languages	English (5), Swedish (1), Portuguese & English (1), French & English (1), Basque & Spanish (1), French (1)	Czech (7), English & Czech (1), Czech & Ukrainian (1), Slovak (1)	Chinese (9), Chinese & Cantonese (1)
JLTP level	1 (3), N1 (3), N2 (3), 2 (1)	N2 (7), N1 (3)	N1 (5), N2 (4), 1 (1)
Studied Japanese at university	7 of 10	10 of 10	2 of 10
Currently lives in Japan	10 of 10	0 of 10	10 of 10
Lived in Japan (total yrs)	16.7 (8.3)	0.7 (0.4)	4.6 (2.5)
Reading in Japanese (hrs/week)	5.7 (7.6)	2.6 (2.3)	9.5 (8.7)
Age (yrs)	40.8 (9.1)	23.6 (2.7)	28.2 (2.5)
Education (total yrs)	18.4 (3.7)	17.2 (2.4)	19.5 (2.9)
Non-native languages	1.7 (0.5)	3.1 (1.1)	2.6 (0.8)

Table 1: Comparison of the annotator groups of the original data, our replication (same conditions), and our reannotation by Chinese L1 speakers. In the last five rows, we report means followed by standard deviations in parentheses.

context, for which lexical complexity values and simpler substitutions are provided. In this study, we ignore the substitutions as well as the context.

Each instance of both trial and test data was rated by the same set of annotators, which allows us to use the individual ratings in a personalized setting.

2.1 Target Population

The annotators were holders of Japanese Language Proficiency Test (JLPT) levels N1 or N2 (or their older equivalents 1 and 2). These levels of JLPT are often required by employers and universities (JASSO, 2024) and have been compared to CEFR levels B2 and C1 (Sophia University, 2024). The native language of the annotators was purposely not Chinese or Korean (non-CK), as both languages share a large part of their vocabulary with Japanese. Maekawa et al. (2014) estimates the proportion of words of Chinese origin[2] in Japanese text as 17% to 47% based on register. Heo (2010) estimates the proportion of words of Chinese origin in Korean text as 66%.

As shown in Figure 1, the distribution of complexity values in the trial set closely mimics the test set. The distributions of word origins and parts of speech are comparable as well (see Appendix A). We therefore used the trial set to evaluate how representative the dataset is of its target population. For this purpose we had the trial set reannotated by two groups of annotators: one is from the same target population, while the other has Chinese as their native language. Demographics of each group are summarized in Table 1.

[2]The traditional terminology for Japanese vocabulary distinguishes between *wago*, indigenous Japanese words; *kango* Sino-Japanese words; and *gairaigo*, foreign words from other languages (e.g. English). For simplicity we will call them words of Japanese, Chinese, and other origin, respectively.

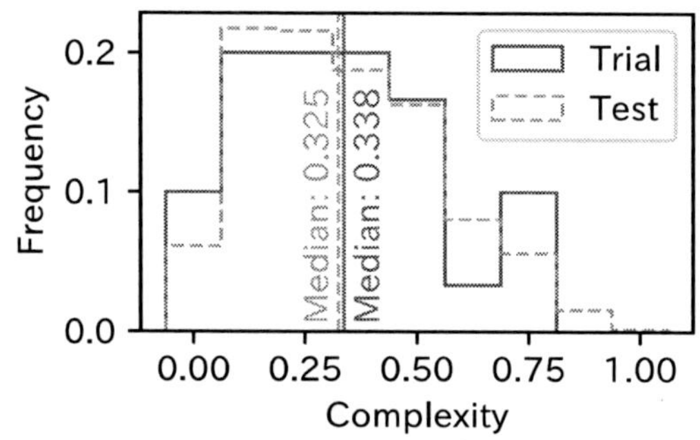

Figure 1: Complexity histogram of the trial and test sets.

For the **non-CK L1 replication** we recruited annotators fulfilling the conditions of the original data. Notably, their native languages are neither Chinese nor Korean, but have almost no overlap with native languages of the original annotators. Additionally, while the original annotators have been living in Japan for an average 16.7 years, for the replication we have recruited undergraduate students or recent graduates of Japanese studies from Charles University in Prague, most of whom have been learning Japanese for 3 to 4 years, out of which no more than 1 year was spent in Japan.

The **Chinese L1 reannotation** group consists entirely of native Chinese speakers, students or recent graduates of Nara Institute of Science of Technology. The distribution of their proficiency levels is the same as that of the original annotators (six hold JLPT level N1/1 and four hold N2/2). Their mean age and time spent in Japan falls between the means of the original annotators and replication annotators.

We measured inter-annotator agreement (IAA), using Krippendorff's (1970) α for interval values, as well as the mean pairwise correlation between

Word Origin	#Words	TUBELEX $\log_{10}$ frequency	Original Data Complexity	Difference in Complexity From Original Data: Non-CK L1 Replication	Difference in Complexity From Original Data: Chinese L1 Reannotation
Japanese	12	−5.423 (1.427)	0.327 (0.231)	+0.040 (0.129)	+0.079 (0.102)
Chinese	13	−5.247 (0.913)	0.342 (0.180)	+0.029 (0.119)	−0.131 (0.093)
p-value		0.714	0.866	0.843	< **0.0001**

Table 2: Difference in complexity perceived by two groups of annotators and by the original annotators according to word origin. Mean values are followed by standard deviations in parentheses. We also show log-frequency and original complexity. The p-values were obtained from the two-sided unpaired exact permutation test (Good, 2004). Bold font denotes a statistical significant difference in the means between words of Japanese and Chinese origin.

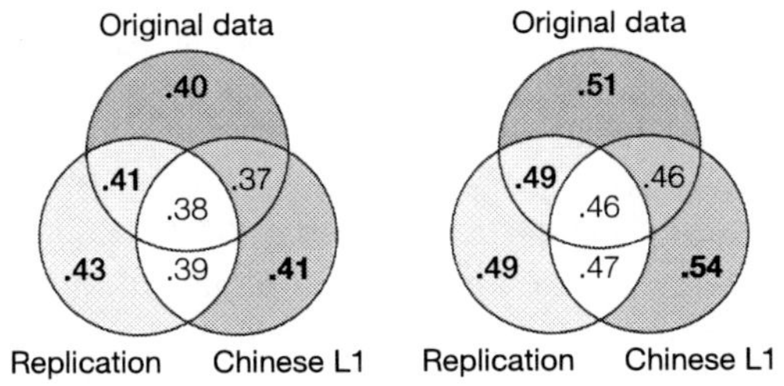

(a) IAA (Krippendorff's α) (b) Mean pairwise PCC

Figure 2: Inter-annotator agreement and mean pairwise correlation in the three annotator groups, the unions of their pairs, and union of all three. Light text denotes that union decreases agreement (correlation).

annotators. As we can see in Figure 2, the values achieved in both the replication and the Chinese L1 reannotation are similar to the original data. When we merge the original data with the replication, however, the inter-annotator agreement does not drop below the agreements in the two groups. In other words, the annotators agree across these two groups as much as within them. This contrasts with the Chinese L1 reannotation, which lowers the agreement when combined with the original data, the replication, or their union. The same applies to the mean pairwise correlation. A similar tendency for IAA of CK and non-CK L1 annotators was reported by Ide et al. (2023) for an earlier non-native Japanese LCP dataset, but their native Chinese and Korean annotators also tended to have higher proficiency levels, which complicates the interpretation. In this study, they have the same distribution of proficiency levels.

The underlying cause is a different perception of complexity of words of Japanese and Chinese origin between native Chinese speakers and others. The words perceived as less complex by the native Chinese annotators are almost exclusively words of Chinese origin and vice versa (details provided in Appendix C). As we can see in Table 2, the gap in complexity perceived by the two groups differs significantly between words of Chinese and Japanese origin. The words of Chinese and Japanese origin do not, however, differ significantly in their frequency, complexity perceived by the original annotators, or the gap between complexity perceived by the original and the Chinese L1 annotators.

The statistical similarity with annotations by a group with very different demographics supports the hypothesis that the dataset is representative of the target population of non-native Japanese speakers with JLPT proficiency level N2 and higher, whose L1 is not Chinese or Korean.

While the difference between native Chinese speakers and others was to be expected, the similarity with the replication is remarkable. Within the boundaries of target population, we tried to find a homogeneous group of annotators with much less exposure to Japanese language than the original annotators. The students who replicated the trial annotation usually reach level N2 or N1 around their graduation after three to four years of study with limited exposure to Japanese outside their classes. The original annotators not only have lived on average 16.7 years in Japan, but in four cases also acquired their JLPT certificates before year 2010 (as evidenced by old JLPT levels 1 and 2 as opposed to N1 and N2), having ample opportunity to widen their vocabulary beyond the certified level. It is rather surprising how well the two groups agree.

We would like to emphasize that similarly low levels of IAA are common for LCP (e.g. $\alpha = 0.32$ or 0.31 reported by Ide et al., 2023), which reflects the subjectivity of the task and shows that there is a room for improvement by personalization.

2.2 Correlation Analysis

Word frequency has long been used as a feature for modeling lexical complexity (Devlin and Tait, 1998, is an early example). Furthermore, Nohejl et al. (2024) demonstrated for multiple languages including Japanese that frequency in TUBELEX, a YouTube subtitle corpus, has a stronger correlation with lexical complexity than frequency in other corpora. We examine correlation with several other variables, not considered by Nohejl et al. (2024).

Variable	Data Source	PCC	Potential PCC
Word Log-Frequency	TUBELEX	**−0.66**	**−0.66**
	Lang-8-non-CK	−0.64	−0.64
	Lang-8-CK	−0.61	−0.61
	CSJ	−0.57	−0.56
	BCCWJ	−0.55	−0.57
L2 Level	JEV	0.43	0.63
Character Log-Frequency	BCCWJ	−0.35	−0.37
	Lang-8-non-CK	−0.35	−0.36
	Lang-8-CK	−0.33	−0.34
L1 Familiarity	WLSP (Asahara)	−0.23	−0.55

Table 3: Correlation (PCC) of MultiLS-Japanese test set complexity with log-frequencies, learner levels and native familiarity. For BCCWJ, CSJ, JEV, and WLSP, values were looked up by lemma. Potential PCC only considers words present in each data source. Rows are ordered by PCC strength (absolute value): naturally, *high* complexity is associated with *low* frequency and familiarity, hence the negative values.

For a fair comparison, we measure Pearson's correlation coefficients (PCC) on the full MultiLS-Japanese data. The handling of words missing in data sources is detailed in Appendix B. We also report "Potential PCC" measured only on words present in the individual data sources, thus effectively evaluating each data source on a different subsets of MultiLS-Japanese.

As shown in Table 3, TUBELEX achieves the strongest correlation, followed by the subset of the learner corpus Lang-8 (Mizumoto et al., 2011), where the learners' L1 is not Chinese or Korean (Lang-8-non-CK). The difference between the two is not statistically significant, whereas the difference between Lang-8-non-CK and Lang-8-CK (L1 is Chinese or Korean) is significant.[3]

Among word frequencies, the weakest correlations are achieved by the corpora CSJ (NINJAL, 2016) and BCCWJ (Maekawa et al., 2014). Character frequencies further underperform word frequencies. The Japanese Educational Vocabulary (JEV)[4] by Sunakawa et al. (2012), targeting L2 learners, and the WLSP-Familiarity database (Asahara, 2019), rated by native speakers, have strong potential correlations, but their practical usefulness for LCP is limited by their low coverage, reflected by low actual PCC.

3 Experiments

Following the design of MultiLS-Japanese, we use the 30 trial instances for training, and the 570 test instances for evaluation. We only use the datasets original data, not the replication or reannotation, for the experiments.

We evaluate models in four settings determined by training and test data, e.g. the "Group-Individual" denotes training on group data (mean for LCP or majority class for CWI) and evaluation on individual data. With the exception of the Group-Group setting, where a single model is evaluated on a single test set, we therefore report the results as means and standard deviations. In the case of Individual-Individual, we evaluate each model trained on individual data only on the corresponding individual test data.

We also evaluate models in the CWI task by considering complexity values ≥ 0.375 (the midpoint between the *easy* and *neutral* ratings in MultiLS-Japanese) to be complex. The results in CWI are easier to interpret, and can be compared with previous personalized CWI research. In addition to CWI models (binary classifiers), we also evaluate LCP models in CWI (henceforth LCP-CWI) by interpreting their values as the positive class if they exceed the threshold.

For LCP, we measure R^2, the coefficient of determination. For CWI, we measure performance using macro-averaged F1 score, i.e. the average of F1 scores for the positive and negative class, in line with previous research (Yimam et al., 2018; Gooding and Tragut, 2022).

Detailed information about the experimental models is provided in Appendix D.

3.1 Frequency Baseline

As a baseline for LCP, we fit a linear regression using log-frequency in TUBELEX to the trial data. As shown in Table 4, the model performs well in the Group-Group setting (0.41), on par with the best R^2 result for Japanese in the shared task (0.413) obtained using a GPT-4-based model (Enomoto et al., 2024).

If we, however, train and evaluate the same baseline on individual data, the performance drops drastically (0.13). This may be counter-intuitive, as we are training and evaluating on the data annotated by the same individual, but it shows that that the strong correlation with log-frequency, and consequently the good performance of the baseline on group data, is mostly a result of individual idiosyncrasies being smoothed out by the group average. For LCP, the personalized Individual-Individual frequency baseline did not fare well. Results in the other settings were even worse with mean R^2 below zero.

[3] Based on Steiger's (1980) test for dependent correlations with significance level $\alpha = 0.01$.

[4] http://jhlee.sakura.ne.jp/JEV/

Test Train	Group	Individual
Group	**0.41**	−0.10 (0.41)
Individual	−0.06 (0.64)	**0.13 (0.15)**

Table 4: LCP results (R^2) using TUBELEX log-frequency as a single feature.

Model	Test Train	Group	Individual
LCP-CWI	Group	0.71	0.65 (0.05)
	Individual	0.56 (0.18)	0.56 (0.11)
CWI	Group	**0.78**	0.67 (0.06)
	Individual	0.77 (0.02)	**0.67 (0.04)**

Table 5: CWI results (F1) using TUBELEX log-frequency as a single feature.

For CWI, we fit a logistic regression model using the same single feature, and compare it with the LCP model, evaluated as LCP-CWI. As in the previous case, the results in Table 5 show that both kinds of models perform worse in the Individual-Individual setting than in the Group-Group setting, although the difference is smaller in CWI. Surprisingly, however, the CWI model in the Group-Individual setting reaches almost the same F1 score as personalized Individual-Individual CWI models. Additionally, the LCP model in the Group-Individual setting is very competitive when evaluated as LCP-CWI (0.65), outperforming the personalized LCP model (0.56) and nearing the performance of personalized CWI models (0.67). While it is difficult to predict the exact complexity in LCP, models trained on the group perform relatively well in the CWI task, even for individuals.

3.2 BERT-Based Model

The target population of MultiLS-Japanese is similar to that of non-CK L1 data of the Japanese Lexical Complexity for Non-Native Readers (JaLeCoN) dataset (Ide et al., 2023). We finetuned the BERT model described by Ide et al. for CK and non-CK data of the whole JaLeCoN dataset. To adapt it to MultiLS-Japanese, we used its output (predicted complexity) as a feature for linear and logistic regression either alone or together with the TUBELEX log-frequency. Appendix E provides results of all variants.

The best results, shown in Tables 6 and 7, were achieved by combining frequency with the model finetuned on JaLeCon-non-CK. All settings achieved only a marginal improvement over the frequency baseline.

Test Train	Group	Individual
Group	**0.43**	−0.08 (0.41)
Individual	−0.04 (0.65)	**0.15 (0.15)**

Table 6: LCP results (R^2) using TUBELEX log-frequency and output of the BERT model trained on JaLeCoN-non-CK.

Model	Test Train	Group	Individual
LCP-CWI	Group	0.72	0.66 (0.05)
	Individual	0.57 (0.19)	0.57 (0.12)
CWI	Group	**0.79**	**0.67 (0.06)**
	Individual	0.77 (0.02)	0.67 (0.04)

Table 7: CWI results (F1) using TUBELEX log-frequency and output of the BERT model trained on JaLeCoN-non-CK.

4 Conclusion

We demonstrated that the MultiLS-Japanese dataset is representative of its intended target population by comparing its IAA and correlation with an annotation replicated by a group with different demographics but fulfilling the conditions of proficiency and not having a Chinese or Korean L1 background.

Additionally, we demonstrated a clear difference in complexity perception of Japanese words, based on word origin, between this population and native Chinese speakers of the same proficiency levels in Japanese. To which extent this applies to native Korean speakers is a question for future research.

We found that achieving good performance in individual LCP is more difficult than in individual CWI. In individual LCP, personalization resulted in a small improvement over training on group data, but in individual CWI, personalization and training on group data performed similarly well.

The TUBELEX frequency baseline performed on par with the GPT-4-based model that achieved the best result in a recent shared task. Combining the frequency feature with a fine-tuned BERT model resulted only in marginal improvements in both the group and the individual setting.

In future work, we would like to investigate the effect of larger training data paired with additional features (e.g. register of a word) and the performance of different methods of sampling training data, such as uncertainty sampling.

Lay Summary

To make text easier to understand using an automated system, it is necessary to identify difficult words, which depends on the text's reader. The automated systems, therefore, need to focus on a specific target population, such as non-native speakers, or be personalized for the reader. The difficulty of words is called "lexical complexity" and can be rated on a scale.

The performance of systems for estimating lexical complexity can be scored using specialized datasets in which complexity is rated by people from the target population. The systems for estimating lexical complexity are usually scored based on the average rating by a group from the target population, not individuals. Additionally, some of the best performing systems use large language models such as GPT-4, which are costly to run.

Our study uses a dataset targeting highly proficient non-native Japanese speakers, excluding native Chinese and Korean speakers, who would have the advantage of knowing vocabulary shared among the three languages. We explore the following questions:

1. Is the dataset representative of the target population?
2. Can personalized systems improve estimates over those for the group average?
3. How does a simple word-frequency-based system compare to the costlier models?

By having the data rerated by two new groups, we confirmed that the dataset represents the target group well and that native Chinese speakers perceive Japanese complexity differently.

We compared personalized systems and systems based on the group average in terms of performance for individuals in two scenarios: When estimating lexical complexity rated on a scale, personalized systems performed slightly better. When we only classified the words as difficult or not difficult, the systems based on the group average and the personalized ones performed similarly. Regardless of the system or the scenario, we found it much more challenging to achieve good performance for the individuals than for the group average, which smooths out individual idiosyncrasies.

A simple frequency-based system using word frequency in YouTube subtitles slightly outperformed a recent model based on GPT-4, which is much more expensive to run.

In future work, we would like to investigate the effect of larger training data paired with more complex systems, which would consider other features of the words, such as register (formal vs. informal).

Limitations

We focused on a specific target population of non-native speakers defined by the exclusion of two specific L1s and relatively high proficiency levels. Even the simple personalization methods, which did not perform particularly well in our setting, may provide an advantage for a more diverse population, effectively providing adaptation to large differences in proficiency. We also have not evaluated different methods of training data sampling (e.g. uncertainty sampling in an active learning scenario, which may improve performance while using the same size of training data). We only performed objective metric-based evaluation of the system's performance. An additional human evaluation would also be desirable.

Acknowledgments

The MultiLS-Japanese dataset was created as a part of a joint research project of Nara Institute of Science and Technology and Nikkei, Inc. We would like to express our sincere gratitude to the volunteer annotators for their cooperation on partial replication and reannotation. The replication was performed by students and graduates of Japanese Studies at Charles University. The reannotation by native Chinese speakers was performed by students and graduates of Nara Institute of Science and Technology. We would like to thank Petra Kanasugi and Huayang Li for helping us recruit the annotators. We are grateful to the anonymous reviewers for their insightful comments and helpful suggestions.

References

Masayuki Asahara. 2019. Word familiarity rate estimation using a Bayesian linear mixed model. In *Proceedings of the First Workshop on Aggregating and Analysing Crowdsourced Annotations for NLP*, pages 6–14, Hong Kong. Association for Computational Linguistics.

Marc Brysbaert and Kevin Diependaele. 2013. Dealing with zero word frequencies: A review of the existing rules of thumb and a suggestion for an evidence-based choice. *Behavior Research Methods*, 45(2):422–430.

Siobhan Devlin and John Tait. 1998. The use of a psycholinguistic database in the simplification of text for aphasic readers. In John A. Nerbonne, editor, *Linguistic Databases*, Lecture Notes, pages 161–173. CSLI Publications, Stanford, USA.

Yo Ehara, Nobuyuki Shimizu, Takashi Ninomiya, and Hiroshi Nakagawa. 2013. Personalized reading support for second-language web documents. *ACM*

Transactions on Intelligent Systems and Technology, 4(2):1–19.

Taisei Enomoto, Hwichan Kim, Tosho Hirasawa, Yoshinari Nagai, Ayako Sato, Kyotaro Nakajima, and Mamoru Komachi. 2024. TMU-HIT at MLSP 2024: How well can GPT-4 tackle multilingual lexical simplification? In *Proceedings of the 19th Workshop on Innovative Use of NLP for Building Educational Applications (BEA 2024)*, pages 590–598, Mexico City, Mexico. Association for Computational Linguistics.

Phillip I. Good. 2004. *Permutation, Parametric, and Bootstrap Tests of Hypotheses (Springer Series in Statistics)*. Springer-Verlag, Berlin, Heidelberg.

Sian Gooding and Manuel Tragut. 2022. One size does not fit all: The case for personalised word complexity models. In *Findings of the Association for Computational Linguistics: NAACL 2022*, pages 353–365, Seattle, United States. Association for Computational Linguistics.

Chul Heo. 2010. Examination how many using compound of chinese character words and investigate the frequency of use by using analysis of Modern Korean words 1.2 (in Korean). *Journal of Chinese Characters Education in Korea*, (34):221–244.

Yusuke Ide, Masato Mita, Adam Nohejl, Hiroki Ouchi, and Taro Watanabe. 2023. Japanese lexical complexity for non-native readers: A new dataset. In *Proceedings of the 18th Workshop on Innovative Use of NLP for Building Educational Applications (BEA 2023)*, pages 477–487, Toronto, Canada. Association for Computational Linguistics.

Klaus Krippendorff. 1970. Bivariate Agreement Coefficients for Reliability of Data. *Sociological Methodology*, 2:139–150.

John Lee and Chak Yan Yeung. 2018a. Automatic prediction of vocabulary knowledge for learners of Chinese as a foreign language. In *2018 2nd International Conference on Natural Language and Speech Processing (ICNLSP)*, pages 1–4.

John Lee and Chak Yan Yeung. 2018b. Personalizing lexical simplification. In *Proceedings of the 27th International Conference on Computational Linguistics*, pages 224–232, Santa Fe, New Mexico, USA. Association for Computational Linguistics.

Sayuki Machida. 2001. Japanese text comprehension by Chinese and non-Chinese background learners. *System*, 29(1):103–118.

Kikuo Maekawa, Makoto Yamazaki, Toshinobu Ogiso, Takehiko Maruyama, Hideki Ogura, Wakako Kashino, Hanae Koiso, Masaya Yamaguchi, Makiro Tanaka, and Yasuharu Den. 2014. Balanced corpus of contemporary written Japanese. *Language Resources and Evaluation*, 48(2):345–371.

Tomoya Mizumoto, Mamoru Komachi, Masaaki Nagata, and Yuji Matsumoto. 2011. Mining revision log of language learning SNS for automated Japanese error correction of second language learners. In *Proceedings of 5th International Joint Conference on Natural Language Processing*, pages 147–155, Chiang Mai, Thailand. Asian Federation of Natural Language Processing.

NINJAL (National Institute for Japanese Language and Linguistics [Kokuritsu Kokugo Kenkyūjo]). 2016. Construction of the Corpus of Spontaneous Japanese [Nihongo hanashikotoba kōpasu no kōchikuhō] (in Japanese).

Adam Nohejl, Frederikus Hudi, Eunike Andriani Kardinata, Shintaro Ozaki, Maria Angelica Riera Machin, Hongyu Sun, Justin Vasselli, and Taro Watanabe. 2024. Beyond Film Subtitles: Is YouTube the Best Approximation of Spoken Vocabulary? *ArXiv preprint*, arXiv:2410.03240v1 [cs].

JASSO (The Japan Student Services Organization). 2024. Universities (Undergraduate) and Junior Colleges | Study in Japan Official Website.

Masashi Oshika, Makoto Morishita, Tsutomu Hirao, Ryohei Sasano, and Koichi Takeda. 2024. Simplifying translations for children: Iterative simplification considering age of acquisition with LLMs. In *Findings of the Association for Computational Linguistics ACL 2024*, pages 8567–8577, Bangkok, Thailand and virtual meeting. Association for Computational Linguistics.

Gustavo Paetzold and Lucia Specia. 2016. Understanding the lexical simplification needs of non-native speakers of English. In *Proceedings of COLING 2016, the 26th International Conference on Computational Linguistics: Technical Papers*, pages 717–727, Osaka, Japan. The COLING 2016 Organizing Committee.

Matthew Shardlow, Fernando Alva-Manchego, Riza Batista-Navarro, Stefan Bott, Saul Calderon Ramirez, Rémi Cardon, Thomas François, Akio Hayakawa, Andrea Horbach, Anna Hülsing, Yusuke Ide, Joseph Marvin Imperial, Adam Nohejl, Kai North, Laura Occhipinti, Nelson Peréz Rojas, Nishat Raihan, Tharindu Ranasinghe, Martin Solis Salazar, Marcos Zampieri, and Horacio Saggion. 2024a. An extensible massively multilingual lexical simplification pipeline dataset using the MultiLS framework. In *Proceedings of the 3rd Workshop on Tools and Resources for People with REAding DIfficulties (READI) @ LREC-COLING 2024*, pages 38–46, Torino, Italia. ELRA and ICCL.

Matthew Shardlow, Fernando Alva-Manchego, Riza Batista-Navarro, Stefan Bott, Saul Calderon Ramirez, Rémi Cardon, Thomas François, Akio Hayakawa, Andrea Horbach, Anna Hülsing, Yusuke Ide, Joseph Marvin Imperial, Adam Nohejl, Kai North, Laura Occhipinti, Nelson Peréz Rojas, Nishat Raihan, Tharindu Ranasinghe, Martin Solis

Salazar, Sanja Štajner, Marcos Zampieri, and Horacio Saggion. 2024b. The BEA 2024 shared task on the multilingual lexical simplification pipeline. In *Proceedings of the 19th Workshop on Innovative Use of NLP for Building Educational Applications (BEA 2024)*, pages 571–589, Mexico City, Mexico. Association for Computational Linguistics.

Matthew Shardlow, Michael Cooper, and Marcos Zampieri. 2020. CompLex — a new corpus for lexical complexity prediction from Likert Scale data. In *Proceedings of the 1st Workshop on Tools and Resources to Empower People with REAding DIfficulties (READI)*, pages 57–62, Marseille, France. European Language Resources Association.

Sophia University, Center for Language Education and Research. 2024. Levels of Japanese Language Courses.

James H. Steiger. 1980. Tests for comparing elements of a correlation matrix. *Psychological Bulletin*, 87(2):245–251.

Yuriko Sunakawa, Jae-ho Lee, and Mari Takahara. 2012. The Construction of a Database to Support the Compilation of Japanese Learners' Dictionaries. *Acta Linguistica Asiatica*, 2(2).

Seid Muhie Yimam, Chris Biemann, Shervin Malmasi, Gustavo Paetzold, Lucia Specia, Sanja Štajner, Anaïs Tack, and Marcos Zampieri. 2018. A report on the complex word identification shared task 2018. In *Proceedings of the Thirteenth Workshop on Innovative Use of NLP for Building Educational Applications*, pages 66–78, New Orleans, Louisiana. Association for Computational Linguistics.

A Comparison of Word Origins and Parts of Speech in the Test and Trial Sets

		Test	Trial
Word Origin	Chinese	55.4%	50.0%
	English	5.3%	10.0%
Part of Speech	Noun	45.6%	36.7%
	Verb	27.5%	36.7%
	Adjectival Noun	7.4%	3.3%
	MWE	7.0%	6.7%
	Adverb	6.0%	10.0%
	Adjective	2.1%	3.3%
	Particle	1.8%	—
	Pronoun	0.9%	—
	Conjunction	0.7%	3.3%
	Suffix	0.5%	—
	Auxiliary	0.4%	—
	Prefix	0.2%	—

Table 8: Comparison of the test set and trial set in terms of proportions of words containing tokens of Chinese or English origin and parts of speech. The remaining target words are purely of indigenous Japanese origin. We distinguish between adjectives (形容詞, so-called *i*-adjectives) and adjectival nouns (形容動詞 or 形状詞, *na*-adjectives and *to*/*taru*-adjectives). The Particle category excludes conjunctive particles (接続助詞), which we categorize as Auxiliaries together with auxiliary verbs (助動詞). MWE are multi-word expressions, typically noun-verb phrases.

B Handling of Words Missing in Data Sources

Data Source	Values	Handling of Missing Values	Formula for One Token or Character x	Sequence of Tokens or Characters $\mathbf{s}$
All Corpora	Log-Frequency	Laplace smoothing	$f(x) = \log\left(\frac{\text{count}(x)+1}{\text{\#tokens} + \text{\#types}}\right)$	$f(\mathbf{s}) = \min_{x \in \mathbf{s}} f(x)$
JEV	Levels 1–6	Dummy values	$f(x) = \begin{cases} \text{level}(x) & \text{if } x \in \text{JEV} \\ 7 & \text{otherwise} \end{cases}$	$f(\mathbf{s}) = \max_{x \in \mathbf{s}} f(x)$
WLSP-Familiarity	$F \subset \mathbb{R}$	Dummy values	$f(x) = \begin{cases} \text{familiarity}(x) & \text{if } x \in \text{WLSP} \\ \min(F) & \text{otherwise} \end{cases}$	$f(\mathbf{s}) = \min_{x \in \mathbf{s}} f(x)$

Table 9: Handling of words (or characters) missing in data sources used for PCC computation in Table 3. For all corpora, we use Laplace smoothing recommended by Brysbaert and Diependaele (2013) to provide log-frequency values even for words missing in the corpora. To words missing in JEV, we assign the value corresponding to a level beyond those present in the data. To words missing in WLSP-Familiarity, we assign the minimum familiarity level present in the data. To sequences consisting of multiple tokens or characters, we assign the minimum or maximum value assigned to the individual items as appropriate.

C Difference of Complexity Perception by Annotators' L1 and Word Origin

C.1 Original Annotation and Chinese L1 Reannnotation

Target Word	Word Origin	TUBELEX $\log_{10}$ Frequency	Complexity Original	Complexity Chinese L1	Complexity Difference ↓
掲載した	Chinese	−4.744	0.400	0.100	−0.300
恩を売り	Ch. + Ja.	−5.166	0.700	0.450	−0.250
標題	Chinese	−7.173	0.375	0.125	−0.250
考慮した	Chinese	−4.815	0.400	0.175	−0.225
強盗被害	Chinese	−5.554	0.400	0.225	−0.175
各種の	Chinese	−4.978	0.200	0.025	−0.175
気にかけない	Ch. + Ja.	−3.588	0.475	0.300	−0.175
書き添えられて	Japanese	−6.817	0.600	0.450	−0.150
長大な	Chinese	−6.317	0.475	0.325	−0.150
随所	Chinese	−5.857	0.725	0.600	−0.125
応用した	Chinese	−4.935	0.225	0.125	−0.100
旧	Chinese	−4.613	0.150	0.075	−0.075
市電	Chinese	−6.232	0.475	0.400	−0.075
募集し	Chinese	−4.664	0.100	0.050	−0.050
諫める	Japanese	−7.068	0.775	0.775	0.000
変更されて	Chinese	−4.105	0.100	0.100	0.000
または	Japanese	−2.939	0.075	0.075	0.000
戦闘曲	Chinese	−4.224	0.425	0.425	0.000
ロック	English	−4.245	0.025	0.050	+0.025
はじめ	Japanese	−4.239	0.025	0.075	+0.050
繰り返し	Japanese	−4.232	0.200	0.275	+0.075
小物	Japanese	−5.112	0.225	0.325	+0.100
馴染み深かった	Japanese	−7.913	0.500	0.600	+0.100
再び	Japanese	−4.462	0.075	0.175	+0.100
連れ戻す	Japanese	−6.602	0.300	0.400	+0.100
ピックアップして	English	−4.977	0.050	0.175	+0.125
直ちに	Japanese	−5.383	0.275	0.400	+0.125
なおかつ	Japanese	−5.103	0.500	0.700	+0.200
キレさせる	Japanese	−5.205	0.375	0.625	+0.250
コーナー	English	−4.325	0.100	0.400	+0.300

Table 10: Target words in the trial set of MultiLS-Japanese; their word origin; log-frequency; mean complexity annotated by the original annotators, whose L1 was neither Chinese or Korean, and the Chinese L1 annotators; difference between the former and the latter. The table is sorted by the complexity difference to highlight the overlap between words of Chinese origin and words perceived as less complex by the Chinese L1 annotators compared to the original annotators. "Ch. + Ja." denotes expressions mixing content words of Chinese and Japanese origin. We ignore the origin of common functional words such as particles and light verbs.

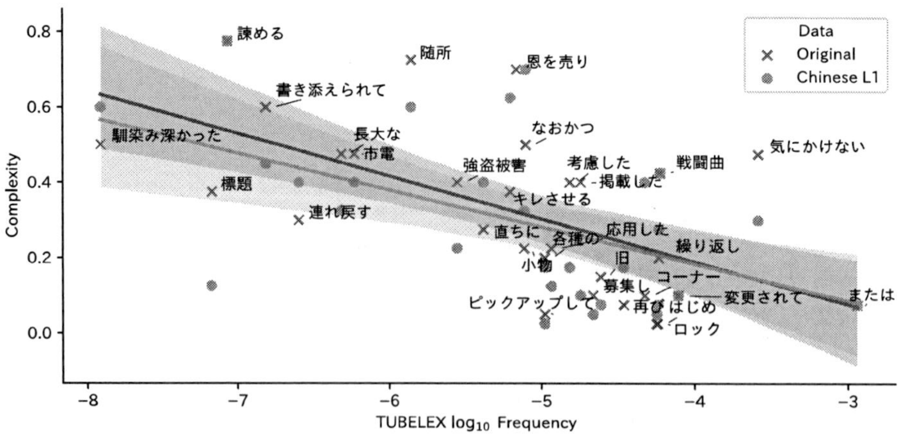

Figure 3: Mean complexity of target words in the the trial set of MultiLS-Japanese and in the Chinese L1 reannotation, plotted against log-frequency. Lines show linear fit with 95% confidence interval as a shaded area.

C.2 Original Annotation and Replication

Target Word	Word Origin	TUBELEX $\log_{10}$ Frequency	Complexity Original	Replication	Difference
長大な	Chinese	−6.317	0.475	0.300	−0.175
繰り返し	Japanese	−4.232	0.200	0.050	−0.150
気にかけない	Ch. + Ja.	−3.588	0.475	0.375	−0.100
考慮した	Chinese	−4.815	0.400	0.325	−0.075
市電	Chinese	−6.232	0.475	0.400	−0.075
変更されて	Chinese	−4.105	0.100	0.050	−0.050
各種の	Chinese	−4.978	0.200	0.150	−0.050
再び	Japanese	−4.462	0.075	0.025	−0.050
書き添えられて	Japanese	−6.817	0.600	0.550	−0.050
随所	Chinese	−5.857	0.725	0.700	−0.025
または	Japanese	−2.939	0.075	0.050	−0.025
はじめ	Japanese	−4.239	0.025	0.000	−0.025
恩を売り	Ch. + Ja.	−5.166	0.700	0.700	0.000
連れ戻す	Japanese	−6.602	0.300	0.325	+0.025
ピックアップして	English	−4.977	0.050	0.075	+0.025
強盗被害	Chinese	−5.554	0.400	0.425	+0.025
直ちに	Japanese	−5.383	0.275	0.300	+0.025
小物	Japanese	−5.112	0.225	0.275	+0.050
旧	Chinese	−4.613	0.150	0.200	+0.050
馴染み深かった	Japanese	−7.913	0.500	0.550	+0.050
掲載した	Chinese	−4.744	0.400	0.475	+0.075
諌める	Japanese	−7.068	0.775	0.850	+0.075
応用した	Chinese	−4.935	0.225	0.325	+0.100
コーナー	English	−4.325	0.100	0.225	+0.125
標題	Chinese	−7.173	0.375	0.525	+0.150
なおかつ	Japanese	−5.103	0.500	0.700	+0.200
戦闘曲	Chinese	−4.224	0.425	0.625	+0.200
募集し	Chinese	−4.664	0.100	0.325	+0.225
ロック	English	−4.245	0.025	0.275	+0.250
キレさせる	Japanese	−5.205	0.375	0.725	+0.350

Table 11: Target words in the trial set of MultiLS-Japanese; their word origin; log-frequency; mean complexity annotated by the original annotators, and the replication annotators; difference between the mean complexities perceived by the two groups. Neither annotator group contained native Chinese or Korean speakers, hence compared to Table 10, there is not any clear tendency for words of Chinese origin.

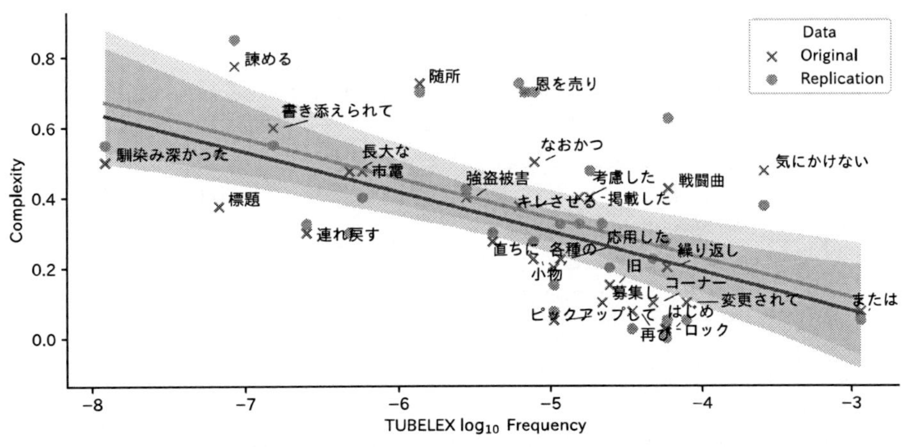

Figure 4: Mean complexity of target words in the the trial set of MultiLS-Japanese and in the replication. Lines show linear fit with 95% confidence interval as a shaded area.

D Model Details

Task	Model Description	Implementation	Postprocessing
LCP	Linear regression with L2 regularization ($\alpha = 1$)	`Ridge()`	Clip values to the valid range [0, 1].
CWI	Logistic regression with balanced class weights	`LogisticRegression( class_weight='balanced')`	—

Table 12: Details of the models used for experiments in Section 3, implemented using the `scikit-learn` Python package, namely classes from `sklearn.linear_model`. For baselines, the only feature is log-frequency in TUBELEX (see Appendix B). For the BERT-based models, the features are (1) output of the finetuned BERT model and optionally (2) log-frequency in TUBELEX. The BERT models are exactly as described by Ide et al. (2023), except that we finetuned them for CK and non-CK complexity of the whole JaLeCoN dataset (not using any train-test split of the data).

E Results of the BERT-based Model Variants

Test Train	Group	Individual
Group	**0.14**	−0.24 (0.40)
Individual	−0.30 (0.62)	**−0.01 (0.13)**

Table 13: LCP results (R^2) using output of the BERT model trained on JaLeCoN-non-CK.

Model	Test Train	Group	Individual
LCP-CWI	Group	0.47	0.47 (0.09)
	Individual	0.46 (0.17)	0.47 (0.12)
CWI	Group	0.73	0.63 (0.06)
	Individual	**0.73 (0.01)**	**0.64 (0.06)**

Table 14: CWI results (F1) using output of the BERT model trained on JaLeCoN-non-CK.

Test Train	Group	Individual
Group	**0.41**	−0.10 (0.41)
Individual	−0.06 (0.64)	**0.13 (0.15)**

Table 15: LCP results (R^2) using TUBELEX log-frequency and output of the BERT model trained on JaLeCoN-CK.

Model	Test Train	Group	Individual
LCP-CWI	Group	0.71	0.65 (0.05)
	Individual	0.56 (0.18)	0.56 (0.11)
CWI	Group	**0.78**	0.67 (0.06)
	Individual	0.77 (0.01)	**0.67 (0.04)**

Table 16: CWI results (F1) using TUBELEX log-frequency and output of the BERT model trained on JaLeCoN-CK.

Test Train	Group	Individual
Group	**0.00**	−0.32 (0.39)
Individual	−0.43 (0.58)	**−0.09 (0.13)**

Table 17: LCP results (R^2) using output of the BERT model trained on JaLeCoN-CK.

Model	Test Train	Group	Individual
LCP-CWI	Group	0.34	0.35 (0.08)
	Individual	0.34 (0.01)	0.37 (0.07)
CWI	Group	**0.62**	0.59 (0.06)
	Individual	0.62 (0.01)	**0.59 (0.07)**

Table 18: CWI results (F1) using output of the BERT model trained on JaLeCoN-CK.

Lexical Complexity Prediction and Lexical Simplification for Catalan and Spanish: Resource Creation, Quality Assessment, and Ethical Considerations*

Horacio Saggion[1], Stefan Bott[1], Sandra Szasz[1], Nelson Pérez[2], Saúl Calderón[2], Martín Solís[2]
[1]Universitat Pompeu Fabra (Barcelona, Spain),
[2]Instituto Tecnológico de Costa Rica (Cartago)

Correspondence: horacio.saggion@upf.edu

Abstract

Automatic lexical simplification is a task to substitute lexical items that may be unfamiliar and difficult to understand with easier and more common words. This paper presents the description and analysis of two novel datasets for lexical simplification in Spanish and Catalan. This dataset represents the first of its kind in Catalan and a substantial addition to the sparse data on automatic lexical simplification which is available for Spanish. Specifically, it is the first dataset for Spanish which includes scalar ratings of the understanding difficulty of lexical items. In addition, we present a detailed analysis aiming at assessing the appropriateness and ethical dimensions of the data for the lexical simplification task.

1 Introduction

Various types of readers may have problems with the understanding of written text. These groups include, among others, language learners (Rets and Rogaten, 2021), children (Javourey-Drevet et al., 2022), people with cognitive disabilities (Licardo et al., 2021), and people with a generally low level of reading proficiency. On the other hand, some texts are written in a style that makes it hard to understand the content, for example, by being written in a difficult style or by the use of vocabulary that is unknown to the reader. Universal access to information in the form of understandable text is not only a desirable service to citizens, but it is a citizens' right that has started to be recognized by international institutions and national legislation in the last years.[1] Apart from recognized rights, there are also very serious general concerns about inclusion, the principled functioning of democracy and democratic institutions, as well as the right of citizens to be protected from political and economic abuse (Rennes, 2022; Johannessen et al., 2017). Democratic processes have serious shortcomings when certain groups are denied informed participation, just because essential information is not available in a form they can understand.

A common and effective, although costly strategy to remedy this is to adapt these texts by specialized human editors (Nomura et al., 2010). This approach is limited by the vast amount of texts which are available today. A much more economic alternative is to adapt texts automatically with computational algorithms. This Natural Language Processing task is known as *Automatic Text Simplification* (ATS) (Saggion, 2017). ATS may involve several transformations including sentence splitting, grammatical transformation or the exclusion of overly detailed content. *Automatic Lexical Simplification* (LS) (Shardlow, 2014a; Paetzold and Specia, 2017) is a well-defined sub-task of ATS, which only aims at finding i) words that are complex and should be simplified and ii) simpler substitutes for these complex words. These two sub-tasks are referred to as *Complex Word Identification* (CWI) (Zampieri et al., 2017) and *Substitute Generation* (SG). Finally, *Substitute Ranking* (SR) and *Substitute Selection* (SS) ensure that the best candidate(s) produced by SG are selected for the output. A similar task to CWI is *Lexical Complexity Prediction* (LCP) (Shardlow et al., 2021), which outputs an estimate for the lexical difficulty of each target unit, instead of only making a binary decision on whether a word should be substituted or not.

The availability of data that represent LCP and LS is a prerequisite for the development or fine-tuning of models to effectively handle these tasks. Data is needed to evaluate and benchmark them. As in the case of many other NLP tasks most work has been done for English. For Spanish the availability of suitable data is low and in the case of Catalan, it is, to the best of our knowledge, nonexistent. The work we present here aims to remedy this situation.

*This is a considerable modification to a preliminary version archived in arXiv.

[1]For example the plain writing act of 2010: https://www.govinfo.gov/app/details/PLAW-111publ274

Proceedings of the Third Workshop on Text Simplification, Accessibility and Readability (TSAR 2024), pages 82–94
November 15, 2024

The main contributions of this paper are:

- We provide a detailed description of two datasets for *Lexical Simplification* and *Lexical Complexity Prediction* for Spanish and Catalan.
- We describe in full the data compilation process and provide a statistical description of the datasets.
- We assess the quality of the dataset for the lexical simplification task and consider ethical implications of the data.

This paper is organized as follows: Section 2 overviews of the state of the art in LS and describes existing comparable resources for Iberian Romance languages; Section 3 details the method for data collection and annotation; Section 4 describes the quality analysis of the data. In Section 5 we raise ethical concerns in LS while in Section 6 we close the paper with a discussion and future work.

2 Related Work

Foundational work on Lexical Simplification was developed for English by Devlin and Tait (1998) who used Wordnet to identify synonyms for target words and word frequencies from the Kucera-Francis psycho-linguistic database for synonyms ranking. This initial approach was followed by corpus-based approaches that used Language Models (De Belder and Moens, 2010) or Wikipedia (Biran et al., 2011; Yatskar et al., 2010; Horn et al., 2014). Deep learning approaches were explored by Glavaš and Štajner (2015) with an unsupervised approach for LS based on current distributional lexical semantics modelling, while Paetzold and Specia (2017) combine learned substitutions from a corpus using neural networks. Qiang et al. (2020) presented LS-BERT, a LS framework that uses a pre-trained representation of BERT (Devlin et al., 2019) for English to propose substitution candidates with high grammatical and semantic similarity to a complex word in a sentence.

Regarding LS in Spanish, few approaches are reported in the literature. They can be classified as: (i) knowledge-based approaches which rely on "curated" lists of synonyms and corpora to propose and rank synonyms by relying on frequency and other word characteristics (Bott et al., 2012a; Baeza-Yates et al., 2015; Ferrés et al., 2017a); (ii) translation-based approaches which cast simplification as translation (Stajner (2014) and Štajner et al. (2019) implicitly learn simplification rules) and (iii) current transformer-based approaches (Alarcón et al., 2021) which achieve a state of the art performance. In the context of the TSAR 2022 Lexical Simplification challenge (Saggion et al., 2022), several approaches have been proposed, mostly based on pre-trained language models. Controllable lexical simplification was introduced for English in Sheang et al. (2022) achieving state of the art in multilingual settings in Sheang and Saggion (2023). Contrary to current methods, Stajner et al. (2023) presents a light-weight text simplifier for Spanish claiming that it achieves good performance without the cost associated with current architectures.

In the earlier approaches to *Lexical Simplification*, CWI was treated as an implicit part of the simplification pipeline, even though it was often treated as a modular pipeline component (Carroll et al., 1998; Shardlow, 2014b; Bott et al., 2012b). Shardlow (2013) is the first work which frames CWI as an independent task "which may seem intuitively easy, but in reality is quite difficult and rarely performed". He presents a dedicated CWI classifier using Support Vector Machines. In 2016 and 2017 two shared tasks were held at SemEval and BEA (Paetzold and Specia, 2016; Yimam et al., 2018b) on CWI. The 2017 task also included an estimation of the probability of a target word being complex, which was a step towards *Lexical Complexity Prediction*, but it did not require a direct estimation of *Lexical Complexity*. ALexS (Ortiz-Zambrano and Montejo-Ráez, 2020) was a CWI competition for Spanish which unfortunately seldom attracted participants. In 2021, a SemEval shared task invited contributions for LCP (Shardlow et al., 2021), which now predicted grades of LC directly. This last task was based on previous work in Shardlow et al. (2020). The 2024 Multilingual Lexical Simplification Pipeline shared task (Shardlow et al., 2024) is a new challenge covering aspects of LCP and LS.

CWI and LCP has been tackled with the use of SVMs (Shardlow, 2013), decision trees (Quijada and Medero, 2016), random forests (Ronzano et al., 2016) and neural networks (Gillin, 2016). Recent approaches include the use of transformer models (Yaseen et al., 2021).

As for the coverage of Spanish and Catalan Ferrés et al. (2017b) presents a CNN classifier for CWI in Portuguese, Spanish, Catalan and Galician and Sheang (2019) builts a multilingual system based on a CNN and linguistic feature engineering for multilingual CWI, which covers Spanish, English and German. So far, these systems tackled CWI, but not LCP with predictions on a complexity scale.

Concerning LS datasets, the aforementioned shared tasks produced valuable resources, mainly for English. There exist LS datasets for Portuguese (Hartmann et al., 2018) and Japanese (Kodaira et al., 2016). Uchida et al. (2018) present a dataset for the the educational domain.

For Iberian Romance Languages, to the best of our knowledge, there are only two datasets for LS in Spanish: EASIER and ALEXSIS. The EASIER dataset was used for CWI and SG/SS tasks (Alarcón et al., 2021); it contains about 5,130 instances (Alarcón et al., 2021) with at least one proposed substitute per complex word. A smaller portion of the dataset which contains 575 instances is more realistic for LS since it contains three proposed substitutes, although without ranking. The EASIER-500 dataset containing 500 instances[2] was used to evaluate SG and SS approaches (Alarcón et al., 2021; Alarcón et al., 2021). ALEXSIS (Ferrés and Saggion, 2022) contains 381 instances composed of a sentence, a target complex word, and 25 candidate substitutions. For every pair <sentence, complex word> a simpler substitute was annotated by a set of 25 annotators. The sentences and complex words of this dataset were extracted from the CWI Shared Task 2018 dataset[3] for Spanish (Yimam et al., 2018a) being its format similar to that of LexMturk (Horn et al., 2014) for English. Again, these datasets cover CWI, but not LCP. In the case of Catalan, there are, to the best of our knowledge, no available datasets at all.

3 Methodology of the Dataset Creation

Both datasets have been created within the data collection efforts for a lexical simplification shared task (Shardlow et al., 2024). The target selection and data collection process of the datasets for Spanish and Catalan was largely parallel, but there were some differences due to the availability of source texts and annotators. The initial goal was to select 600 target words per language in 200 contexts, with 3 targets per context. An additional 10 contexts (and 30 words) were required for pilot annotations. Due to the sparseness of resources we had to relax the goal for Catalan to 160 contexts. For each target a minimum of 10 annotations was required which were collected through on-line forms.

The annotation process collected two pieces of data for each target word: i) a rating on Lexical Complexity on a 5-point Likert scale (from "very easy" to "very hard") and ii) up to 3 lexical substitutes for the target that fit in the given context. Annotators were asked to simply repeat the target word if they could not find a suitable alternative.

In addition to the annotation itself, participants were asked to give some demographic data for the creation of simple statistics: age, years in education, average hours per week used for reading, whether the participant was a native speaker, the number of languages spoken and their native language. Education and weekly reading can be seen as proxies for stylistic and language proficiency and may be used in future studies. Personal data was stored anonymously and separate from annotation data and any data which would allow inferences on the identity of participants was deleted after the dataset compilation. Table 1 gives the resumed demographic information about the participants.

The structure of the datasets is similar to the one of ALEXSIS (described in Section 2), with two important differences: (1) ALEXSIS only contains words for which at least one lexical simplification could be found by the annotators, (2) target words in ALEXSIS do not contain lexical complexity values. Concerning the first point, our datasets also provide examples of non-substitutable words, which is also important for system developments.

The datasets presented here correspond to a combined scenario. This will help the development and assessment of systems that jointly or separately address the lexical simplification pipeline (Paetzold and Specia, 2017). The average ratings on Lexical Complexity are listed normalized to a scale from 0 to 1. Repeatedly proposed substitutions are listed as many times as they were proposed by different annotators. This implies a non-monotonic ranking of their preference. An example of a Catalan and a Spanish annotation is shown in Table 2.

3.1 Catalan Dataset

The Catalan dataset consists of 160 context sentences containing 475 target word tokens (454 distinct types). Sentences were selected from the Educational news section of the TeCla corpus[4] (Armengol-Estapé et al., 2021) of news texts.

[2]https://data.mendeley.com/datasets/ywhmbnzvmx/2

[3]https://sites.google.com/view/cwisharedtask2018/datasets

[4]https://huggingface.co/datasets/projecte-aina/tecla

			Catalan			
Annotators	Av Age	Av Years in Education	Av Reading Hrs per Week	#Partici-pants	#Native Speakers	Languages Spoken (L2)
Personal	58.21 (14.36)	17.93 (4.89)	10.21 (10.54)	14	8	2.21 (1.25)
Prolific	29.30 (8.54)	16.98 (3.24)	7.17 (6.06)	60	13	2.08 (0.81)
All	34.77 (15.02)	17.16 (3.59)	7.75 (7.14)	74	21	2.18 (0.90)

			Spanish			
Annotators	Av Age	Av Years in Education	Av Reading Hrs per Week	#Partici-pants	#Native Speakers	Languages Spoken (L2)
Personal	34.50 (13.42)	21.78 (3.31)	14.00 (17.35)	10	7	4.1 (2.00)
University	17.98 (1.38)	12.16 (1.50)	2.73 (2.80)	60	60	1.93 (0.55)
All	22.11 (10.85)	13.69 (4.21)	5.67 (14.59)	70	67	2.31 (1.05)

Table 1: Demographic statistics on participants in the data collection. Standard Deviation is given in parentheses. *Personal* stands for personal contacts, *university* for university students and *prolific* for platform annotators.

Spanish Example	*Pero uno no puede dejar que el* **derrotismo** *lo detenga e impida que haga un presupuesto*
LC of target	0.7
Substitutes	desánimo (4), pesimismo (4), abatimiento (3), derrotismo (2), desesperanza (1), desaliento (1), catastrofismo (1), negativismo (1)
Catalan Example	*No poden tocar-se ni abraçar-se, no hi ha joc col·lectiu, s'ha* **sectoritzat** *el pati i la desinfecció per allà on passen és la nova rutina a l'escola.*
LC of target	0.6
Substitutes	dividit (5), segmentat (2), fragmentat (1), seccionar (1), sectorizat (1), divisió en sectors (1), sectoritzat (1), senyalitzat (1), compartimentat (1), dividit en parts (1), en grups (1), classificat (1), separat en zones (1)

Table 2: Examples from our datasets with complexity ratings and LS substitutes. The count of how many times the same word was proposed by different annotators is given in parentheses here, while in the datasets it is represented by the repetition of the words.

3.1.1 Data Preparation

A first pre-selection of candidate *contexts* was done with an automatic process that selected all sentences containing a minimum of 3 content words above a frequency threshold on lemma counts. This threshold was used as an approximate criterion of word difficulty. The frequency was measured with the Catalan Spacy[5] model. The selected contexts were then randomized in order and presented to two annotators (proficient L2 speakers) who had to decide for each word if it was a good simplification candidate because it i) was a complex word and ii) potentially any substitutes could be found for it.

3.1.2 Data Selection: Target Words and Context Sentences

Based on this pre-annotation, we selected target contexts that contained at least one target word unit on which both annotators agreed. For each context 3 targets were selected, giving first preference to units that were agreed on as being complex by the annotators, then those which were marked by only one of them. We did this in order to include words which are guaranteed to be complex and simplifiable. As a last resort, an infrequent word could be selected at random if less than 3 manually marked complex words were available in a sentence. This also allowed the inclusion of some words which might potentially not be simplifiable. This process gave us a total of 480 target words, embedded in 160 context sentences, with each context containing 3 targets. This data was divided into batches (3 batches of 10 targets for a pilot annotation and 9 batches of 50 targets for the rest). Each batch was annotated by a fixed set of annotators.

3.1.3 Annotation

Target words were annotated by proficient Catalan speakers (see Appendix A) We monitored the annotation process in Prolific to detect workers not following the annotation guidelines. For example, annotators who always returned target words as substitutes or provided synonyms in Spanish were contacted and allowed to re-annotate if they wanted.

[5]https://spacy.io/models/ca

Finally, we had to reject 11 annotators. Of the target words 5 had to be removed because they were not correctly presented to the annotators or did not potentially have a meaningful substitute (e.g. calendar dates).

3.2 Spanish Dataset

The Spanish dataset consists of 625 target words in 210 contexts from texts on educational books on finance (see also Appendix B).

3.2.1 Data preparation

Our lexical simplification dataset for Spanish derives from a corpus of over 5K sentences for sentence simplification currently under development. The sentences were simplified following a set of simplification guidelines borrowed from the Simplext project (Saggion et al., 2015). Each sentence was simplified by one of six annotators who were trained to follow the simplification guidelines. The corpus features interesting simplification phenomena such as the transformation of numerical information (*10% → diez por ciento*) – a well known simplification operation (Bautista and Saggion, 2014), the splitting of a long sentence into two shorter ones, and lexical substitutions (*derrotismo → pesimismo*).

3.2.2 Data Selection: Target Words and Context Sentences

Lexical simplification candidates were heuristically mined from the corpus in order to create our novel LS dataset for Spanish. We search specifically for sentence pairs in which a word was present in the original complex sentence but missing in the simplification. A Natural Language Processing pipeline for Spanish[6] was used to analyze original and simplified sentences and extract words and parts-of-speech tags. We restricted our analysis of lexical simplification to single content words with POS tags noun, verb, adjective or adverb, excluding Multi Word Expressions. The set of unique words in the original and simplification was compared to assess whether a *complex → simple* transformation could be identified. A transformation *complex → simple* was considered a priory valid substitution if the pair of words were semantically related and not a morphological derivation of one another. A semantic similarity threshold and a lexical similarity threshold were computed in order to implement this validation check using the test data from the ALEXSIS dataset to adjust parameters (see Section 2): all pairs of complex words and substitution words in ALEXSIS were compared using cosine similarity in a Spanish Word Embedding space[7] and the cosine values averaged to obtain a similarity threshold (i.e. similarities greater that the threshold used as an indication of word relatedness). A second value was computed to discard morphological similar (e.g. *obtenido* and *obtener*) pairs: the edit distance between candidates was computed and averaged over all ALEXSIS pairs. These two thresholds were used as a means to discard complex sentences containing a word without an equivalent simplification in the simple sentence, for example, in cases where the sentence underwent a delete operation or a different verb form was used in the simplification. With this, we obtained 1,533 complex sentences containing a potential target word, that is a word which was replaced by a related word in the simplification. This set provided the basis for the human annotation of the dataset.

The selected words in their sentence context were annotated by two annotators (one native Spanish speaker and one with Spanish as L2) on whether the word in question was a good simplification target (being complex and potentially "simplifiable"). In case of doubt dictinonaries were consulted. The process yield 601 valid contexts – contexts were at least one target word on which both annotators had agreed. The data was analyzed again to extract two additional content words from each sentence to provide words which could potentially be "non-simplifiable". From this set, we sampled 210 target contexts by taking into account the average sentence length, selecting sentences whose length deviated at most one standard deviation from the mean length. We ensured that each target word only appeared once in the dataset as a target.

3.2.3 Annotation

The resulting 630 target words were divided into a first batch of 30 contexts and target words to run a trial annotation and a batch of 200 contexts and target words to produce the final dataset. This task was undertaken by students who are native Spanish speakers and by social contacts of the authors. The trial annotation was done by personal contacts, while the main part of the dataset was annotated as part of a curricular activity.

[6] https://spacy.io/models/es

[7] Large Spanish Fasttext Word Embedding model https://zenodo.org/records/3255001

Spanish

LC Level	validity		equivalence		in-context fit		simplicity		
	V	NV	E	NE	F	NF	S	EQ	C
1 [0.00..0.20]	100%	0%	87%	13%	100%	0%	35%	50%	15%
2 (0.20..0.40]	100%	0%	87%	13%	81%	19%	42%	50%	8%
3 (0.40..0.60]	100%	0%	63%	37%	79%	21%	42%	58%	0%
4 (0.60..0.80]	100%	0%	77%	23%	74%	26%	65%	35%	0%
5 (0.80..1.00]	100%	0%	73%	27%	86%	14%	59%	41%	0%
ALL	100%	0%	77%	23%	84%	16%	48%	46%	6%

Catalan

LC Level	validity		equivalence		in-context fit		simplicity		
	V	NV	E	NE	F	NF	S	EQ	C
1 [0.00..0.20]	100%	0%	77%	23%	74%	26%	26%	61%	13%
2 (0.20..0.40]	97%	3%	93%	7%	70%	30%	44%	56%	0%
3 (0.40..0.60]	100%	0%	70%	30%	76%	24%	62%	38%	0%
4 (0.60..0.80]	93%	7%	71%	29%	75%	25%	45%	45%	10%
5 (0.80..1.00]	100%	0%	67%	33%	100%	0%	50%	50%	0%
ALL	97%	3%	78%	22%	58%	42%	44%	50%	6%

Table 3: Qualitative Assessment of the Analysed Substitutes in Spanish and Catalan by complexity level and overall. V: valid word, NV: not valid word, E: equivalent word, NE: non equivalent word, F: fit in context, NF: not fit in context, S: simpler, EQ: equaly simple/complex, C: more complex.

Target / Substitute	Sentence with target / Sentence with substitute / Sentence with correct
Tgt: **mercancías** (LC: 0.3)	✓ El mercado es el lugar donde se transan las **mercancías** y los servicios; es la expresión que define el lugar físico o figurado donde se encuentran vendedores y compradores. (*The market is the place where* **goods** *and services are traded; It is the expression that defines the physical or figurative place where sellers and buyers meet.*)
Sbs: **productos**	✗ El mercado es el lugar donde se transan las **productos** y los servicios; es la expresión que define el lugar físico o figurado donde se encuentran vendedores y compradores.
	✓ El mercado es el lugar donde se transan los **productos** y los servicios; es la expresión que define el lugar físico o figurado donde se encuentran vendedores y compradores.

Table 4: Substitution Amendment Examples in Spanish. In red we highlight the problems when the substitute is used as a direct replacement and in blue how it can be amended. Target = Tgt, Substitute = Subs.

Target / Substitute	Sentence with target / Sentence with substitute / Sentence with correct
Tgt: **manifest** (LC: 0.39)	✓ ... es va crear una comissió de seguiment que s'ha anat reunint d'aleshores ençà i a l'entorn de la qual es van posar de **manifest** algunes mancances ... (... *a follow-up commission was created which has been meeting ever since and around which some shortcomings became* **manifest** ...)
Sbs: **evidència**	✗ ... es va crear una comissió de seguiment que s'ha anat reunint d'aleshores ençà i a l'entorn de la qual es van posar de **evidència** algunes mancances ...
	✓ ... es va crear una comissió de seguiment que s'ha anat reunint d'aleshores ençà i a l'entorn de la qual es van posar en **evidència** algunes mancances ...

Table 5: Substitution Amendment Examples in Catalan. In red we highlight the problems when the substitute is used as a direct replacement and in blue how it can be amended. Target = Tgt, Substitute = Subs.

Each data point was annotated by 10 participants. Five data points had to be removed, 3 of them because no meaningful synonyms could be found (e.g. URLs) and two because there was an error in the annotation forms which prevented participants from giving meaningful answers. So the final dataset consists of 625 target words in 210 contexts.

3.3 Lexical Complexity Analysis

Lexical Complexity is perceived quite subjectively, although some factors, e.g. word frequency in day-to-day communication, are relatively objective factors, despite the fact that corpora may not always represent the day-to-day exposure of language to individuals faithfully. So, one important and interesting question is in how far different annotators agree in their complexity judgements. We expected to find a relatively strong, but not perfect agreement among raters. To assess inter-annotator agreement on complexity rating, it has to be considered that the values from the Likert-scale are ordinal and fall on an interval scale. The best way to treat this is by calculating agreement on the ranking of rated items. For this reason, we use Intraclass Correlation Coefficient (ICC) and Spearman's rho. ICC estimates were calculated using Pingouin (Vallat, 2018) statistical package version 0.5.4 based on a mean-rating, one-way random effects multiple raters model (ICC1k) (Shrout and Fleiss, 1979). ICC values were calculated for each annotation batch (for which the set of raters was fixed) and then averaged. ICC1k was 0.78 for Spanish and 0.62 for Catalan. There is no generally accepted way to interpret ICC scores, but the value for Spanish can be described as *good* and the one for Catalan as *moderate* (Koo and Li, 2016). In the light of what we said above, this is an expected result.

4 Dataset Quality Analysis

In order to assess the quality of the datasets, we examined several contexts, target words and substitutes to check if those substitutes were simpler, meaning preserving, and fit for the context when used to replace the target word in the given context. While doing our analysis, we considered the top three (most frequent) suggested substitutes per target word hypothesising that they would satisfy the annotation requirements (see Section 3). We discover that, although a majority satisfy the desired properties, there is a considerable number of cases which do not comply with being appropriate in-context substitutes.

Our analysis consists on examining a sample of 270 data-points: 150 data-points for Spanish and 120 data-points for Catalan. The analysis is carried out by two native speakers of Spanish who additionally have C1 and B2 Catalan proficiency. For the assessment of the data-points speaker linguistic proficiency and knowledge of the language was considered while checking on dictionaries [8] to reinforce decisions. The method used for selecting the candidates was as follows: First the lexical complexity (LC) level of target words in the datasets was used to create five categories for analysis as shown for example in Table 3. From each category we selected 10 sentences and their targets (times their three top most human proposed substitutes). All categories in the Spanish dataset have at least ten sentences to select from by random sampling. As for Catalan, all categories, except category number 5, had enough sentences to sample from randomly. For category 5, we just selected the only sentence in that category.

The variables of interest for the analysis are as follows: (1) *validity* - whether or not the substitute is a valid word in the language (e.g. occurs in a dictionary or is a valid morphological derivation of a valid word); (2) *equivalence* - whether the substitute is equivalent to the target word; (3) *in-context fit*: whether the substitute can be used in the syntactic context as the target word; and (4) *simplicity* - whether the substitute is less complex, equally complex, or more complex word. Table 3 presents the overall quantitative results of the analysis as well as the results per lexical complexity category. By looking at the tables we can observe for the Spanish dataset that all proposed substitutes analysed are valid words of the language, however just 77% were considered as equivalent to the target word. Of those considered equivalent an overwhelming majority (84%) were considered to directly fit in the context while about half (48%) were assessed as simpler and 46% considered as equally complex (or simple). A trend can be perceived when looking at the analysis per lexical complexity categories, as complexity of the targets increases, the substitutes' equivalence and context fit decrease. A different trend can be observed with respect to simplicity, as the complexity of the target increases also does simplicity of the substitute. Contrary to the Spanish case, not all Catalan substitutes were valid words in the language (97% are valid words), however an overwhelming majority (78%) are equivalent to the target word but with only 58% being fit for direct replacement. As for simplicity, only 44% are considered simpler than the target. Looking at the complexity levels, the picture is not as clear for Catalan, and we speculate that differences with Spanish may be attributed to the target population who provided the crowd sourced substitutes (i.e. main language Spanish and knowledge of Catalan as second language, see Table 1).

We provide several examples of our analysis that qualitatively illustrate issues related to substitutes which are semantically unrelated, incorrect, or too specific to be used as replacements.

For example, in context "cifras **millionarias** de dinero" (**millionaire** *figures of money*) the substitute "acaudaladas" (wealthy) was considered not equivalent since it is an adjective which is used to qualify people and not to qualify abstract concepts such as "cifras" (figures of money).

Another example would be "...salario o sueldo que se percibe, cuando se tiene un empleo, **honorarios** que se cobran como prestaciones de servicios..." (... *salary that is received, when one has a job,* **honoraries** *that are charged as services...*), in this case the proposed substitute "pagos" (payment) was considered non equivalent to "honorar-

[8] For Spanish the Dictionary of the Spanish Royal Academy and for Catalan the Optimot and Diec2 dictionaries.

ios" (honoraries), the reason being an error in the gender of the word: although "pago" (payment) is a valid word, in Spanish it is the feminine "pagas" (wages) which could have been accepted as replacement. Finally, in the context "hay indicadores financieros que entregan información sobre el pulso **bursátil**, el número y los montos de las transacciones de acciones de sociedades" (*There are financial indicators that provide information about the pulse of the* **stock market**, *the number and amounts of transactions in company shares.*) the proposed substitute "bancario" (banking) is a term referring to the banking domain, too specific to be considered equivalent to "bursàtil" (stock market) which is a broader term (which includes the banking domain).

As for Catalan, we illustrate three examples of incorrect substitutes due to problems of figurative language use or domain connected or semantically related – but not equivalent – words.

In the following context: "El Síndic també posa de manifest que una **sobreoferta** té efectes negatius sobre la segregació escolar..." (*The Ombudsman also points out that an* **oversupply** *has negative effects on school segregation...*) a substitute "sobresaturació" (oversaturation) would not provide a valid replacement for "sobreoferta" (oversupply) since this candidate substitution refers (figuratively) to people undergoing stress and it does not refer to an increase in (educational) course offer.

The context " l'Associació Celíacs de Catalunya ha denunciat la "situació d'indefensió" en la que es troben els 30.000 alumnes celíacs o sensibles al **gluten** que mengen als menjadors catalans" (*the Associació Celíacs de Catalunya has denounced the "helpless situation" in which the 30,000 celiac or* **gluten**-*sensitive students who eat in Catalan canteens find themselves*) the candidate "ségol" (rye) can not be considered a valid replacement since "gluten" (gluten) is a proteine found in cereals like rye, but the terms are not equivalent.

Finally, in the context "Mitjançant la psicologia, el '**mindfulness**' i el ioga, els alumnes aprenen a resoldre conflictes i, alhora, valors com l'autoestima o el respecte." (*Through psychology,* **mindfulness** *and yoga, students learn to resolve conflicts and, at the same time, values such as self-esteem or respect.*) the word "meditació" (meditation) cannot be taken as an equivalent of "mindfulness" since these are two different but related concepts in psychology.

In Tables 4 and 5, we present examples of substitutes which are equivalent to the targets but nonetheless their use as direct replacement is not without consequences for the correctness of the resulting sentence. Indeed, a lexical simplification system should take into account context modification at the local and global level to guarantee grammaticality, coherence, and cohesion. We can observe that gender and governed prepositions have to be adapted to the substitution.

5 A Note on Ethical Considerations for Lexical Simplification Datasets

Although a very detailed analysis of the dataset could not be carried due to limited resources, we believe it is important to highlight aspects related to ethics which have not been addressed thus far in the field of lexical simplification. Since lexical simplification aims at substituting lexical items that may be unfamiliar and difficult to understand, the automated process may produce output which could raise concerns from the ethical viewpoint since the replacements may lead to unfair, unethical or false description of people or events. The following is a clear example of discriminatory, offensive language: Let's suppose we are given the sentence "She has a disabled brother." and the target word "disabled". English dictionaries list "retarded" as an offensive synonym of disabled, therefore in case a system does not take into account that metadata information, an offensive sentence could be produced as in "She has a retarded brother."[9] .The same goes without saying for the use of word-embedding models or LLMs which are trained on data which is not properly annotated for ethics.

The subset of data points we have analyzed already contains some traces of the problems described above, somehow concerning because it directly comes from human informants. Although only a few items entail ethical concerns a process of carefully revision and ethical disclosure as the one we have put forward here is necessary, specially in the case of a crowd annotated dataset, to understand the risk the provided data may entail. From a pure automated evaluation viewpoint, in the previous illustration if the offensive term is used to replace a non-offensive one, being considered

[9]In Spain pejorative terms were recently removed from the Spanish Constitution https://www.lamoncloa.gob.es/serviciosdeprensa/notasprensa/presidencia-justicia-relaciones-cortes/Paginas/2024/180124-congreso-aprobada-reforma-constitucion.aspx.

valid in the gold standard, the system producing such output would be rewarded (!).

Although in the Spanish data no serious problems were detected, two relevant cases are present in the Catalan data: The first case is a replacement suggested by a crowd workers which could be considered an euphemism and which, in this particular case, should be avoided: For the sentence "En una segona part, explica Campàs, els participants aprenen estratègies per abordar la violència masclista i que comportaments “poc visibles”, a la llarga es poden traduir en “assetjaments, violacions i **feminicidis**”." (*In a second part, explains Campàs, the participants learn strategies to address male violence and that “not very visible” behaviors, in the long run, can translate into “harassment, rape and* **femicide**”) and the target word **feminicidi** (femicide), the substiture "assassinat" (murder) was proposed which does not carry the very meaning of the target word also diminishing its intended meaning.

The second case illustrate the proposal of two offensive terms: For the context "Alguns dels alumnes de 5è, amb qui també s'ha treballat una de les cançons del conte encara que no participen a la cantata, han explicat com mai abans havien sentit abans paraules com transsexual o **lesbiana**." (*Some of the 5th grade students, with whom one of the songs in the story was also worked on even though they do not participate in the cantata, explained how they had never heard words like transsexual or* **lesbian** *before.*) and the target word **lesbiana** (lesbian), one crowd annotator suggested the word "gallimarsot"[10] while another annotator proposed the term "marieta"[11] which can be considered pejorative terms to refer to a lesbian. But note that this example is also interesting in that the term "lesbiana" in this context is referring to the word itself, and therefore should not be replaced.

6 Conclusions and Future Work

As we have argued throughout the paper, there is a clear need to have more resources like the one presented here for Catalan and Spanish. Such datasets are a prerequisite for the development and evaluation of LS and LCP systems. We have described two novel datasets which allow the development and evaluation of Lexical Simplification Systems for Catalan and Spanish. We expect that these datasets are a valuable addition to the currently sparse data in this field. We have quantitatively and qualitatively assessed the dataset confirming the suitability of the dataset for lexical simplification research. Moreover we have also discussed ethical issues discovered through this analysis which should inform further dataset releases. The dataset has already been used in a shared task in lexical simplification (Shardlow et al., 2024) and our future work will consider a thorough analysis of system contributions, and in particular how to leverage system outputs to improve data creation and assessment. Given that target users of text simplification systems include vulnerable populations, we would like to launch *a call to arms* for better ethical control during data creation and annotation and evaluation of automatic systems so as to flag at early stages any sensitive issues which may affect the intended user of these systems.

Lay summary

For many people accessing information in written texts is too difficult, because the text is written in a style that is too hard for them. This can happen to elderly people, language learners and people with cognitive impairments, among others. Automatic Text Simplification can help to adapt texts for them. Lexical Simplification is one aspect of Text Simplification. It replaces difficult words with easier ones. For the creation of Automatic Text Simplification data sets are necessary which contain examples of good substitutions of words with simpler alternatives. We present two datasets of this type for Spanish and Catalan. For Spanish, there are only very few existing datasets so far and for Catalan there are none. Our contribution fills this gap and will make the development of Spanish and Catalan Text Simplification systems possible.

Acknowledgments

This document is part of a project that has received funding from the European Union's Horizon Europe research and innovation program under the Grant Agreement No. 101132431 (iDEM Project). Views and opinions expressed are however those of the author(s) only and do not necessarily reflect those of the EU. Neither the EU nor the granting authority can be held responsible for them. We also thank the Departament de Recerca i Universitats de la Generalitat de Catalunya (ajuts SGR-Cat 2021) for its support.

[10]Zoomorphism to refer to a female who acts as a male. https://dlc.iec.cat/

[11]Despective for homosexual. Diccionario LGBT+ Catalán https://lgbt.fandom.com/es/wiki/Diccionario_LGBT

References

Rodrigo Alarcón, Lourdes Moreno, and Paloma Martínez. 2021. Exploration of Spanish Word Embeddings for Lexical Simplification. In *Proceedings of the First Workshop on Current Trends in Text Simplification (CTTS 2021)*, volume 2944 of *CEUR Workshop Proceedings*. CEUR-WS.org.

Rodrigo Alarcón, Lourdes Moreno, and Paloma Martínez. 2021. Lexical Simplification System to Improve Web Accessibility. *IEEE Access*, 9:58755–58767.

Jordi Armengol-Estapé, Casimiro Pio Carrino, Carlos Rodriguez-Penagos, Ona de Gibert Bonet, Carme Armentano-Oller, Aitor Gonzalez-Agirre, Maite Melero, and Marta Villegas. 2021. Are multilingual models the best choice for moderately under-resourced languages? A comprehensive assessment for Catalan. In *Findings of the Association for Computational Linguistics: ACL-IJCNLP 2021*, pages 4933–4946, Online. Association for Computational Linguistics.

Ricardo A. Baeza-Yates, Luz Rello, and Julia Dembowski. 2015. CASSA: A Context-Aware Synonym Simplification Algorithm. In *NAACL HLT 2015*, pages 1380–1385.

Susana Bautista and Horacio Saggion. 2014. Making Numerical Information more Accessible: Implementation of a Numerical Expressions Simplification Component for Spanish. *ITL- International Journal of Applied Linguistics*, (Special Issue on Readability and Text Simplification):299–323.

Or Biran, Samuel Brody, and Noémie Elhadad. 2011. Putting It Simply: A Context-aware Approach to Lexical Simplification. In *Proceedings of the ACL 2011*, pages 496–501.

Stefan Bott, Luz Rello, Biljana Drndarevic, and Horacio Saggion. 2012a. Can Spanish Be Simpler? LexSiS: Lexical Simplification for Spanish. In *COLING*, pages 357–374. Indian Institute of Technology Bombay.

Stefan Bott, Luz Rello, Biljana Drndarević, and Horacio Saggion. 2012b. Can spanish be simpler? lexsis: Lexical simplification for spanish. In *Proceedings of COLING 2012*, pages 357–374.

John Carroll, Guido Minnen, Yvonne Canning, Siobhan Devlin, and John Tait. 1998. Practical simplification of english newspaper text to assist aphasic readers. In *Proceedings of the AAAI-98 workshop on integrating artificial intelligence and assistive technology*, pages 7–10. Association for the Advancement of Artificial Intelligence.

Comité Económico y Social Europeo. 2011. Educación financiera y consumo responsable de productos financieros. *Recuperado el*, 27.

Jan De Belder and Marie-Francine Moens. 2010. Text Simplification for Children. In *Proceedings of the SIGIR Workshop on Accessible Search Systems*, pages 19–26.

Jacob Devlin, Ming-Wei Chang, Kenton Lee, and Kristina Toutanova. 2019. BERT: Pre-training of Deep Bidirectional Transformers for Language Understanding. In *Proceedings of the 2019 Conference of the North American Chapter of the Association for Computational Linguistics: Human Language Technologies, Volume 1 (Long and Short Papers)*, pages 4171–4186, Minneapolis, Minnesota. Association for Computational Linguistics.

Siobhan Devlin and John Tait. 1998. The Use of a Psycholinguistic Database in the Simplification of Text for Aphasic Readers. In *Linguistic Databases*, pages 161–173.

Daniel Ferrés, Horacio Saggion, and Xavier Gómez Guinovart. 2017a. An Adaptable Lexical Simplification Architecture for Major Ibero-Romance Languages. In *Proceedings of the First Workshop on Building Linguistically Generalizable NLP Systems*, pages 40–47, Copenhagen, Denmark. Association for Computational Linguistics.

Daniel Ferrés, Horacio Saggion, and Xavier Gómez Guinovart. 2017b. An adaptable lexical simplification architecture for major ibero-romance languages. In *Proceedings of the First Workshop on Building Linguistically Generalizable NLP Systems*, pages 40–47.

Daniel Ferrés and Horacio Saggion. 2022. ALEXSIS: A Dataset for Lexical Simplification in Spanish. In *Language Resources and Evaluation Conference (LREC-2022)*.

Nat Gillin. 2016. Sensible at semeval-2016 task 11: Neural nonsense mangled in ensemble mess. In *Proceedings of the 10th International Workshop on Semantic Evaluation (SemEval-2016)*, pages 963–968.

Goran Glavaš and Sanja Štajner. 2015. Simplifying Lexical Simplification: Do We Need Simplified Corpora? In *Proceedings of the 53rd Annual Meeting of the Association for Computational Linguistics and the 7th International Joint Conference on Natural Language Processing (Volume 2: Short Papers)*, pages 63–68, Beijing, China. Association for Computational Linguistics.

Nathan S Hartmann, Gustavo H Paetzold, and Sandra M Aluísio. 2018. Simplex-pb: A lexical simplification database and benchmark for portuguese. In *Computational Processing of the Portuguese Language: 13th International Conference, PROPOR 2018, Canela, Brazil, September 24–26, 2018, Proceedings 13*, pages 272–283. Springer.

Colby Horn, Cathryn Manduca, and David Kauchak. 2014. Learning a Lexical Simplifier Using Wikipedia. In *Proceedings of the 52nd Annual Meeting of the Association for Computational Linguistics*

(Volume 2: Short Papers), pages 458–463, Baltimore, Maryland. Association for Computational Linguistics.

Ludivine Javourey-Drevet, Stéphane Dufau, Thomas François, Núria Gala, Jacques Ginestié, and Johannes C Ziegler. 2022. Simplification of literary and scientific texts to improve reading fluency and comprehension in beginning readers of french. *Applied Psycholinguistics*, 43(2):485–512.

Marius Rohde Johannessen, Lasse Berntzen, and Ansgar Ødegård. 2017. A review of the norwegian plain language policy. In *Electronic Government: 16th IFIP WG 8.5 International Conference, EGOV 2017, St. Petersburg, Russia, September 4-7, 2017, Proceedings 16*, pages 187–198. Springer.

Tomonori Kodaira, Tomoyuki Kajiwara, and Mamoru Komachi. 2016. Controlled and balanced dataset for japanese lexical simplification. In *Proceedings of the ACL 2016 Student Research Workshop*, pages 1–7.

Terry K Koo and Mae Y Li. 2016. A guideline of selecting and reporting intraclass correlation coefficients for reliability research. *Journal of chiropractic medicine*, 15(2):155–163.

Marta Licardo, Nina Volčanjk, and Dragica Haramija. 2021. Differences in communication skills among elementary students with mild intellectual disabilities after using easy-to-read texts. *The new educational review*, 64:236–246.

Misako Nomura, Gyda Skat Nielsen, and Bror Tronbacke. 2010. *Guidelines for easy-to-read materials*. International Federation of Library Associations and Institutions (IFLA).

Jenny A Ortiz-Zambrano and Arturo Montejo-Ráez. 2020. Overview of ALexS 2020: First workshop on lexical analysis at SEPLN. In *Proceedings of the Iberian Languages Evaluation Forum (IberLEF 2020)*, volume 2664, pages 1–6.

Gustavo Paetzold and Lucia Specia. 2016. Semeval 2016 task 11: Complex word identification. In *Proceedings of the 10th International Workshop on Semantic Evaluation (SemEval-2016)*, pages 560–569.

Gustavo Paetzold and Lucia Specia. 2017. Lexical Simplification with Neural Ranking. In *Proceedings of the 15th Conference of the European Chapter of the Association for Computational Linguistics: Volume 2, Short Papers*, pages 34–40, Valencia, Spain. Association for Computational Linguistics.

Jipeng Qiang, Yun Li, Yi Zhu, Yunhao Yuan, and Xindong Wu. 2020. LSBert: A Simple Framework for Lexical Simplification. *arXiv preprint arXiv:2006.14939*.

Maury Quijada and Julie Medero. 2016. Hmc at semeval-2016 task 11: Identifying complex words using depth-limited decision trees. In *Proceedings of the 10th International Workshop on Semantic Evaluation (SemEval-2016)*, pages 1034–1037.

Evelina Rennes. 2022. *Automatic Adaptation of Swedish Text for Increased Inclusion*. Ph.D. thesis, Linköping University Electronic Press.

Irina Rets and Jekaterina Rogaten. 2021. To simplify or not? facilitating english l2 users' comprehension and processing of open educational resources in english using text simplification. *Journal of Computer Assisted Learning*, 37(3):705–717.

Francesco Ronzano, Luis Espinosa Anke, Horacio Saggion, et al. 2016. Taln at semeval-2016 task 11: Modelling complex words by contextual, lexical and semantic features. In *Proceedings of the 10th International Workshop on Semantic Evaluation (SemEval-2016)*, pages 1011–1016.

Horacio Saggion. 2017. *Automatic Text Simplification*. Synthesis Lectures on Human Language Technologies. Morgan & Claypool Publishers.

Horacio Saggion, Sanja Štajner, Stefan Bott, Simon Mille, Luz Rello, and Biljana Drndarevic. 2015. Making it Simplext: Implementation and Evaluation of a Text Simplification System for Spanish. *TACCESS*, 6(4):14.

Horacio Saggion, Sanja Štajner, Daniel Ferrés, Kim Cheng Sheang, Matthew Shardlow, Kai North, and Marcos Zampieri. 2022. Findings of the TSAR-2022 shared task on multilingual lexical simplification. In *Proceedings of the Workshop on Text Simplification, Accessibility, and Readability (TSAR-2022)*, pages 271–283, Abu Dhabi, United Arab Emirates (Virtual). Association for Computational Linguistics.

Matthew Shardlow. 2013. A comparison of techniques to automatically identify complex words. In *51st annual meeting of the association for computational linguistics proceedings of the student research workshop*, pages 103–109.

Matthew Shardlow. 2014a. A Survey of Automated Text Simplification. *International Journal of Advanced Computer Science and Applications*, 4.

Matthew Shardlow. 2014b. Out in the open: Finding and categorising errors in the lexical simplification pipeline. In *LREC*, pages 1583–1590.

Matthew Shardlow, Fernando Alva-Manchego, Riza Batista-Navarro, Stefan Bott, Saul Calderon Ramirez, Rémi Cardon, Thomas François, Akio Hayakawa, Andrea Horbach, Anna Hülsing, Yusuke Ide, Joseph Marvin Imperial, Adam Nohejl, Kai North, Laura Occhipinti, Nelson Peréz Rojas, Nishat Raihan, Tharindu Ranasinghe, Martin Solis Salazar, Sanja Štajner, Marcos Zampieri, and Horacio Saggion. 2024. The BEA 2024 shared task on the multilingual lexical simplification pipeline. In *Proceedings of the 19th Workshop on Innovative Use of NLP for Building Educational Applications (BEA 2024)*, pages 571–589, Mexico City, Mexico. Association for Computational Linguistics.

Matthew Shardlow, Michael Cooper, and Marcos Zampieri. 2020. Complex: A new corpus for lexical complexity prediction from likert scale data. *arXiv preprint arXiv:2003.07008*.

Matthew Shardlow, Richard Evans, Gustavo Henrique Paetzold, and Marcos Zampieri. 2021. Semeval-2021 task 1: Lexical complexity prediction. *arXiv preprint arXiv:2106.00473*.

Kim Cheng Sheang. 2019. Multilingual complex word identification: Convolutional neural networks with morphological and linguistic features. In *Proceedings of the Student Research Workshop (RANLPStud 2019); 2019 Sep 2-4; Varna, Bulgaria.[Varna]: ACL; 2019. p. 83-9*. ACL (Association for Computational Linguistics).

Kim Cheng Sheang, Daniel Ferrés, and Horacio Saggion. 2022. Controllable lexical simplification for English. In *Proceedings of the Workshop on Text Simplification, Accessibility, and Readability (TSAR-2022)*, pages 199–206, Abu Dhabi, United Arab Emirates (Virtual). Association for Computational Linguistics.

Kim Cheng Sheang and Horacio Saggion. 2023. Multilingual controllable transformer-based lexical simplification. *Proces. del Leng. Natural*, 71:109–123.

Patrick E Shrout and Joseph L Fleiss. 1979. Intraclass correlations: uses in assessing rater reliability. *Psychological bulletin*, 86(2):420.

Sanja Stajner. 2014. Translating Sentences from Original to Simplified Spanish. *Procesamiento del lenguaje natural*, 53:61–68.

Sanja Stajner, Daniel Ibanez, and Horacio Saggion. 2023. Less: A computationally-light lexical simplifier for spanish. In *Proceedings of the 14th International Conference on Recent Advances in Natural Language Processing, RANLP 2023, Varna, Bulgaria, 4-6 September 2023*, pages 1132–1142. INCOMA Ltd., Shoumen, Bulgaria.

Satoru Uchida, Shohei Takada, and Yuki Arase. 2018. Cefr-based lexical simplification dataset. In *Proceedings of International Conference on Language Resources and Evaluation*, volume 11, pages 3254–3258. European Language Resources Association.

Raphael Vallat. 2018. Pingouin: statistics in python. *J. Open Source Softw.*, 3(31):1026.

Bruno Bastos Vieira de Melo, Mónica Silveira-Maia, and Sandra Barbosa Ribeiro. 2023. Full financial education programmes for people with disabilities: a scoping review. *Revista Brasileira de Educação Especial*, 29:e0222.

Tuqa Bani Yaseen, Qusai Ismail, Sarah Al-Omari, Eslam Al-Sobh, and Malak Abdullah. 2021. Just-blue at semeval-2021 task 1: Predicting lexical complexity using bert and roberta pre-trained language models. In *Proceedings of the 15th international workshop on semantic evaluation (SemEval-2021)*, pages 661–666.

M. Yatskar, B. Pang, C. Danescu-Niculescu-Mizil, and L. Lee. 2010. For the Sake of Simplicity: Unsupervised Extraction of Lexical Simplifications from Wikipedia. In *Proceedings of HLT-NAACL 2010*.

Seid Muhie Yimam, Chris Biemann, Shervin Malmasi, Gustavo H. Paetzold, Lucia Specia, Sanja Stajner, Anaïs Tack, and Marcos Zampieri. 2018a. A Report on the Complex Word Identification Shared Task 2018. *CoRR*, abs/1804.09132.

Seid Muhie Yimam, Chris Biemann, Shervin Malmasi, Gustavo H Paetzold, Lucia Specia, Sanja Štajner, Anaïs Tack, and Marcos Zampieri. 2018b. A report on the complex word identification shared task 2018. *arXiv preprint arXiv:1804.09132*.

Marcos Zampieri, Shervin Malmasi, Gustavo Paetzold, and Lucia Specia. 2017. Complex word identification: Challenges in data annotation and system performance. *arXiv preprint arXiv:1710.04989*.

Sanja Štajner, Horacio Saggion, and Simone Paolo Ponzetto. 2019. Improving Lexical Coverage of Text Simplification Systems for Spanish. *Expert Systems with Applications*, 118:80–91.

Appendix A: Selection criteria for annotators

For Catalan, annotators were in part recruited from persons of the social environment of the authors and in part from workers recruited over the Prolific[12] crowdsourcing platform.[13] All trial data was annotated by social contacts, as well as a part of the main annotations. In the case of Catalan it is difficult to select a pool of participants that consists only of native speakers because Catalonia is a largely bilingual territory. However, since Catalan has been used as the main vehicular language in the school system for several decades, most people who had their education in Catalonia have a high level of Catalan proficiency. Also a large part of the population grew up bilingually.

For Spanish, the trial annotation was done by personal contacts, while the main part of the dataset was annotated as part of a curricular activity within a course on written communication. This course was designed to foster the development of skills necessary for writing scientific and academic texts that are comprehensible to a broad audience. It required the texts to adhere to standards of clarity, precision, coherence, and readability, aligning with the principles of effective scientific communication. The primary intent behind this task was to enhance the student's ability to identify and modify the use

[12]https://www.prolific.com/

[13]Annotators received a fair pay.

of complex terminology, opting for more accessible alternatives without compromising the accuracy or depth of the content. This approach facilitates widespread dissemination and understanding.

The annotators recruited from personal contacts were mostly speakers of European Spanish , while the rest were speakers of the Costa Rican variety of Spanish.

Since the availability of annotators was limited, the main criterion for the recruitment of annotators from the personal contacts of the authors was their availability, both for Spanish and for Catalan. We made sure that all of them were proficient speakers of the language, either native or L2 speakers which use the language on a daily basis. Even without having any stricter selection criteria, in practice their annotations were much more reliable than annotations from crowdsourcing workers. For Catalan we had to discard 11 crowdsourcing annotators.

Appendix B: Selection criteria for texts

Both of datasets have been created within the context of the MLSP24 (Multilingual Lexical Simplification Pipeline) shared task (Shardlow et al., 2024), in which comparable datasets for 10 languages were created. In the guidelines for the data selection it was strongly suggested to use texts from the educational domain.

For Catalan, we could not find a sufficiently large corpus of educational text. So, entences were selected from the Educational news section of the TeCla corpus (Armengol-Estapé et al., 2021) of news texts.

For Spanish, we selected educational texts on finance due to their social relevance and the pressing need to make this knowledge accessible to vulnerable populations. Financial literacy, recognized as an essential tool for economic empowerment and inclusion, especially among individuals with disabilities, remains underexplored in text simplification (Vieira de Melo et al., 2023). Learning about personal finance is critical in fostering autonomy and improving decision-making. The specialized nature of these texts, characterized by domain-specific terminology and conceptual density, requires careful consideration in simplification approaches to maintain accessibility and accuracy (Comité Económico y Social Europeo, 2011). Our research addresses these challenges by focusing on this area, aligning with broader efforts to promote financial competence and social inclusion for underserved communities. The Spanish texts originate from publications in South America.

SciGisPy: a Novel Metric for Biomedical Text Simplification via Gist Inference Score

Chen Lyu
University of Warwick
chen.lyu@warwick.ac.uk

Gabriele Pergola
University of Warwick
gabriele.pergola.1@warwick.ac.uk

Abstract

Biomedical literature is often written in highly specialized language, posing significant comprehension challenges for non-experts. Automatic text simplification (ATS) offers a solution by making such texts more accessible while preserving critical information. However, evaluating ATS for biomedical texts is still challenging due to the limitations of existing evaluation metrics. General-domain metrics like SARI, BLEU, and ROUGE focus on surface-level text features, and readability metrics like FKGL and ARI fail to account for domain-specific terminology or assess how well the simplified text conveys core meanings (*gist*). To address this, we introduce *SciGisPy*, a novel evaluation metric inspired by Gist Inference Score (GIS) from Fuzzy-Trace Theory (FTT). SciGisPy measures how well a simplified text facilitates the formation of abstract inferences (gist) necessary for comprehension, especially in the biomedical domain. We revise GIS for this purpose by introducing domain-specific enhancements, including semantic chunking, Information Content (IC) theory, and specialized embeddings, while removing unsuitable indices. Our experimental evaluation on the Cochrane biomedical text simplification dataset demonstrates that *SciGisPy* outperforms the original GIS formulation, with a significant increase in correctly identified simplified texts (84% versus 44.8%). The results and a thorough ablation study confirm that *SciGisPy* better captures the essential meaning of biomedical content, outperforming existing approaches.

1 Introduction

Biomedical literature is often written in highly specialized language, making it challenging for non-experts to understand. The 2022 World Health Organization (WHO) report identifies low public health literacy as a significant global issue, affecting disease prevention and management (Osborne et al., 2022). Automatic text simplification (ATS)

Complex Medical Abstract – ABS

Technical abstract: The pooled evidence derived from trials of gabapentin suggests that it is not efficacious for the prophylaxis of episodic migraine in adults. Since adverse events were common among the gabapentin-treated patients, it is advocated that gabapentin should not be used in routine clinical practice. Gabapentin enacarbil is not efficacious for the prophylaxis of episodic migraine in adults. There is no published evidence from controlled trials of pregabalin for the prophylaxis of episodic migraine in adults.
GisPy score: -0.417
SciGisPy score: -5.596

Plain-Language Summary - PLS

Plain-language summary: The studies showed that neither gabapentin nor gabapentin enacarbil was more effective than placebo at reducing the frequency of migraine headaches. Gabapentin commonly caused side effects, especially dizziness and somnolence (sleepiness). No studies of pregabalin were identified, and research on this drug is desirable.
GisPy score: 0.348
SciGisPy score: 3.599

Figure 1: An example of excerpts from a technical abstract (top) and its corresponding plain-language summary (bottom) from the Cochrane text simplification dataset (Devaraj et al., 2021). SciGisPy demonstrates better ability in distinguishing between ABS and PLS.

offers a potential solution by transforming complex biomedical language into simpler, more accessible text while preserving essential details. However, evaluating the effectiveness of ATS on biomedical texts remains a challenge.

Existing metrics for biomedical text simplification are still limited. General-domain ATS metrics, such as SARI (Xu et al., 2016), BLEU (Papineni et al., 2002), and ROUGE (Lin, 2004), focus on surface-level word edits and n-gram overlaps, relying heavily on the quality and variety of reference texts. Similarly, referenceless metrics, like BERTScore (Zhang et al., 2019a), Flesch-Kincaid Grade Level (FKGL) (Kincaid et al., 1975), and Automated Readability Index (ARI) (Senter and Smith, 1967), focus on syntactic and lexical simplicity (e.g., shortening sentences, simplifying vocabulary), but fail to capture domain-specific terminology, and more importantly, they cannot ensure that the core meaning (or *gist*) is easily understood.

Proceedings of the Third Workshop on Text Simplification, Accessibility and Readability (TSAR 2024), pages 95–106
November 15, 2024

(a) Original Gist Inference Score (GIS) formula by (Wolfe et al., 2019)

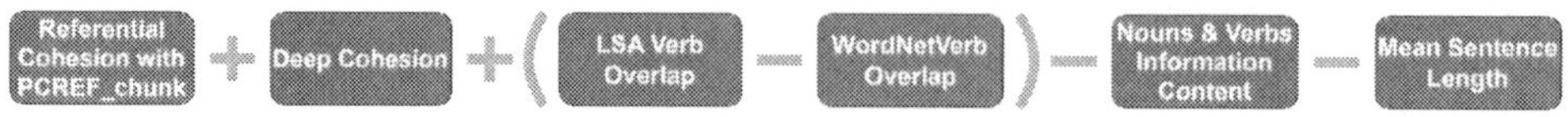

(b) Enhanced GIS formula for Biomedical Text Simplification: SciGisPy

Figure 2: Original and enhanced GIS formula

These limitations are especially critical for biomedical texts because they do not provide an adequate measure of whether the text is effective in facilitating comprehension of complex medical concepts despite its linguistic simplicity.

To address this gap, we propose a novel, task-specific evaluation score, SciGisPy, based on the Gist Inference Score (GIS), inspired by the Fuzzy-Trace Theory (FTT). FTT posits that human cognition operates through two parallel representations: gist (the essential meaning) and verbatim (exact details) (Reyna, 2021). GIS measures how effectively a text conveys this *gist*, supporting decision-making. While previous GIS formulations have been explored in general domains (Hosseini et al., 2022), none have been optimized for the complexities of biomedical documents.

In this work, we introduce SciGisPy, the first GIS formulation for biomedical text. Figure 2 shows the original GIS formula and our enhanced version, which incorporates domain-specific adaptations. These include new indices and improvements, based on semantic-based chunking, Information Content (IC) theory, specialised embeddings, and an overall revision of the original GIS formulation.

Our contribution can be summarized as follows:

- We introduce SciGisPy, a novel GIS formulation specifically designed for biomedical text simplification, revising existing indices and eliminating those unsuitable for the biomedical domain.

- We introduce newly designed indices for SciGisPy, based on semantic-driven chunking, Information Content (IC) theory, and linguistic features of biomedical sentences.

- We conduct a comprehensive experimental evaluation of GIS as a metric for biomedical text simplification, analyzing the relevance of each index and its correlation with established simplification metrics.

2 Related Work

Text Simplification Metrics The development of automatic evaluation metrics tailored specifically for biomedical ATS remains under-explored. Due to the scarcity of specialized metrics, existing studies often rely on general-domain ATS metrics, which are insufficient for capturing the characteristics of biomedical text. Reference-based metrics, such as BLEU (Papineni et al., 2002) and ROUGE (Lin, 2004), compare simplified outputs to human-generated references, focusing on n-gram precision and recall. These metrics heavily depend on the quality of reference texts and may penalize valid simplifications that use different wording (Pergola et al., 2019, 2021a; Zhu et al., 2021). SARI (Xu et al., 2016), designed for text simplification, evaluates word-level edits but similarly focuses on surface-level features like n-gram overlaps, missing the deeper semantic aspects crucial for biomedical comprehension (Sulem et al., 2018; Pergola et al., 2021b; Alva-Manchego et al., 2021). BERTScore (Zhang et al., 2019a), leveraging contextual embeddings from BERT, improves semantic similarity evaluation but still underperforms in biomedical contexts (Sun et al., 2022; Zhu et al., 2022, 2023; Lu et al., 2023).

Readability metrics, such as Flesch-Kincaid Grade Level (FKGL) (Kincaid et al., 1975) and Automated Readability Index (ARI) (Senter and Smith, 1967), are reference-less and rely on surface features like sentence length and word complexity. However, these metrics do not account for the accurate use of domain-specific terminology or semantic nuances critical to biomedical texts. Consequently, they often fail to effectively evaluate the readability and accuracy of simplified medical content, underscoring the need for more advanced evaluation methods in this domain.

Gist and GIS According to Fuzzy-Trace Theory (FTT) (Reyna, 2021), individuals encode multiple mental representations when processing text, ranging from verbatim, which captures surface-level details, to gist, which conveys the core meaning. In FTT, "gist" refers to the essential idea of a matter. Prior research (Reyna, 2021) suggests that gist representations significantly influence decision-making processes more than verbatim representations. Therefore, assessing gist representation can help measure a document's ability to generate clear and actionable mental models and effectively communicate its message.

The Gist Inference Score (GIS) was first introduced by Wolfe et al. (Wolfe et al., 2019) to evaluate how well a text enables readers to form gist inferences. Before the development of the GisPy library (Hosseini et al., 2022), which automated GIS evaluation, research on GIS was still developing (Reyna, 2021; Wolfe et al., 2019). GIS was initially proposed by leveraging Coh-Metrix, a multilevel linguistic framework analyzing over 100 variables related to text simplicity, such as referential cohesion, lexical diversity, and latent semantic analysis (LSA) (Wolfe et al., 2019; Graesser et al., 2011; Sun et al., 2024). However, Coh-Metrix lacks batch processing and efficiency. The GisPy library, building on these earlier methods and leveraging advanced NLP techniques, provides the first open-source solution for computing GIS across multiple documents. In GisPy (Hosseini et al., 2022), GIS is composed of seven indices: Referential Cohesion, Deep Cohesion, Verb Overlap, Word Concreteness, Word Imageability, and Hypernymy Nouns & Verbs, each associated with either a positive or negative coefficient. This work extends the GisPy library by modifying, removing, and adding to these indices for better alignment with biomedical simplification tasks.

2.1 GisPy and Other Text Simplification Metrics

GIS, as a reference-less metric, is more closely related and comparable to the readability metrics, such as FKGL and ARI. However, we argue that GIS captures different information from the text compared to FKGL and ARI.

While FKGL and ARI focus on surface-level "verbatim" features of text, GIS aims to measure the likelihood that readers will develop meaningful "gist inferences" from the text. Specifically, FKGL assesses readability based solely on surface-level features using sentence length and word syllable count, whereas GIS captures the underlying abstract meaning by considering more complex dimensions of text features such as cohesion and word concreteness. To validate this argument, we calculated the Pearson correlation coefficients between the reference-less metrics shown in A.3, where the results are all close to zero, proving that GIS is uncorrelated with these metrics.

3 Method

In this section, we first review the indices in the original GisPy formulation (Hosseini et al., 2022) and assess their suitability for biomedical text simplification. For each index, we propose adaptations by either (i) introducing novel approaches, (ii) improving the existing indices with more specialized methods, or (iii) removing them if unsuitable for the biomedical domain.

3.1 Enhancing GIS indices for Biomedical Document Simplification

As shown in Figure 2, the original GIS formula includes seven indices, with some positively and others negatively weighted. These indices cover five dimensions of text features. Through analysis, we posit that only four dimensions are beneficial for evaluating biomedical text simplicity – *Referential Cohesion, Deep Cohesion, Verb Overlap, Hypernymy Nouns & Verbs*, while *Word Concreteness and Imageability* is not.

Hypernymy Nouns & Verbs: This index measures word specificity, based on the idea that more specific words are harder to understand for a general audience without specialized knowledge. Simplifying biomedical texts often requires translating technical terms into concepts that are accessible to a broader audience, thus making this metric valuable for evaluating simplified biomedical documents.

To achieve this, the index (`WRDHYPnv`) uses WordNet's hierarchy of concepts and penalizes words with greater depth in the hierarchy, as these represent more specialized terms. In particular, the specificity is quantified by the average hypernym path length of synonym sets.

In the original GIS formula, this index evaluates word specificity by listing all nouns and verbs in a document, identifying their synonym sets in WordNet, and calculating the average hypernym path length. Instead, we propose three more fine-grained alternatives to address limitations when applied to specialized texts: (i) the first ensures proper comparison of noun and verb paths via normalisation (WRDHYP_norm), (ii) the second introduces and adapts the concept of Information Content WRDIC, and (iii) the third resolves a development issue found in the original GisPy library.

i. Hypernym Root Normalisation: In WordNet, unlike noun synsets that all trace back to the hypernym root '*entity*', verb synsets can trace back to different hypernym roots, with some synsets having multiple roots. For example, in the biomedical domain, the verb *administer* could trace back to *apply* (in the context of giving treatment) or *manage* (in the context of overseeing care). Consequently, the GisPy approach of averaging hypernym paths for all synsets can lead to incomparable path lengths if the roots are different, as these roots may have hypernym hierarchies of varying scales.

To address this issue, we propose an alternative approach, where instead of averaging all hypernym paths, we group the paths that lead to the same root and apply L1 normalization within each group to balance the scales of the hypernym hierarchies. For synsets with multiple hypernym roots, we select the longest hypernym path and its corresponding root as the representative. Finally, we compute the average of the normalized path lengths across all groups to obtain the final result. We indicate this new index with WRDHYP_norm, where the suffix stands for "*root normalization*", formalised as follows:

$$\text{WRDHYP\_norm} = \frac{1}{n}\sum_{i=1}^{n}\frac{L_i}{||L_i||_1}$$

Where L_i is the path length for the i-th hypernym path group, $||L_i||_1$ is the L1 normalization of the path length for each root group, and n is the total number of hypernym path groups.

ii. Information Content: To improve the GIS metric for biomedical text simplification, we propose to replace the Wordnet hypernym-based solution WRDHYP with a new approach based on Information Content (IC) (Cover and Thomas, 2006), namely WRDIC. Simple hypernym path counting can be insufficient in some cases, as it fails to account for the frequency and relevance of terms within specific domains. For instance, two biomedical terms may have the same path length but differ significantly in importance or specificity within a corpus. Information Content addresses this issue by considering the probability of encountering a term in a given corpus. In information theory, IC is a measure derived from the probability of a specific event occurring from a random variable (Cover and Thomas, 2006). In this context, the IC of a word can be defined as $-\log(P(c))$, where $P(c)$ is the probability of encountering a hypernym of word c in a corpus.

To compute the new index, similar to the strategy in WRDHYP, we first identify all nouns and verbs in the text. Then, we calculate the average of their IC values to generate the final result. IC provides a more accurate measure of word specificity, with higher IC values indicating more specialized words. This approach enhances the ability to measure text simplification by considering both the structure of the language and its actual use in the domain, making it particularly suitable for specialized domains.

iii. Mean Hypernym Paths Length: The original GisPy score (Hosseini et al., 2022) uses WordNet (Miller, 1995) and its Synset objects from the NLTK library[1] to compute hierarchical paths (WRDHYP). However, for some verb synsets, there are multiple hypernym roots, resulting in several hypernym paths leading to different roots. This issue is critical because having different roots makes the hypernym paths non-comparable, as the hierarchical structures vary in depth and scope.

The original GisPy paper assumes a single hypernym path per root and does not account for this issue. We addressed this by modifying the index to use the mean length of all available hypernym paths for a given synset when multiple paths are available, which we call WRDHYP_mean [2].

Verb Overlap: According to the FFT, abstract verb overlaps promote the formation of gist representations, aiding readers in understanding the text's core meaning. To capture this, the GisPy score uses two indices: SMCAUSe (positively weighted) and SMCAUSwn (negatively weighted) (Hosseini et al., 2022). For biomedical text simplification, SMCAUSe is important because it promotes simplicity by emphasizing abstract overlaps between verbs, while SMCAUSwn penalizes the redundant repetition of identical or similar verbs.

In its original implementation, this index is based

[1] https://www.nltk.org

[2] We flagged the issue regarding multiple hypernym paths for verb synsets on the GisPy GitHub repository. The authors implemented a solution using the maximum path length, but our preliminary experiments indicated that averaging the path lengths offers a more balanced measure of specificity.

on the *en_core_web_trf*[3] from SpaCy, a RoBERTa-based pre-trained language model (Liu et al., 2021), to generate token vector embeddings for each verb, and then computes cosine similarity of the embeddings. To better suit the characteristics of biomedical texts, often featuring technical and compound terminology, we propose a simple yet effective modification, adopting embedding models specialised for technical documents. We identify two embedding models for this index, fastText (Bojanowski et al., 2017) and BioWordVec (Zhang et al., 2019b).

FastText (Bojanowski et al., 2017) is a widely used word embedding library, particularly suitable for technical documents. It learns word embeddings on a sub-word basis, which allows it to represent out-of-vocabulary words. This is particularly useful for dealing with biomedical language characterized by many compound words (Pergola et al., 2018). We adopt pre-trained embeddings provided by fastText and name this index `SMCAUSf`.

Our second alternative is BioWordVec (Zhang et al., 2019b), based on a benchmark biomedical word embedding library. BioWordVec combines subword information from unlabeled biomedical text with the widely-used Biomedical Subject Headings (MeSH) vocabulary (Lipscomb, 2000). Pre-trained using FastText embeddings, BioWordVec is the most commonly used biomedical word embedding model in the recent literature. We adopt it to improve the `SMCAUS` index, and name it `SMCAUSb`.

Referential Cohesion: Referential Cohesion measures word and idea overlaps across sentences, making it a suitable metric to characterise simplicity in the biomedical text. In Hosseini et al. (2022) this dimensions is captured with two indices: `PCREF` and `CoREF` (both positively weighted). `PCREF` calculates cosine similarity between sentence embeddings, while the `CoREF` focuses on coreference resolution across sentences. A high overlap in both indices typically indicates that the text maintains consistent ideas and vocabulary, which helps readers follow complex biomedical content more easily, thus promoting text simplicity. To improve the detection of referential cohesion in biomedical texts, we introduce (i) a novel index based on *semantic chunking*, which posits that a lower number of semantic chunks indicates stronger coherence, and (ii) more suitable sentence embedding models designed for technical and biomedical documents.

i. Semantic Chunking: We introduce an alternative solution for measuring Referential Cohesion to substitute `PCREF`. This new approach is based on the concept of *semantic chunking*[4]. Unlike traditional methods that chunk text using a fixed size, semantic chunking adaptively determines breakpoints between sentences based on embedding similarity of customizable window size. This ensures that each chunk contains sentences that are semantically related. Similar to `PCREF`, the semantic chunking method uses cosine similarity between sentences to represent overlap across sentences.

We argue that a higher number of chunks indicates more diverse semantics and topics within the text. Therefore, minimizing the number of chunks ensures textual coherence and enhances simplicity. Inspired by this, we designed a new index, `PCREF_chunk`, built using a semantic chunker to replace the original `PCREF`. We selected BioSimCSE (Kanakarajan et al., 2022) as the sentence embedding model, as its biomedical-domain embeddings capture semantics more accurately. We apply a negative coefficient to this index, indicating that fewer semantic chunks correspond to higher coherence and simplicity.

ii. Specialized Sentence Embeddings The original index *PCREF* calculates cosine similarity between sentences using the pretrained MPNet model [5] from Hugging Face as the sentence embedding model.

We experimented with five state-of-the-art sentence embedding models. First, we adopted two leading general-purpose models from the Massive Text Embedding Benchmark (MTEB) Leaderboard mxbai-embed-large-v1 (Li and Li, 2023) and the e5-mistral-7b-instruct (Jiang et al., 2023; Wang et al., 2023, 2022) embedding models. Additionally, we utilized three state-of-the-art biomedical domain embedding models based on BERT: BioSimCSE (Kanakarajan et al., 2022) and BioBERT (Lee et al., 2020), which generate contextual embeddings, and a context-free embedding model, BioSentVec (Chen et al., 2019). These models are known for their robustness in biomedical text processing.

Detailed implementation information is provided in Section 4, where a thorough ablation study highlights the impact of each of them. Each model

[3]`https://spacy.io/models/en#en_core_web_trf`

[4]LlamaIndex Semantic Chunking Documentation

[5]`https://huggingface.co/sentence-transformers/all-mpnet-base-v2`

is indicated by a suffix to the index name (e.g., PCREF_mxbai) specifying the embedding used.

Deep Cohesion: Indicated by the *PCDC* index (positively weighted), it measures the extent to which a text uses causal and intentional connectives, detected using regular expression patterns. The index is still highly relevant to biomedical text comprehension, as it supports logical relationships between sentences, crucial for ensuring that readers can follow complex biomedical information. Therefore, we retain the original design of this index as in Hosseini et al. (2022).

Mean Sentence Length: FTT suggests that people extract both verbatim (exact details) and gist (core meaning) from texts. Longer or more complex sentences may increase cognitive load, making it harder to focus on gist and potentially promoting reliance on verbatim processing. In contrast, shorter sentences with clear structures could help readers extract gist more easily because the underlying meaning is more accessible. Research in readability and health communication has shown that shorter sentences enhance readability by making information more accessible (Rudd et al., 2023), reducing cognitive load (Graesser et al., 2011), improving comprehension (National Institutes of Health, 2012), and maintaining consistency and focus (Weiss, 2007).

To address this gap within the original GIST score, we propose a new composite index called Mean Sentence Length (MSL) . This index, rewards the reduction of the average sentence length. Concretely, we calculate the mean sentence length by counting the number of words in each sentence and averaging these counts across the entire text. Despite its simplicity, preliminary exploration on this index showed promising results, with a more detailed assessment presented in Section 4.

3.2 Removing Word Concreteness and Imageability

Unlike the previous indices, the dimension we find potentially detrimental to representing biomedical text simplicity is *Word Concreteness and Imageability*. In the original GisPy score, *Word Concreteness* (PCCNCz) measures how concrete and image-evoking words are, while *Imageability* (WRDIMGc) indicates how easily a word can evoke a mental image. For instance, high imageability words like "hammer" are more specific and easily visualized compared to low imageability words like "reason". These indices are negatively weighted in the GIS formula, suggesting its promotion of abstractness. However, we argue that words with high concreteness and imageability (such as "heart") help understand scientific and biomedical texts, are easier to visualize and thus improve comprehension and make it easier to follow for diverse audiences. Therefore, we hypothesize that removing this concreteness-penalizing index from GIS formula could enhance its performance in biomedical text simplification task.

In conclusion, while the GIS formula promotes abstractness in text to generate Gist, this may not align with promoting simplicity, especially in biomedical texts. Relevant indices may need to be modified or removed to better evaluate simplicity in biomedical documents.

4 Experiments

In this section, we present an experimental evaluation to assess the effectiveness of the GIS metric and our proposed index enhancements in the biomedical domain, using a Cochrane Library dataset (Devaraj et al., 2021) containing technical documents paired with simplified versions, firstly detailed in Section 4.1. In Section 4.2, we report the results of our evaluation on this dataset, exploring the impact of different index combinations on simplified texts. Specifically, we analyze which index combinations produce the most significant improvements in gist abstraction by measuring the GIS differences between the technical and simplified documents. Finally, we assess the generalization of our findings by testing on several benchmark datasets from previous GIS literature to evaluate how well our GIS enhancements can be applied beyond the biomedical domain.

4.1 Datasets

We conducted GIS analysis and tested our indices enhancement on the Cochrane paragraph-level biomedical text simplification dataset (Devaraj et al., 2021), which is sourced from the Cochrane library[6] of systematic reviews. The Cochrane text simplification dataset comprises 4,459 parallel pairs of technical abstracts (ABS) and their plain-language summaries (PLS) crafted by domain experts, where the PLS texts are simplified versions of original technical abstracts. Figure 1 presents a sample excerpt of a technical abstract

[6]https://www.cochranelibrary.com/

Index		Mean GIS Diff	% + GIS Diff	% inc GIS Diff	% - to +
Original GisPy (Hosseini et al., 2022)		-0.461	43.38%	N/A	N/A
Without *PCCNC* & *WRDIMG*		-0.022	49.91%	60.94%	**12.87%**
Hypernymy Nouns & Verbs	*WRDHYP_mean*	0.158	52.85%	74.54%	11.58%
	WRDHYP_norm	-1.355	31.25%	17.56%	1.27%
	WRDIC	0.211	51.38%	**78.77%**	9.74%
Verb Overlap	*SMCAUSe*	-0.728	39.25%	41.36%	3.95%
	SMCAUSb	-0.678	40.53%	43.38%	4.78%
Referential Cohesion	*PCREF_mxbai*	-0.328	45.59%	61.12%	4.41%
	PCREF_BioSimCSE	-0.629	40.53%	37.87%	2.48%
	PCREF_BioBERT	-0.655	40.99%	43.75%	3.68%
	PCREF_mistral	-0.503	44.39%	53.22%	3.86%
	PCREF_BioSentVec	-0.686	40.99%	37.04%	2.57%
	PCREF_chunk	**0.418**	**54.32%**	61.12%	5.97%
Mean Sentence Length (MSL)		0.321	52.94%	76.93%	11.40%
SciGisPy (Our)		**2.312**	**85.39%**	**85.57%**	**44.21%**

Table 1: Results of GIS Enhancements on Cochrane simplification development set. The second column displays the average GIS difference across the entire dataset. The third column indicates the percentage of documents with a positive GIS difference. The fourth column shows the percentage of documents where the GIS difference increased following the enhancement. The fifth column reports the percentage of documents that initially had a negative GIS difference but shifted to a positive value.

and its corresponding PLS. Since GIS score computation does not require any training, we sample 4,334 document pairs as our *development set* to determine the best index configurations; while the remaining additional subset, used as *test set*, will be introduced in the following sections. Since SciGisPy does not involve any training, no training set is required.

In previous literature, three benchmark general-domain datasets have been used for evaluating GIS metrics: News Reports vs. Editorials, Journal Article Methods vs. Discussion, and Disneyland Measles Outbreak Data (Wolfe et al., 2019; Hosseini et al., 2022). This subset serves as our *test set* to assess the generalisation of our biomedical-specialized GIS.

4.2 Results and Discussion

To investigate the effectiveness of applying GisPy GIS in evaluating the simplicity of biomedical text, we first computed GIS values for all Abstracts (ABS)s and Plain Language Summaries (PLS)s in the development set using the best configuration reported for the GisPy library, following the evaluation process outlined in Hosseini et al. (2022). After we obtained the GIS score for all documents, we calculated the *GIS difference* between each pair of ABS and PLS:

$$\text{GIS Difference} = \text{GIS}_{\text{PLS}} - \text{GIS}_{\text{ABS}}$$

In the rest part of this paper, "GIS difference" refers to the difference calculated using the above equation. A *positive GIS difference* for a pair of documents suggests that audiences will more easily abstract the gist from the simplified text (PLS) compared to the original text (ABS), subsequently showing that GIS can be a good indicator of simplification. Consistent with previous literature, we compare the average GIS difference among all documents under the different GIS formulations to determine the more effective alternatives, namely mean GIS difference.

To evaluate the impact of each individual enhancement, we ran GisPy with each enhancement applied separately, while keeping all other indices identical to those in the original formula. Additionally, when testing combinations of enhancements that modify the same index, for those that modify the same index, we ensured that only one change was applied at a time to prevent overlapping calculations.

4.2.1 GIS for Biomedical Text Simplification

First, we report the GIS scores resulting from the original GisPy on the development set of the Cochrane Simplification Dataset in Table 1. The average GIS for ABS texts is 0.225, while for PLS texts, the mean GIS is -0.225, resulting in a mean GIS difference of -0.450; only 43% of document pairs have a positive GIS difference. These results show that the original GIS formulation struggles to distinguish between simplified and unsimplified

Index	Mean GIS Diff	% + GIS Diff	% inc GIS Diff	% - to +
Original GisPy (Hosseini et al., 2022)	-0.311	44.8%	N/A	N/A
SciGisPy (Our)	2.295	84%	79.2%	45.6%

Table 2: Results of GIS Enhancements on Cochrane simplification test set. See Table 1 for column descriptions.

texts for most biomedical documents.

We proceed to discuss the impact of the enhancements proposed in this work; for each index enhancement listed, Table 1 reports the results obtained by running GisPy with only the corresponding enhancements while keeping the rest of the formula unchanged.

Removing Word Concreteness and Imageability: To test our hypothesis that removing word concreteness and imageability promotes biomedical text easier to comprehend (Sec. 3.2), we ran GIS without *PCCNC* and *WRDIMG* and observed positive results, as reported in Table 1: the average GIS difference increased from -0.450 to -0.022, with **49.91%** of documents now exhibiting a positive GIS difference, compared to 43.38% with the original GIS formula. This finding supports our initial analysis and confirms the need to tailor the roles of the indices when dealing with specialised domains.

Semantic Chunking: As mentioned earlier, the mean GIS difference is our primary metric for evaluating the performance of new GIS formula. A larger difference indicates better distinction between simplified and original documents. Based on the experiment results shown in Table 1, most of our enhancements produced positive outcomes. The enhancement *PCREF_chunk* achieved the most significant improvement, leading to the mean GIS difference increase from -0.461 to 0.418. This enhancement also led to 54.32% of documents obtaining a positive GIS difference, an increase of 10.94% compared to the original GisPy, which achieved 43.38%.

In addition, we tracked the impact of each enhancement on individual documents. The fourth column in Table 1 presents the percentage of documents where the GIS difference increased after the enhancement. This indicates that the enhanced GIS formula can better distinguish between the original ABS text and the simplified PLS text compared to the original GIS. The table's last column also shows the percentage of documents that originally had a negative GIS difference but switched to positive; this represents cases where the original GIS failed to evaluate simplicity, but the new GIS succeeded.

Looking at ABS-PLS pairs in Table 1, more than half of our indices enhancements yielded positive results. Some indices demonstrated significant improvements, with *WRDIC* by achieving the highest increase with 78.77% of documents in the development set transiting to a positive GIS difference.

Best Formulation: Based on the experimental results on the development set, we identified the best combination of our enhanced GIS formula, as shown in Figure 2. We adopted the enhancements of Referential Cohesion with Semantic Chunking (`PCREF_chunk`), Hypernyms with Information Content (IC) (`WRDIC`), and Mean Sentence Length (`MSL`), together with the removal of indices `PCCNC` and `WRDIMG`. The significant results of this biomedical text simplification-targeted GIS formula are presented in the last row of Table 1.

Generalisation: To test the generalisation of this finding, we also applied the enhanced formula to the Cochrane test set. The results, presented in the last row of Table 2, demonstrate a significant improvement, with the new GIS successfully identifying 84% of simplified texts, doubling the original number. This confirms the effectiveness of our new GIS for evaluating biomedical text simplification.

4.2.2 Gist Inference Benchmarks

To assess whether our enhancements improve the evaluation of Gist abstraction in the general domain, the original objective of GIS, we tested all index enhancements on the benchmark datasets used in the original GisPy paper. The News Reports vs. Editorials dataset comprises 50 pairs of documents per category, totaling 100 documents. The Journal Article Methods vs. Discussion dataset includes 25 pairs, amounting to 50 documents. The Disneyland dataset consists of 191 articles in total. To ensure comparability with these datasets, we randomly sampled 125 document pairs from the Cochrane dataset.

The experimental results were less significant compared to the previous results on the Cochrane simplification dataset since our enhancements were targeted at biomedical text simplification. However, we still identified a combination of index en-

Benchmark	Approach	Distance	t-statistic	p-value
Reports vs. Editorials	GisPy with *PCREF_mistral & MSL*	**3.260**	4.068	$*2 \times 10^{-4}$
	GisPy (Hosseini et al., 2022)	2.551	3.643	$*7 \times 10^{-4}$
	Coh-Metrix (Graesser et al., 2011)	2.535	3.826	$*3 \times 10^{-4}$
	(Wolfe et al., 2019)	0.368	-	-
Methods vs. Discussion	GisPy with *SCAUSf*	**5.200**	5.916	$*3 \times 10^{-7}$
	GisPy	5.012	7.188	$*3 \times 10^{-9}$
	Coh-Metrix	5.010	6.331	$*7 \times 10^{-8}$
	(Wolfe et al., 2019)	0.747	-	-
Disney	GisPy with *MSL*	**2.442**	3.492	$*6 \times 10^{-4}$
	GisPy	2.418	3.440	$*7 \times 10^{-4}$
	Coh-Metrix	0.998	1.878	6×10^{-2}

Table 3: Comparison of GIS scores generated by GisPy with our enhancement indices vs. original GisPy vs. other methods for all benchmarks

hancements that outperformed the original GisPy formula on the benchmark dataset. The results are presented in Table 3, where we also performed a student's t-test with the null hypothesis following GisPy (Hosseini et al., 2022) paper, which shows how good a GIS score can significantly distinguish these ABS texts and PLS texts. This positive result demonstrates that our proposed solutions are not only beneficial for simplification evaluation, but also enhance the measure of how easily GIS can be inferred.

5 Conclusion

In this study, we addressed the challenge of evaluating biomedical automatic text simplification by introducing a novel referenceless evaluation metric, SciGisPy, inspired by the Gist Inference Score (GIS) from Fuzzy-Trace Theory. This metric was specifically adapted and enhanced for biomedical text simplification through rigorous feasibility analysis and domain-specific enhancements. Our comprehensive experimental assessment on the Cochrane text simplification dataset demonstrates that SciGisPy significantly outperforms the original GIS metric in assessing the simplicity of biomedical texts.

6 Limitations

A limitation of this study is the reliance on a single benchmark, the Cochrane simplification dataset, due to the limited availability and suitability of biomedical text simplification datasets at the document level. Validating our methodology across multiple datasets would strengthen its robustness.

Additionally, while we introduced several improvements to the individual GIS indices, the coefficient magnitudes currently remain fixed at 1. Developing an automated method to dynamically adjust these coefficients based on text distributions could further improve the accuracy and versatility of SciGisPy in text simplification.

Lay Summary

Medical research papers are often written in very complex and technical language, which makes it difficult for non-experts to understand. To solve this problem, automatic text simplification (ATS) systems try to rewrite these texts in a simpler way while keeping the important information intact. However, it's hard to evaluate how well these systems simplify medical texts because current tools focus too much on the surface details, like word counts and sentence length, without considering whether the text still conveys the core meaning (the *gist*).

In this study, the researchers developed a new evaluation tool called SciGisPy, designed specifically to measure how well simplified medical texts communicate the essential meaning. It builds on an existing concept called the *Gist Inference Score* (GIS), which measures how easily a reader can understand the gist of a text. SciGisPy adds new features like focusing on medical terms, simplifying complex sentences, and improving coherence between ideas. The study shows that SciGisPy significantly improves the evaluation of simplified medical texts compared to existing methods, helping to make complex medical information more accessible to a broader audience.

References

Fernando Alva-Manchego, Carolina Scarton, and Lucia Specia. 2021. The (un)suitability of automatic evaluation metrics for text simplification. *Computational Linguistics*, 47(4):861–889.

Piotr Bojanowski, Edouard Grave, Armand Joulin, and Tomas Mikolov. 2017. Enriching word vectors with subword information. *Transactions of the association for computational linguistics*, 5:135–146.

Qingyu Chen, Yifan Peng, and Zhiyong Lu. 2019. Biosentvec: creating sentence embeddings for biomedical texts. In *2019 IEEE International Conference on Healthcare Informatics (ICHI)*, pages 1–5. IEEE.

Thomas M. Cover and Joy A. Thomas. 2006. *Elements of Information Theory (Wiley Series in Telecommunications and Signal Processing)*. Wiley-Interscience, USA.

Ashwin Devaraj, Byron C Wallace, Iain J Marshall, and Junyi Jessy Li. 2021. Paragraph-level simplification of medical texts. In *Proceedings of the conference. Association for Computational Linguistics. North American Chapter. Meeting*, volume 2021, page 4972. NIH Public Access.

Arthur C Graesser, Danielle S McNamara, and Jonna M Kulikowich. 2011. Coh-metrix: Providing multilevel analyses of text characteristics. *Educational researcher*, 40(5):223–234.

Pedram Hosseini, Christopher Wolfe, Mona Diab, and David Broniatowski. 2022. GisPy: A tool for measuring gist inference score in text. In *Proceedings of the 4th Workshop of Narrative Understanding (WNU2022)*, pages 38–46, Seattle, United States. Association for Computational Linguistics.

Albert Q Jiang, Alexandre Sablayrolles, Arthur Mensch, Chris Bamford, Devendra Singh Chaplot, Diego de las Casas, Florian Bressand, Gianna Lengyel, Guillaume Lample, Lucile Saulnier, et al. 2023. Mistral 7b. *arXiv preprint arXiv:2310.06825*.

Kamal Raj Kanakarajan, Bhuvana Kundumani, Abhijith Abraham, and Malaikannan Sankarasubbu. 2022. Biosimcse: Biomedical sentence embeddings using contrastive learning. In *Proceedings of the 13th International Workshop on Health Text Mining and Information Analysis (LOUHI)*, pages 81–86.

Peter Kincaid, Robert P. Fishburne, Richard L. Rogers, and Brad S. Chissom. 1975. Derivation of new readability formulas (automated readability index, fog count and flesch reading ease formula) for navy enlisted personnel.

Jinhyuk Lee, Wonjin Yoon, Sungdong Kim, Donghyeon Kim, Sunkyu Kim, Chan Ho So, and Jaewoo Kang. 2020. Biobert: a pre-trained biomedical language representation model for biomedical text mining. *Bioinformatics*, 36(4):1234–1240.

Xianming Li and Jing Li. 2023. Angle-optimized text embeddings. *arXiv preprint arXiv:2309.12871*.

Chin-Yew Lin. 2004. Rouge: A package for automatic evaluation of summaries. In *Text summarization branches out*, pages 74–81.

C.E. Lipscomb. 2000. Medical Subject Headings (MeSH). *Bulletin of the Medical Library Association*, 88(3):265.

Zhuang Liu, Wayne Lin, Ya Shi, and Jun Zhao. 2021. A robustly optimized bert pre-training approach with post-training. In *China National Conference on Chinese Computational Linguistics*, pages 471–484. Springer.

Junru Lu, Jiazheng Li, Byron Wallace, Yulan He, and Gabriele Pergola. 2023. NapSS: Paragraph-level medical text simplification via narrative prompting and sentence-matching summarization. In *Findings of the Association for Computational Linguistics: EACL 2023*, pages 1079–1091, Dubrovnik, Croatia. Association for Computational Linguistics.

George A Miller. 1995. Wordnet: a lexical database for english. *Communications of the ACM*, 38(11):39–41.

National Institutes of Health. 2012. Clear communication: An NIH health literacy initiative. *http://www.nih. gov/clearcommunication/healtHealth Literacyiteracy. htm.*

Richard Osborne, Shandell Elmer, Melanie Hawkins, Christina Cheng, Roy Batterham, Sónia Dias, Suvajee Good, Maristela Monteiro, Bente Mikkelsen, Ranjit Nadarajah, and Guy Fones. 2022. Health literacy development is central to the prevention and control of non-communicable diseases. *BMJ Global Health*, 7.

Kishore Papineni, Salim Roukos, Todd Ward, and Wei-Jing Zhu. 2002. Bleu: a method for automatic evaluation of machine translation. In *Proceedings of the 40th annual meeting of the Association for Computational Linguistics*, pages 311–318.

Gabriele Pergola, Lin Gui, and Yulan He. 2019. TDAM: A topic-dependent attention model for sentiment analysis. *Information Processing & Management*, 56(6):102084.

Gabriele Pergola, Lin Gui, and Yulan He. 2021a. A disentangled adversarial neural topic model for separating opinions from plots in user reviews. In *Proceedings of the 2021 Conference of the North American Chapter of the Association for Computational Linguistics: Human Language Technologies*, pages 2870–2883, Online. Association for Computational Linguistics.

Gabriele Pergola, Yulan He, and David Lowe. 2018. Topical phrase extraction from clinical reports by incorporating both local and global context. In *The 2nd AAAI Workshop on Health Intelligence*, pages 499–506. Association for the Advancement of Artificial

Intelligence. 2018 Workshop on Health Intelligence (W3PHIAI 2018).

Gabriele Pergola, Elena Kochkina, Lin Gui, Maria Liakata, and Yulan He. 2021b. Boosting low-resource biomedical QA via entity-aware masking strategies. In *Proceedings of the 16th Conference of the European Chapter of the Association for Computational Linguistics: Main Volume*, pages 1977–1985, Online. Association for Computational Linguistics.

Valerie F Reyna. 2021. A scientific theory of gist communication and misinformation resistance, with implications for health, education, and policy. *Proceedings of the National Academy of Sciences*, 118(15):e1912441117.

Rima E Rudd, Jennie Epstein Anderson, Sarah Oppenheimer, and Charlotte Nath. 2023. Health literacy: an update of medical and public health literature. In *Review of Adult Learning and Literacy, Volume 7*, pages 175–204. Routledge.

RJ Senter and Edgar A Smith. 1967. Automated readability index. Technical report, Technical report, DTIC document.

Elior Sulem, Omri Abend, and Ari Rappoport. 2018. BLEU is not suitable for the evaluation of text simplification. In *Proceedings of the 2018 Conference on Empirical Methods in Natural Language Processing*, pages 738–744, Brussels, Belgium. Association for Computational Linguistics.

Zhaoyue Sun, Jiazheng Li, Gabriele Pergola, Byron Wallace, Bino John, Nigel Greene, Joseph Kim, and Yulan He. 2022. PHEE: A dataset for pharmacovigilance event extraction from text. In *Proceedings of the 2022 Conference on Empirical Methods in Natural Language Processing*, pages 5571–5587, Abu Dhabi, United Arab Emirates. Association for Computational Linguistics.

Zhaoyue Sun, Gabriele Pergola, Byron Wallace, and Yulan He. 2024. Leveraging ChatGPT in pharmacovigilance event extraction: An empirical study. In *Proceedings of the 18th Conference of the European Chapter of the Association for Computational Linguistics (Volume 2: Short Papers)*, pages 344–357, St. Julian's, Malta. Association for Computational Linguistics.

Liang Wang, Nan Yang, Xiaolong Huang, Binxing Jiao, Linjun Yang, Daxin Jiang, Rangan Majumder, and Furu Wei. 2022. Text embeddings by weakly-supervised contrastive pre-training. *arXiv preprint arXiv:2212.03533*.

Liang Wang, Nan Yang, Xiaolong Huang, Linjun Yang, Rangan Majumder, and Furu Wei. 2023. Improving text embeddings with large language models. *arXiv preprint arXiv:2401.00368*.

Barry D Weiss. 2007. *Health literacy and patient safety: Help patients understand. Manual for clinicians.* American Medical Association Foundation.

Christopher R Wolfe, Mitchell Dandignac, and Valerie F Reyna. 2019. A theoretically motivated method for automatically evaluating texts for gist inferences. *Behavior research methods*, 51:2419–2437.

Wei Xu, Courtney Napoles, Ellie Pavlick, Quanze Chen, and Chris Callison-Burch. 2016. Optimizing statistical machine translation for text simplification. *Transactions of the Association for Computational Linguistics*, 4:401–415.

Tianyi Zhang, Varsha Kishore, Felix Wu, Kilian Q Weinberger, and Yoav Artzi. 2019a. Bertscore: Evaluating text generation with bert. *arXiv preprint arXiv:1904.09675*.

Yijia Zhang, Qingyu Chen, Zhihao Yang, Hongfei Lin, and Zhiyong Lu. 2019b. Biowordvec, improving biomedical word embeddings with subword information and mesh. *Scientific data*, 6(1):52.

Lixing Zhu, Zheng Fang, Gabriele Pergola, Robert Procter, and Yulan He. 2022. Disentangled learning of stance and aspect topics for vaccine attitude detection in social media. In *Proceedings of the 2022 Conference of the North American Chapter of the Association for Computational Linguistics: Human Language Technologies*, pages 1566–1580, Seattle, United States. Association for Computational Linguistics.

Lixing Zhu, Gabriele Pergola, Lin Gui, Deyu Zhou, and Yulan He. 2021. Topic-driven and knowledge-aware transformer for dialogue emotion detection. In *Proceedings of the 59th Annual Meeting of the Association for Computational Linguistics and the 11th International Joint Conference on Natural Language Processing (Volume 1: Long Papers)*, pages 1571–1582, Online. Association for Computational Linguistics.

Lixing Zhu, Runcong Zhao, Gabriele Pergola, and Yulan He. 2023. Disentangling aspect and stance via a Siamese autoencoder for aspect clustering of vaccination opinions. In *Findings of the Association for Computational Linguistics: ACL 2023*, pages 1827–1842, Toronto, Canada. Association for Computational Linguistics.

A Appendix

A.1 Original GIS distribution on Cochrane dataset

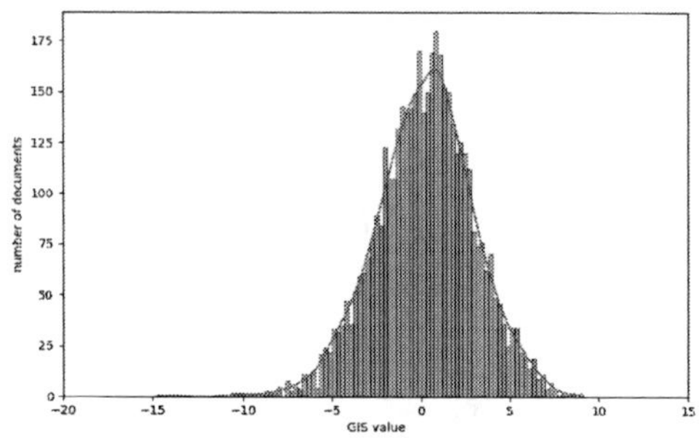

(a) GIS distribution for ABS

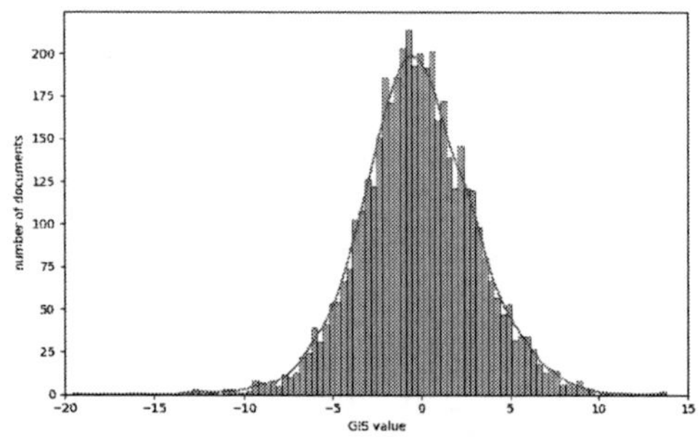

(b) GIS distribution for PLS

Figure A1: GIS distribution histogram and KDE for Cochrane text simplification dataset

The GIS distributions of ABS and PLS are jointly shown in Figure A1. Both distributions resemble Gaussian distributions, since all indices in GIS were transformed into z-scores, which were subsequently summed up with coefficients to GIS.

A.2 GIS correlation with other TS metrics

This is initially illustrated in Figure A2, where ABS and PLS from a subset of Cochrane simplification dataset (1000 samples) are plotted on corresponding scatter plots, with GIS on the vertical axis and the respective text simplification metric on the horizontal axis. Here we sampled 1000 documents from the development set due to the difficulty to visualize the original large amount of data. If there were a correlation, the points would roughly form a line, however this is not observed in any of the plots.

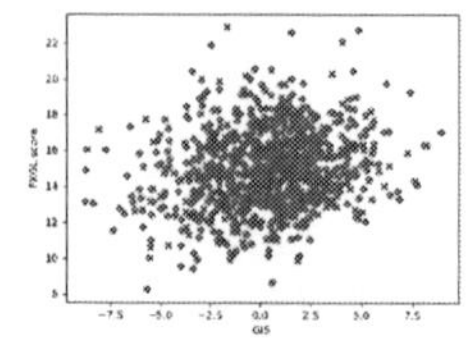

(a) GIS vs. FKGL for ABS

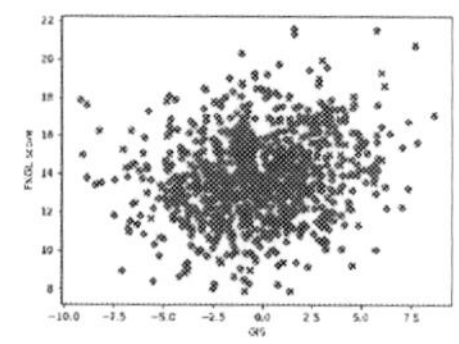

(b) GIS vs. FKGL for PLS

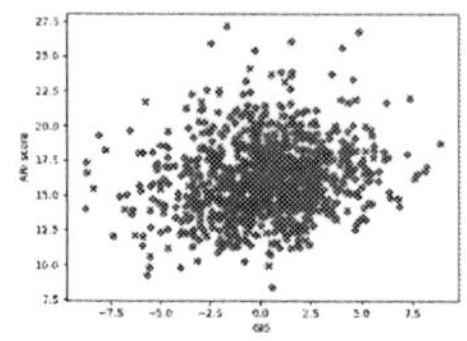

(c) GIS vs. ARI for ABS

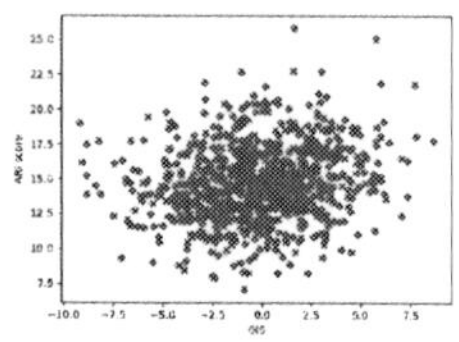

(d) GIS vs. ARI for PLS

Figure A2: Scatter plot for GIS and other metrics on Cochrane simplification dataset, on ABS and PLS documents separately

A.3 GisPy and Other Text Simplification Metrics

In this section, we demonstrate that there is no overlap between the aspects evaluated by GIS and other automatic text simplification metrics (FKGL and ARI), with highlighting the unique advantages of using GIS for this task.

Documents	GIS vs. FKGL	GIS vs. ARI
ABS	0.17	0.14
PLS	0.18	0.18

Table A1: Pearson correlation coefficients between GIS and FKGL, and between GIS and ARI

To validate the above argument, we calculated the Pearson correlation coefficients between the reference-less metrics shown in A1, where the results are all close to zero: for between GIS and KFGL, the numbers are 0.17 for ABS texts and 0.18 for PLS texts; for between GIS and ARI, the coefficient is 0.14 for ABS texts, and 0.18 for PLS texts. Note that the Pearson correlation coefficient would suggest no linear correlation if the value between two distributions is close to 0. These results further prove that GIS is uncorrelated with these metrics.

EASSE-DE & EASSE-multi:
Easier Automatic Sentence Simplification Evaluation for German & Multiple Languages

Regina Stodden
Department of Computational Linguistics
Faculty of Arts and Humanities
Heinrich Heine University Düsseldorf, Germany
regina.stodden@hhu.de

Abstract

In this work, we propose EASSE-multi, a framework for easier automatic sentence evaluation for languages other than English. Compared to the original EASSE framework, EASSE-multi does not focus only on English. It contains tokenizers and versions of text simplification evaluation metrics which are suitable for multiple languages. In this paper, we exemplify the usage of EASSE-multi for German TS resulting in EASSE-DE. Further, we compare text simplification results when evaluating with different language or tokenization settings of the metrics. Based on this, we formulate recommendations on how to make the evaluation of (German) TS models more transparent and better comparable. Additionally, we present a benchmark on German TS evaluated with EASSE-DE and make its resources (i.e., test sets, system outputs, and evaluation reports) available. The code of EASSE-multi and its German specialisation (EASSE-DE) can be found at https://github.com/rstodden/easse-multi and https://github.com/rstodden/easse-de.

1 Introduction

Automatic text simplification (TS) is a natural language processing (NLP) task that involves the development of algorithms and models to automatically transform complex textual content into more straightforward and accessible language. Manual or automatic evaluation is required to measure the quality of the generated simplifications. A good simplification should be grammatically correct, more simple and better readable than the original text and preserve the original meaning of it. For manual evaluation, people are asked to rate the extent of these three aspects for the generated simplification with respect to the original sentence. Because manual evaluation is very time-consuming, automatic metrics are used for a first quality check of sentence simplification models (Alva-Manchego et al., 2020). Compared to manual evaluation methods, automatic evaluation methods facilitate a quick assessment the output of various text simplification models, making it feasible to compare and iterate on different approaches efficiently. Further, with the increasing mass of evaluation data of different model approaches, it becomes challenging to evaluate this large number of generated texts manually. Automatic evaluation methods allow researchers to scale up their assessments to handle large datasets effectively (Alva-Manchego et al., 2020).

Alva-Manchego et al. (2019) proposed an evaluation framework for easier automatic sentence simplification evaluation, called EASSE, to facilitate a comparison of TS models on existing test sets and on the same evaluation metrics as well as to unify the implementation of the evaluation metrics. EASSE is nowadays the common standard for evaluating English TS models. Although it is specified for only English TS evaluation, it is often also used to evaluate TS models of other languages, e.g., German (see, e.g., Trienes et al. 2022), Spanish (see, e.g., Gonzalez-Dios et al. 2022), French (see, e.g., Cardon and Grabar 2020), Swedish (see, e.g., Holmer and Rennes 2023) or on a multi-lingual benchmark (Ryan et al., 2023). However, using EASSE on non-English texts raises some problems, e.g., the tokenizer is not adapted to the language of interest, the BERT-Score is evaluated on an English-only BERT model, and the readability scores are only designed for English.

In this paper, we present EASSE-multi, an adaptation of EASSE for languages other than English (i.e., more than 70 languages, these that are supported by SpaCy), to make the evaluation of non-English TS easier and more robust. We exemplify its usage for one language with several TS resources, i.e., German and the German EASSE variant, EASSE-DE. We further analyze the effects of different settings in EASSE-DE on TS metrics when evaluating German texts and presenting a German TS benchmark build with EASSE-DE.

2 Related Work

2.1 Automatic Evaluation

In order to automatically evaluate text simplification, SARI (Xu et al., 2016) is the primary metric to measure the overall simplicity quality. In more detail, SARI compares a generated simplification sentence with the source sentence and several references to estimate the quality of the lexical simplification. Further, most often BLEU (Papineni et al., 2002) and BERT-Score-Precision (Zhang* et al., 2020) are utilized to measure the similarity or meaning preservation between the original text and the system-generated simplification. Following Alva-Manchego et al. (2021), BERT-Score-Precision can also

Proceedings of the Third Workshop on Text Simplification, Accessibility and Readability (TSAR 2024), pages 107–116
November 15, 2024

measure overall simplicity even if not implemented for this use case. Recently, the LENS score (Maddela et al., 2023) has been proposed to measure the overall simplification quality of English simplifications; it is a trainable score trained on human assessments and English complex-simple pairs. However, human assessments are often missing for TS system outputs in other languages, hence, it is difficult to reproduce for other languages.

Readability formulas such as, FRE or FKGL (Flesch, 1948), are also often used to estimate the readability of the system output (Alva-Manchego et al., 2021). For a syntactical simplification evaluation, SAMSA (Sulem et al., 2018b) has been proposed: SAMSA is a referenceless metric based on the annotation of semantic structures.

The reliability of these metrics for English TS evaluation has been questioned in research, e.g., see Sulem et al. (2018a), Tanprasert and Kauchak (2021), or Alva-Manchego et al. (2021). Another issue with automatic metrics is that the reliability of the scores has only been evaluated against human annotations of English annotations and that the correlations are not yet reproduced or repeated in other languages. Therefore, the suitability of the scores is unclear for other languages than English. Stodden and Kallmeyer (2020) have indeed shown that the way how English sentences are simplified differs from the German or Spanish ways.

Hence, different simplification metrics might be required per language. An approach in this direction could be learnable metrics (per language) as LENS (Maddela et al., 2023), BETS (Zhao et al., 2023) or MeaningBERT (Beauchemin et al., 2023), which are currently only applied to English texts. But, as long as SARI, BLEU, and BERT-Score are still common practices in TS research, we will use them in our analysis but we are also open to replacing or extending the metrics in our evauluation framework, if available.

2.2 Original EASSE Package

The original EASSE package (Alva-Manchego et al., 2019) is designed to ease the automatic evaluation of English sentence simplification. It contains the implementation of automatic evaluation metrics, including SARI, BLEU, SAMSA, FKGL, and BERT-Score, as well as a linguistic feature analysis on the simplification pairs utilizing the TS-eval package by Martin et al. (2018). EASSE also stores English TS test sets and outputs of English TS systems, as well as builds an evaluation report regarding all specified metrics of all specified TS models to facilitate the whole evaluation process. It is commonly used to evaluate TS system outputs in English and other languages. In this work, we will adapt EASSE in order to be better suitable for evaluation in other languages than English.

3 System Overview: EASSE-multi

In order to make EASSE language-independent and more robust for evaluating texts of languages other than English, we are proposing EASSE-multi (and its German variant EASSE-DE in the next section).

Therefore, we add a language constant to EASSE-multi to specify the currently evaluated language (e.g., "DE" for German in EASSE-DE). We also add SpaCy to the list of possible tokenizers to allow tokenization specified for languages other than English (see subsection 3.1).

The language constant also allows to choose language-specific evaluation metrics, e.g., readability metrics (see subsection 3.3), different models for BERT-Score (see subsection 3.2) and multi-lingual linguistic feature extraction (see subsection 3.4).

3.1 Tokenization

The original EASSE version currently supports 13a tokenization or white-space split tokenization (presuming pre-tokenized data). To include the language component into tokenization, we added the tokenizers of SpaCy (Montani et al., 2023) and the extension Spacy-Stanza (Qi et al., 2020)[1] as they currently support the tokenization of roughly 70 languages and also support linguistic annotations, e.g., part-of-speech tagging and dependency parsing, which will be relevant for the linguistic feature extraction.

3.2 Metrics

Evaluation metrics for TS are mostly language-independent, e.g., SARI, or BLEU, as they are n-gram-based methods. However, the n-grams depend on tokenization, which differs from language to language (see previous section). On the other hand, there are also language-specific evaluation metrics: Following Zhang* et al. (2020), BERT-Score can be used for a specific language (e.g., using the English-only model RoBERTa (Liu et al., 2019)) or in a multi-lingual setting (e.g., using a multi-lingual model such as BERT-multilingual (Devlin et al., 2019)).

In EASSE-multi, the usage of the metrics is optimized regarding the evaluated language, as based on the language constant, the tokenizer and the BERT-model are chosen to fit non-English languages better.

3.3 Readability

Readability scores and the LENS-Score (Maddela et al., 2023) are language-dependent, for the first due to included language-specific averages of word and sentence lengths and for the second due to training an evaluation score exclusively on English.

As an extension of EASSE, we also added readability formulas for languages other than English to EASSE-multi, which have already been implemented in the textstat package – a package for measuring readability and complexity in different languages. For example, common readability scores for German are the Amstad's adaption on the Flesch Reading Ease (FRE) or the Vienna non-fictional text formulas (Bamberger and

[1]https://github.com/explosion/spacy-stanza

Vanecek, 1984). LENS has not been reproduced for other languages due to missing required human assessment labels; hence, it makes no sense to include it in EASSE-multi.

Following the criticism of Tanprasert and Kauchak (2021) regarding readability metrics for TS evaluation, we follow their recommendation and include average sentence length, number of syllables and number of splits in our report. Hence, we add these features to the default report.

3.4 Multi-lingual Feature Extraction

As argued in Tanprasert and Kauchak (2021) and Alva-Manchego et al. (2019), we include a few linguistic features to get more insights into the system-generated simplification. For this, we are using the feature extraction toolkit of the reference-less quality estimation tool (further called TS-eval) by Martin et al. (2018) for the English analysis and its extended language-independent version TS-eval-multi by Stodden and Kallmeyer (2020). We decided to use TS-eval-multi for feature extraction and not the similar language-independent feature extraction toolkit called LFTK (Lee and Lee, 2023) as both versions of TS-eval focus more on features for text simplification, whereas LFTK focuses more on features for readability assessment. The TS-eval package has also already been integrated into the evaluation package EASSE, which facilitates its extension to the multilingual TS-eval. Further, most of LFTK's implemented features only apply to English. In future work, TS-eval-multi could be extended with features of LFTK. TS-eval-multi contains, for example, the parse tree height, cosine similarity between source and output based on pre-trained word embeddings, and length of phrases and clauses.

3.5 Additional Resources

The original EASSE framework also includes resources of English TS, i.e., English TS test sets, word lists, and system outputs of English TS models. With EASSE-multi, this component can be extended to the language of interest. We exemplify this with EASSE-DE and add only German resources (see section 4). However, the German resources can be easily replaced with resources of other languages.

3.6 Recommended Setting

At the moment, we cannot provide recommended settings per language except specifying the language constant, using SpaCy for tokenization, and using the multilingual BERT-Score. Further recommendations, for example, if case sensitivity is useful for the language of interest or determining which BERT version is more suitable for the language of interest, require more analysis which is out of the scope of this work. However, we recommend always naming which kind of settings have been used during evaluation as it can greatly influence the TS metrics. The settings should be reported in detail to ensure that the effect on the metric is due to the TS system and not the evaluation metrics' settings.

Furthermore, it could be helpful to report the results of the baselines, e.g., src2src (i.e., source-to-source or using the original complex sentence as input and output) or tgt2tgt (target-to-target or using the simple sentence as input and output). If the system outputs cannot be made available, it could help to verify on the gold data whether the applied evaluation method (e.g., in a replication experiment) is the same as the evaluation method used for an original experiment, as the results should be identical. Additionally, it could be helpful to re-evaluate the data comparing to. Therefore, we recommend making the system outputs publicly available (if the data is not restricted by license or copyright), e.g., as part of the EASSE-DE resources.

3.7 Usage

In order to customize EASSE-multi for a specific language (e.g., EASSE-DE for German or EASSE-ES for Spain), a few steps are necessary. First, the framework needs to be updated with language-specific data, i.e., TS test sets, (optionally) system outputs, and a SpaCy model[2] in the language of interest. Next, the settings[3] should be edited to fit the language, i.e., a) set the language constant, b) decide on considering or ignoring casing, c) edit metric scores (e.g., add language-specific readability scores), and d) (optionally) specify test set names and paths. Then, you can either run EASSE-multi to evaluate one single model or generate a report of scores for several models. More instructions on how to use EASSE-multi can be found in the GitHub repository[4].

4 EASSE-DE: Using EASSE-multi for German TS Evaluation

We will exemplify the usage of EASSE-multi for one language, i.e., German, resulting in EASSE-DE[5]. We have decided on German, as it is well-researched language in the research field of TS and enough resources (i.e., TS models, test sets, and system outputs) are available for a reasonable showcase project.

Therefore, we add German resources to EASSE-DE (see subsection 4.1), i.e., German sentence simplification test sets (see subsubsection 4.1.1), and available outputs of German TS systems regarding these test sets (see subsubsection 4.1.2). Further, we analyze whether and to what extent differences exist when evaluating German TS with the original evaluation framework EASSE or its adaptation EASSE-DE (see subsection 4.2).

[2]https://spacy.io/usage/models

[3]You can find the settings file here: https://github.com/rstodden/easse-multi/blob/master/easse/utils/constants.py

[4]https://github.com/rstodden/easse-multi

[5]https://github.com/rstodden/easse-de

name	target group	domain	size	# ref.	n:m	complex FRE↓	complex sent. len.↑	complex word len.↑	simple FRE↑	simple sent. len.↓	simple word len.↓
ABGB	non-experts	law	448	2	40%	42.75	24.85	1.83	44.6	22.39	1.89
APA_LHA-or-a2	Non-native speaker	news	500	1	6 %	44.7	20.2	1.92	69.55	11.27	1.78
APA_LHA-or-b1	Non-native speaker	news	500	1	8 %	43.7	20.48	1.93	62.6	12.82	1.83
BiSECT	people w. reading problems	politics	753	1	100 %	**8.55**	**30.24**	2.01	35.85	15.72	1.98
DEplain-APA	Non-native speaker	news	1,231	1	27 %	58.75	11.92	1.86	65.8	10.55	1.79
DEplain-web	mixed	web/mixed	1,846	1	57 %	62.95	19.13	1.64	**77.9**	10.76	**1.57**
GEOlino	children	encyclopedia	663	1	40 %	61.5	13.31	1.7	66.0	9.94	1.66
simple-german-corpus	mixed	web/mixed	391	1	73 %	41.15	13.96	2.0	65.4	**9.31**	1.83
TextComplexityDE	Non-native speaker	encyclopedia	250	1	83 %	28.1	27.75	**2.08**	51.2	14.17	1.9

Table 1: Overview Test Sets for German Sentence Simplification which are included in EASSE-DE. Including the target group, domain, size in sentence pairs, number of references, percentage of $n : m$ alignments, word length measured in syllables, and sentence length measured in words.

System Name	Reference	Type	Training Data	# Simp. Pairs	URL
hda-etr	Siegel et al. (2019)	rule-based	-	-	https://github.com/hdaSprachtechnologie/easy-to-understand_language
sockeye-APA-LHA	Spring et al. (2021) & Ebling et al. (2022)	seq2seq	APA-LHA OR-A2 & APA-LHA OR-B1	8,455 & 9,268	https://github.com/ZurichNLP/RANLP2021-German-ATS
sockeye-DEplain-APA	Stodden (2024)	seq2seq	DEplain-APA	10,660	https://huggingface.co/DEplain
mBART-DEplain-APA	Stodden et al. (2023)	fine-tuned seq2seq	DEplain-APA	10,660	https://huggingface.co/DEplain/trimmed_mbart_sents_apa
mBART-DEplain-APA+web	Stodden et al. (2023)	fine-tuned seq2seq	DEplain-APA+web	10,660 + 1,594	https://huggingface.co/DEplain/trimmed_mbart_sents_apa_web
mT5-DEplain-APA	Stodden (2024)	fine-tuned seq2seq	DEplain-APA	10,660	https://huggingface.co/DEplain
mT5-SGC	Stodden (2024)	fine-tuned seq2seq	SGC	4,430	https://huggingface.co/DEplain
BLOOM-zero	Ryan et al. (2023)	zero-shot AR model	-	-	https://github.com/XenonMolecule/MultiSim
BLOOM-sim-10	Ryan et al. (2023)	few-shot AR model	TCDE19 & GEOlino	200 & 959	https://github.com/XenonMolecule/MultiSim
BLOOM-random 10	Ryan et al. (2023)	few-shot AR model	TCDE19 & GEOlino	200 & 959	https://github.com/XenonMolecule/MultiSim
custom-decoder-ats	Anschütz et al. (2023)	AR model + fine-tuned seq2seq	Simplified, monolingual German data & 20Minuten	544,467 & 17,905	https://huggingface.co/josh-oo/custom-decoder-ats

Table 2: Overview of German TS models including training details (i.e., training data and size of training samples). Each line separates different model types. Adaptation from Stodden (2024).

4.1 German TS Resources

4.1.1 German TS Test Sets

For a better overview of available test sets for German sentence simplification, we have added gold data, i.e., manually simplified complex-simple sentence pairs, to EASSE-DE. In more detail, EASSE-DE refers to nine test sets, i.e., ABGB (Meister, 2023), APA-LHA-OR-A2 (Spring et al., 2021), APA-LHA-OR-B1 (Spring et al., 2021), BiSECT (Kim et al., 2021), DEplain-APA (Stodden et al., 2023), DEplain-web (Stodden et al., 2023), TextComplexityDE (Naderi et al., 2019), GEOlino (Mallinson et al., 2020), and Simple-German-Corpus (Toborek et al., 2023). We refer to Table 1 for more meta data of the test sets.

4.1.2 German TS Models

For German TS, a few models are available or reproducible, e.g., ZEST, by Mallinson et al. (2020), sockeye by Spring et al. (2021), custom-decoder-ats by Anschütz et al. (2023), the few-shot approaches on BLOOM by Ryan et al. (2023), or the mBART models by Stodden et al. (2023). A more detailed description and analysis of German TS models, including their reproduction, has been recently proposed by Stodden (2024). The system outputs of all reproduced German TS models (see Table 2) have been added to EASSE-DE to facilitate a better comparison between existing models and models which will be newly proposed in future.

4.2 Comparison of EASSE and EASSE-DE

In the following section, we present and analyse the metric scores when using either the original EASSE or the adapted version EASSE-DE, including different settings on three German test sets of one German TS model.

4.2.1 Method

Evaluation Settings. In the comparative analysis, we focus on the settings in EASSE regarding i) language specification (i.e., English vs. German), ii) tokenization method (i.e., none vs 13a vs SpaCy), iii) BERT model version (i.e., RoBERTa-large vs BERT-base-multilingual-cased), iv) FRE version (English vs German). Due to their n-gram-based approach, we expect the tokenization method to have an effect on SARI and BLEU but not on BERT-Score-Precision.

German TS Test Sets. In the analysis, we evaluate on three available German TS test sets: DEplain-APA (Stodden et al., 2023), DEplain-web (Stodden et al., 2023), and TextComplexityDE (Naderi et al., 2019).

These test sets are all manually simplified and manually aligned, and, therefore, we expect a higher simplification quality for them as for other test sets, e.g., BiSECT (Kim et al., 2021)[6] or APA-LHA (Spring et al., 2021)[7]. Further, these three test sets include texts of different domains (news, web, and Wikipedia), and their simplification addresses different target groups (non-native speakers and people with cognitive disabilities). Hence, they represent different kinds of simplifications and therefore seem to be a good choice for our analysis.

German TS Model. Further, we have selected the generated simplifications of one model, i.e., mBART-DEplain-APA+web. Reasons for the choice of this model are that it is ready-to-use without additional examples, and, following Stodden (2024), this model achieves the best BERT-Scores across several test sets. In comparison, the BLOOM models by Ryan et al. (2023) are few-shot models that require additional complex-simple pairs to generate simplifications.

4.2.2 Results

The results of the mBART-APA+web model with different settings are presented in Table 3.[8] In the following, we analyse the differences regarding tokenization, readability scores, multi-lingual BERT-Score, and system rankings.

	Tok.	Lang.	BLEU↑	SARI↑	BS-P↑	FRE↑
TCDE19 (n = 250)	spacy	EN	**18.56**	**37.69**	0.39	**57.37**
	spacy	DE	17.75	37.37	**0.55**	43.65
	13a	DE	18.04	37.41	**0.55**	43.55
	none	DE	16.04	37.47	**0.55**	43.65
DEplain-APA (n = 1231)	spacy	EN	**30.59**	**34.79**	0.48	**78.25**
	spacy	DE	28.03	33.81	**0.64**	65.2
	13a	DE	28.37	33.92	**0.64**	65.2
	none	DE	24.69	32.88	**0.64**	65.2
DEplain-web (n = 1846)	spacy	EN	18.37	**34.21**	0.27	**76.52**
	spacy	DE	17.99	34.07	**0.44**	69.05
	13a	DE	18.17	34.10	**0.44**	69.05
	none	DE	15.97	33.67	**0.44**	69.05

Table 3: Scores of trimmed-mbart-DEplain-APA+web when using different language settings and tokenizers.

Tokenization. As expected, different tokenization methods (including language specification) affect the calculation of metrics used for TS evaluation. The last three rows in each block of Table 3 show the differences in the scores when using different tokenization strategies. We can see that the BERT-score is always the same for all settings due to the sub-word tokenization in BERT. The FRE scores are also robust across all test sets when looking at the trimmed-mBART results, but in Appendix A Table 5, we see slightly more differences. The SARI scores also change slightly, i.e., to less than 1 point in all settings, whereas the differences in the BLEU scores range between 2 to 3 points in all test sets. In conclusion, when comparing one model against another with a slightly different evaluation setting (here, the tokenizer), even these small changes can be wrongly interpreted as an improvement of the model idiosyncrasy. However, it is only due to the different settings. Therefore, we recommend stating all settings chosen for evaluation for a more reliable comparison.

Readability Metrics. As can be seen in Table 3, the scores are quite different wrt. to FRE for the English and German settings (see first two rows in each block). The results are different due to the different constants of the formulas and their dependency on different tokenization and syllable splitting. When interpreting the readability scores, they also result in different categories: Following (Amstad, 1978), the simplifications with the English setting on DEplain-APA and DEplain-web can be described as "ease" whereas they are categorized as "simple" using the German setting. In summary, the language adaptation of readability scores can make a noticeable difference when interpreting the simplification results.

BERT-Score. As shown in the first two rows of each row-block in Table 3, changing the transformer model of the BERT-Score significantly affects the BERT-Score. The scores using the multi-lingual model are much higher than those using the only-English model. Hence, the choice of the BERT model seems to have a high effect on the TS evaluation.

System Rankings. When evaluating TS systems, often their ranks are compared to each other instead of the exact scores. Therefore, we have analysed whether the ranks changes when evaluating 11 German TS systems (and 2 baselines) either with the original EASSE or with EASSE-DE.[9] As can be seen in Table 4, the ranks of the models wrt. BLEU, and BERT-Score-Precision are slightly changing depending on the EASSE version whereas the ranks for SARI are constant. Contrary to the ranks, changes are visible wrt. the scores. When evaluating more similar systems (e.g., during hyperparameter tuning) the differences might get more meaningful and relevant also with respect to the ranks. Therefore, it is important to specify the settings used for evaluation to have a reliable comparison.

5 Benchmark for German TS

EASSE-DE facilitates modeling German text simplification by providing a unified evaluation framework as well as storing data of several German test sets (see Table 1). Additionally with the provided system outputs of reproduced German TS systems (Stodden, 2024), a

[6]BiSECT is generated using machine translation of English texts. Due to this augmentation strategy, the German version includes encoding errors.

[7]The training and validation sets of APA-LHA are automatically aligned, and, hence, more faulty compared to manually aligned corpora.

[8]To ensure that the effects are not due to the system but to the evaluation changes, we also add the results of the identity baseline (see Table 5).

[9]The system outputs, which have been used for this analysis, are available upon request at `https://doi.org/10.5281/zenodo.13891495`.

	BLEU↑		SARI↑		BS-P↑	
	S	R	S	R	S	R
hda_LS	22.3	5	26.06	12	0.55	7
sockeye-APA-LHA	11.84	11	40.16	3	0.37	12
sockeye-DEplain-APA	19.58	7	44.14	1	0.53	9
mbart_DEplain_apa	28.49	1	38.72	5	0.64	1
mbart_DEplain_apa_web	28.03	2	33.81	10	0.64	1
mT5-DEplain-APA	22.32	4	39.41	4	0.61	4
mt5-simple-german-corpus	8.12	12	37.92	6	0.48	11
BLOOM-zero	16.14	9	35.43	9	0.53	9
BLOOM-10-random	17.97	8	35.93	8	0.57	5
BLOOM-10-similarity	20.97	6	41.27	2	0.57	5
custom-decoder-ats	1.24	13	36.42	7	0.16	13
Identity baseline	26.89	3	15.25	13	0.63	3
Truncate baseline	16.11	10	27.2	11	0.55	7

(a) Evaluated with default settings of EASSE-DE, i.e., no lower-casing and SpaCy tokenizer.

	BLEU↑		SARI↑		BS-P↑	
	S	R	S	R	S	R
hda_LS	23.77	4	26.82	12	0.38	7
sockeye-APA-LHA	12.42	11	40.27	3	0.13	12
sockeye-DEplain-APA	20.97	7	44.89	1	0.36	9
mbart_DEplain_APA	30.01	1	39.12	5	0.47	1
mbart_DEplain_APA_web	29.62	2	34.44	10	0.47	1
mT5-DEplain-APA	23.7	5	39.8	4	0.46	3
mt5-simple-german-corpus	8.92	12	38.2	6	0.29	11
BLOOM-zero	17.23	10	35.19	9	0.36	9
BLOOM-10-random	19.23	8	35.52	8	0.38	7
BLOOM-10-similarity	22.21	6	41.21	2	0.39	6
custom-decoder-ats	1.29	13	36.65	7	-0.13	13
Identity baseline	28.5	3	15.88	13	0.45	4
Truncate baseline	18.94	9	28.31	11	0.41	5

(b) Evaluated with default settings of original EASSE, i.e., lower-casing and 13a tokenizer.

Table 4: Scores (S) and ranks (R) of German TS models on the DEplain-APA test set.

benchmark for German TS can be easily build and updated using EASSE-DE. In Appendix B, we provide a German TS benchmark including results of 7 German TS models (see Table 2) on 7 German test sets of the domains of news, web, and Wikipedia texts.

As discussed in Stodden (2024), there is no clear picture regarding best performing models across all domains or test sets. As expected, models achieve the best scores if they are evaluated and trained on the same corpus. However, corresponding to the ranks following the metrics' scores the models are ranked differently, e.g., a model gets the highest SARI score but lower BS_P scores and vice versa. For a reliable interpretation of the metrics, there is more research to be done regarding finding new evaluation metrics and checking the suitability of existing metrics on languages other than English.

6 Discussion & Conclusion

We have proposed EASSE-multi, which facilitates easy evaluation of sentence simplification in multiple languages. Therefore, we have extended the original EASSE package with a language-constant tokenizer, language-dependent version of BERT-Score, and language-wise readability scores.

Further, we have exemplified using EASSE-multi for German TS evaluation in the form of EASSE-DE. In comparing the results generated by EASSE and EASSE-DE, we have shown that it is important to consider the text's language when evaluating. Following that, we recommend using EASSE-DE over EASSE when evaluating German sentence simplification models as it includes language-sensitive evaluation metrics. Even if the scores per metric might be lower when using EASSE-DE than EASSE, we argue that these are more reliable due to the language-sensitive metrics.

Further, we argue that it is unreliable to compare scores (maybe originating from different papers) as they might be generated by using different evaluation settings. Before making a comparison, we recommend verifying whether the same settings of the metric have been used in both experiments (the referenced and the new one). Otherwise, the differences in the scores might not be dependent on the model changes (which is the question of interest) but on, for example, different kinds of tokenization. Therefore, we strongly recommend always specifying the settings or, even better, the implementation of the metrics used for the evaluation, as it can have a huge impact on the reported scores. We identified the following aspects which should be reported accompanied with automatic evaluation: 1. language setting (e.g., EN, or DE) for features (e.g., BERT-Score, FRE, or word length), 2. tokenizer (e.g., none, 13a, or SpaCy), 3. lower casing (True or False), 4. BERT-Score model (e.g., RoBERTa-large, mT5, or BERT-base-multilingual-cased)

7 Future Work

Even if most of the scores are language-independent or can be easily adapted to work for other languages, as shown previously, there still might be problems in using the same scores for different languages due to language idiosyncrasies and different simplification operations per language. Approaches in the direction of language-wise evaluation of non-English TS could be learnable metrics (per language) as already proposed for English, e.g., LENS, BETS, or MeaningBERT. In future work, we want to investigate learnable metrics for non-English languages to fit the language idiosyncrasies better and add them to EASSE-DE.

Further, we would like to extend EASSE-DE to include more German TS resources. We hope that EASSE-DE will be useful for German TS researchers and invite them to contribute their test sets or system outputs to EASSE-DE.

Acknowledgements

First, we want to thank the authors of the original EASSE paper, without their highly valuable contribution (openly licensed code, and clearly structured and easy adaptable code) this extension would have not been possible. We also want to thank the reviewers for their valuable feedback, which has helped to strengthen the paper.

Lay Summary

The process of automatically rewriting texts is also called "automatic text simplification". Automatic text simplification can be defined as: the change of word choice in a text and/or the restructuring of a sentence to be better understandable for a given target group. Often, research in text simplification focuses on the simplification of English texts. In this work, we facilitate the research on text simplification in multiple languages. In more detail, we have focused on the evaluation of automatic text simplification systems for multiple languages. Therefore, we have provided an evaluation toolkit which can be used to evaluate the output of text simplification systems.

Additionally, we have showcased the usage of this toolkit for German. We are providing an easy-to-use framework for German text simplification including a selection of test sets, system outputs of several German TS models and a report regarding their quality.

Limitations

In this work, we have just showcased the usage of EASSE-multi for German, although it is also applicable to other languages. Furthermore, we have focused on openly licensed TS models and, hence, we have not included proprietary language models, e.g., ChatGPT.

References

Fernando Alva-Manchego, Louis Martin, Carolina Scarton, and Lucia Specia. 2019. EASSE: Easier automatic sentence simplification evaluation. In *Proceedings of the 2019 Conference on Empirical Methods in Natural Language Processing and the 9th International Joint Conference on Natural Language Processing (EMNLP-IJCNLP): System Demonstrations*, pages 49–54, Hong Kong, China. Association for Computational Linguistics.

Fernando Alva-Manchego, Carolina Scarton, and Lucia Specia. 2020. Data-driven sentence simplification: Survey and benchmark. *Computational Linguistics*, 46(1):135–187.

Fernando Alva-Manchego, Carolina Scarton, and Lucia Specia. 2021. The (un)suitability of automatic evaluation metrics for text simplification. *Computational Linguistics*, 47(4):861–889.

Toni Amstad. 1978. *Wie verständlich sind unsere Zeitungen?* Studenten-Schreib-Service. PhD Thesis.

Miriam Anschütz, Joshua Oehms, Thomas Wimmer, Bartłomiej Jezierski, and Georg Groh. 2023. Language models for German text simplification: Overcoming parallel data scarcity through style-specific pre-training. In *Findings of the Association for Computational Linguistics: ACL 2023*, pages 1147–1158, Toronto, Canada. Association for Computational Linguistics.

Richard Bamberger and Erich Vanecek. 1984. *Lesen - Verstehen - Lernen - Schreiben. Die Schwierigkeitsstufen von Texten in deutscher Sprache.* Jugend u. Volk Sauerlaender, Wien.

David Beauchemin, Horacio Saggion, and Richard Khoury. 2023. Meaningbert: Assessing meaning preservation between sentences. *Frontiers in Artificial Intelligence*, 6.

Rémi Cardon and Natalia Grabar. 2020. French biomedical text simplification: When small and precise helps. In *Proceedings of the 28th International Conference on Computational Linguistics*, pages 710–716, Barcelona, Spain (Online). International Committee on Computational Linguistics.

Jacob Devlin, Ming-Wei Chang, Kenton Lee, and Kristina Toutanova. 2019. BERT: Pre-training of deep bidirectional transformers for language understanding. In *Proceedings of the 2019 Conference of the North American Chapter of the Association for Computational Linguistics: Human Language Technologies, Volume 1 (Long and Short Papers)*, pages 4171–4186, Minneapolis, Minnesota. Association for Computational Linguistics.

Sarah Ebling, Alessia Battisti, Marek Kostrzewa, Dominik Pfütze, Annette Rios, Andreas Säuberli, and Nicolas Spring. 2022. Automatic text simplification for german. *Frontiers in Communication*, 7.

Rudolph Flesch. 1948. A new readability yardstick. *Journal of applied psychology*, 32(3):221.

Itziar Gonzalez-Dios, Iker Gutiérrez-Fandiño, Oscar m. Cumbicus-Pineda, and Aitor Soroa. 2022. IrekiaLFes: a new open benchmark and baseline systems for Spanish automatic text simplification. In *Proceedings of the Workshop on Text Simplification, Accessibility, and Readability (TSAR-2022)*, pages 86–97, Abu Dhabi, United Arab Emirates (Virtual). Association for Computational Linguistics.

Daniel Holmer and Evelina Rennes. 2023. Constructing pseudo-parallel Swedish sentence corpora for automatic text simplification. In *Proceedings of the 24th Nordic Conference on Computational Linguistics (NoDaLiDa)*, pages 113–123, Tórshavn, Faroe Islands. University of Tartu Library.

Joongwon Kim, Mounica Maddela, Reno Kriz, Wei Xu, and Chris Callison-Burch. 2021. BiSECT: Learning to split and rephrase sentences with bitexts. In *Proceedings of the 2021 Conference on Empirical Methods in Natural Language Processing*, pages 6193–6209, Online and Punta Cana, Dominican Republic. Association for Computational Linguistics.

Bruce W. Lee and Jason Lee. 2023. LFTK: Handcrafted features in computational linguistics. In *Proceedings of the 18th Workshop on Innovative Use of NLP for Building Educational Applications (BEA 2023)*, pages 1–19, Toronto, Canada. Association for Computational Linguistics.

Yinhan Liu, Myle Ott, Naman Goyal, Jingfei Du, Mandar Joshi, Danqi Chen, Omer Levy, Mike Lewis, Luke Zettlemoyer, and Veselin Stoyanov. 2019. Roberta: A robustly optimized BERT pretraining approach. *CoRR*, abs/1907.11692.

Mounica Maddela, Yao Dou, David Heineman, and Wei Xu. 2023. LENS: A learnable evaluation metric for text simplification. In *Proceedings of the 61st Annual Meeting of the Association for Computational Linguistics (Volume 1: Long Papers)*, pages 16383–16408, Toronto, Canada. Association for Computational Linguistics.

Jonathan Mallinson, Rico Sennrich, and Mirella Lapata. 2020. Zero-shot crosslingual sentence simplification. In *Proceedings of the 2020 Conference on Empirical Methods in Natural Language Processing (EMNLP)*, pages 5109–5126, Online. Association for Computational Linguistics.

Louis Martin, Samuel Humeau, Pierre-Emmanuel Mazaré, Éric de La Clergerie, Antoine Bordes, and Benoît Sagot. 2018. Reference-less quality estimation of text simplification systems. In *Proceedings of the 1st Workshop on Automatic Text Adaptation (ATA)*, pages 29–38, Tilburg, the Netherlands. Association for Computational Linguistics.

Fabian Meister. 2023. ABGB-TextSimplification-Datasets. GitHub repository: `https://github.com/MeisterFa/ABGB-TextSimplification-Datasets`. Visited on 2023-12-01.

Ines Montani, Matthew Honnibal, Matthew Honnibal, Adriane Boyd, Sofie Van Landeghem, and Henning Peters. 2023. explosion/spaCy: v3.7.2: Fixes for APIs and requirements.

Babak Naderi, Salar Mohtaj, Kaspar Ensikat, and Sebastian Möller. 2019. Subjective assessment of text complexity: A dataset for german language. *CoRR*, abs/1904.07733.

Kishore Papineni, Salim Roukos, Todd Ward, and Wei-Jing Zhu. 2002. Bleu: a method for automatic evaluation of machine translation. In *Proceedings of the 40th Annual Meeting of the Association for Computational Linguistics*, pages 311–318, Philadelphia, Pennsylvania, USA. Association for Computational Linguistics.

Peng Qi, Yuhao Zhang, Yuhui Zhang, Jason Bolton, and Christopher D. Manning. 2020. Stanza: A python natural language processing toolkit for many human languages. In *Proceedings of the 58th Annual Meeting of the Association for Computational Linguistics: System Demonstrations*, pages 101–108, Online. Association for Computational Linguistics.

Michael Ryan, Tarek Naous, and Wei Xu. 2023. Revisiting non-English text simplification: A unified multilingual benchmark. In *Proceedings of the 61st Annual Meeting of the Association for Computational Linguistics (Volume 1: Long Papers)*, pages 4898–4927, Toronto, Canada. Association for Computational Linguistics.

Melanie Siegel, Dorothee Beermann, and Lars Hellan. 2019. Aspects of linguistic complexity: A german - norwegian approach to the creation of resources for easy-to-understand language. In *11th International Conference on Quality of Multimedia Experience QoMEX 2019, Berlin, Germany, June 5-7, 2019*, pages 1–3. IEEE.

Nicolas Spring, Annette Rios, and Sarah Ebling. 2021. Exploring German multi-level text simplification. In *Proceedings of the International Conference on Recent Advances in Natural Language Processing (RANLP 2021)*, pages 1339–1349, Held Online. INCOMA Ltd.

Regina Stodden. 2024. Reproduction & Benchmarking of German Text Simplification Systems. In *Proceedings of the Workshop on DeTermIt! Evaluating Text Difficulty in a Multilingual Context @ LREC-COLING 2024*, pages 1–15, Torino, Italia. ELRA and ICCL.

Regina Stodden and Laura Kallmeyer. 2020. A multilingual and cross-domain analysis of features for text simplification. In *Proceedings of the 1st Workshop on Tools and Resources to Empower People with REAding DIfficulties (READI)*, pages 77–84, Marseille, France. European Language Resources Association.

Regina Stodden, Omar Momen, and Laura Kallmeyer. 2023. DEplain: A German parallel corpus with intralingual translations into plain language for sentence and document simplification. In *Proceedings of the 61st Annual Meeting of the Association for Computational Linguistics (Volume 1: Long Papers)*, pages 16441–16463, Toronto, Canada. Association for Computational Linguistics.

Elior Sulem, Omri Abend, and Ari Rappoport. 2018a. BLEU is not suitable for the evaluation of text simplification. In *Proceedings of the 2018 Conference on Empirical Methods in Natural Language Processing*, pages 738–744, Brussels, Belgium. Association for Computational Linguistics.

Elior Sulem, Omri Abend, and Ari Rappoport. 2018b. Semantic structural evaluation for text simplification. In *Proceedings of the 2018 Conference of the North American Chapter of the Association for Computational Linguistics: Human Language Technologies, Volume 1 (Long Papers)*, pages 685–696, New Orleans, Louisiana. Association for Computational Linguistics.

Teerapaun Tanprasert and David Kauchak. 2021. Flesch-kincaid is not a text simplification evaluation metric. In *Proceedings of the 1st Workshop on Natural Language Generation, Evaluation, and Metrics (GEM 2021)*, pages 1–14, Online. Association for Computational Linguistics.

Vanessa Toborek, Moritz Busch, Malte Boßert, Christian Bauckhage, and Pascal Welke. 2023. A new aligned simple German corpus. In *Proceedings of the 61st Annual Meeting of the Association for Computational Linguistics (Volume 1: Long Papers)*, pages

11393–11412, Toronto, Canada. Association for Computational Linguistics.

Jan Trienes, Jörg Schlötterer, Hans-Ulrich Schildhaus, and Christin Seifert. 2022. Patient-friendly clinical notes: Towards a new text simplification dataset. In *Proceedings of the Workshop on Text Simplification, Accessibility, and Readability (TSAR-2022)*, pages 19–27, Abu Dhabi, United Arab Emirates (Virtual). Association for Computational Linguistics.

Wei Xu, Courtney Napoles, Ellie Pavlick, Quanze Chen, and Chris Callison-Burch. 2016. Optimizing statistical machine translation for text simplification. *Transactions of the Association for Computational Linguistics*, 4:401–415.

Tianyi Zhang*, Varsha Kishore*, Felix Wu*, Kilian Q. Weinberger, and Yoav Artzi. 2020. Bertscore: Evaluating text generation with bert. In *International Conference on Learning Representations*.

Xinran Zhao, Esin Durmus, and Dit-Yan Yeung. 2023. Towards reference-free text simplification evaluation with a BERT Siamese network architecture. In *Findings of the Association for Computational Linguistics: ACL 2023*, pages 13250–13264, Toronto, Canada. Association for Computational Linguistics.

A Results of Identity Baseline

	Tok.	Lang.	BLEU↑	SARI↑	BS-P↑	FRE↑
TCDE19 (n = 250)	spacy	EN	**28.22**	15.31	0.37	**39.16**
	spacy	DE	27.31	14.99	**0.55**	28.1
	13a	DE	27.49	15.05	**0.55**	28.0
	none	DE	24.43	13.78	**0.55**	28.1
DEplain-APA (n = 1231)	spacy	EN	**29.28**	**16.17**	0.45	**77.64**
	spacy	DE	26.89	15.25	**0.63**	58.75
	13a	DE	27.25	15.35	**0.63**	64.6
	none	DE	23.33	13.75	**0.63**	58.75
DEplain-web (n = 1846)	spacy	EN	21.24	12.09	0.25	**70.33**
	spacy	DE	20.85	11.93	0.42	62.95
	13a	DE	20.89	11.94	0.42	62.95
	none	DE	18.82	10.9	0.42	62.95

Table 5: Scores of identity baseline on three test sets when using different language settings and tokenizers.

B German TS Benchmark

B.1 Evaluation on News Corpora

	BLEU↑	SARI↑	BS_P↑	FRE↑	Compr. ratio↓	Sent. splits↑
hda_LS	3.02	14.02	0.12	37.55	1.14	1.04
sockeye-APA-LHA	**13.59**	**51.77**	**0.35**	68.65	0.64	0.99
sockeye-DEplain-APA	4.79	40.32	0.25	**70.25**	0.71	1.25
mBART-DEplain-APA	4.73	30.28	0.23	57.55	0.85	1.33
mBART-DEplain-APA+web	4.56	25.89	0.23	56.35	0.84	1.16
mT5-DEplain-APA	4.65	34.47	0.24	58.10	0.58	1.09
mT5-SGC	2.78	39.79	0.28	**70.25**	**0.48**	1.00
BLOOM-zero	2.44	26.83	0.19	51.85	0.82	1.29
BLOOM-10-random	2.64	33.05	0.24	57.95	0.64	0.98
BLOOM-10-similarity	5.10	38.05	0.29	64.60	0.59	0.98
custom-decoder-ats	0.28	37.05	0.08	52.60	3.16	**2.91**
Identity baseline	3.50	3.90	0.18	44.70	1.00	1.00
Reference baseline	100	100	1.00	69.55	0.60	0.97
Truncate baseline	2.60	17.49	0.19	54.25	0.79	1.00

Table 6: Evaluation on APA-LHA-OR-A2 (copied from Stodden (2024)).

	BLEU↑	SARI↑	BS_P↑	FRE↑	Compr. ratio↓	Sent. splits↑
hda_LS	4.54	15.49	0.15	36.15	1.15	1.10
sockeye-APA-LHA	**11.00**	**44.93**	**0.32**	61.90	0.70	0.97
sockeye-DEplain-APA	3.57	39.4	0.25	**70.65**	0.68	1.26
mBART-DEplain-APA	5.32	30.94	0.26	57.65	0.86	1.37
mBART-DEplain-APA+web	5.81	26.61	0.25	56.05	0.85	1.19
mT5-DEplain-APA	4.92	35.70	0.26	57.70	0.57	1.10
mT5-SGC	2.54	39.36	0.29	70.45	**0.48**	1.00
BLOOM-zero	3.41	27.56	0.21	56.80	0.84	1.34
BLOOM-10-random	5.18	32.43	0.26	56.25	0.71	0.98
BLOOM-10-similarity	6.21	37.22	0.27	62.00	0.72	0.98
custom-decoder-ats	0.52	37.59	0.07	49.70	3.78	**3.51**
Identity baseline	5.47	4.89	0.22	43.70	1.00	1.00
Reference baseline	100	100	1.00	62.60	0.68	0.98
Truncate baseline	4.59	18.36	0.22	53.85	0.79	1.00

Table 7: Evaluation on APA-LHA-OR-B1 (copied from Stodden (2024)).

	BLEU↑	SARI↑	BS_P↑	FRE↑	Compr. ratio↓	Sent. splits↑
hda_LS	22.3	26.06	0.55	64.60	1.00	1.00
sockeye-APA-LHA	11.84	40.16	0.37	63.70	0.94	0.97
sockeye-DEplain-APA	19.58	**44.14**	0.53	71.45	0.94	1.09
mBART-DEplain-APA	**28.49**	38.72	**0.64**	65.30	0.99	1.07
mBART-DEplain-APA+web	28.03	33.81	**0.64**	65.20	0.98	1.05
mT5-DEplain-APA	22.32	39.41	0.61	63.20	0.87	1.04
mt5-SGC	8.12	37.92	0.48	**71.65**	**0.74**	1.00
BLOOM-zero	16.14	35.43	0.53	65.10	0.87	1.14
BLOOM-10-random	17.97	35.93	0.57	65.50	0.91	1.00
BLOOM-10-similarity	20.97	41.27	0.57	65.70	0.93	1.07
custom-decoder-ats	1.24	36.42	0.16	53.00	7.41	**5.07**
Identity baseline	26.89	15.25	0.63	58.75	1.00	1.00
Reference baseline	100.00	100.00	1.00	65.80	1.03	1.20
Truncate baseline	16.11	27.20	0.55	66.10	0.80	1.01

Table 8: Evaluation on DEplain-APA (copied from Stodden (2024)).

B.2 Evaluation on Web Corpora

	BLEU↑	SARI↑	BS_P↑	FRE↑	Compr. ratio↓	Sent. splits↑
sockeye-APA-LHA	0.24	32.41	0.13	69.55	0.74	0.90
sockeye-DEplain-APA	3.44	36.24	0.24	76.7	0.76	1.32
mBART-DEplain-APA	13.50	33.11	0.40	69.65	0.90	1.30
mBART-DEplain-APA+web	**17.99**	34.07	**0.44**	69.05	0.85	1.16
mT5-DEplain-APA	6.80	**37.15**	0.36	70.90	0.63	1.10
mt5-SGC	2.50	36.56	0.37	**78.10**	**0.47**	0.93
BLOOM-zero	10.88	30.58	0.35	70.30	0.85	1.28
BLOOM-10-random	11.06	30.90	0.39	68.55	0.69	0.98
BLOOM-10-similarity	11.62	37.03	0.42	70.05	0.63	0.98
custom-decoder-ats	0.72	34.92	0.10	57.15	5.41	**3.79**
Identity baseline	20.85	11.93	0.42	62.95	1.00	1.00
Reference baseline	100.00	100.00	1.00	77.90	0.94	1.84
Truncate baseline	17.28	24.58	0.40	67.05	0.82	1.02

Table 9: Evaluation on DEplain-web (copied from Stodden (2024)).

	BLEU↑	SARI↑	BS_P↑	FRE↑	Compr. ratio↓	Sent. splits↑
hda_LS	6.34	20.22	0.25	41.15	1.00	1.03
sockeye-APA-LHA	0.33	35.50	0.13	63.70	0.80	0.82
sockeye-DEplain-APA	1.35	37.86	0.18	**71.05**	0.79	1.01
mBART-DEplain-APA	5.70	32.77	0.31	58.15	0.97	1.00
mBART-DEplain-APA+web	6.56	29.80	0.33	44.95	1.61	1.09
mT5-DEplain-APA	2.81	35.92	0.30	51.45	0.76	0.88
mt5-SGC	3.30	43.62	0.37	58.55	**0.61**	0.85
BLOOM-zero	3.76	31.95	0.25	53.55	0.81	1.07
BLOOM-10-random	4.64	33.16	0.30	51.50	0.75	0.92
BLOOM-10-similarity	**13.32**	**44.66**	**0.38**	58.65	0.92	1.13
custom-decoder-ats	0.44	36.53	0.06	32.05	8.83	**3.68**
Identity baseline	7.46	6.51	0.29	41.15	1.00	1.00
Reference baseline	100.00	100.00	1.00	65.40	1.25	1.81
Truncate baseline	4.66	20.12	0.28	50.50	0.81	0.87

Table 10: Evaluation on SGC (copied from Stodden (2024)).

B.3 Evaluation on Knowledge Acquiring Corpora

	BLEU↑	SARI↑	BS_P↑	FRE↑	Compr. ratio ↓	Sent. splits ↑
hda_LS	55.22	34.20	0.76	61.50	1.00	1.00
sockeye-APA-LHA	0.69	18.94	0.15	69.45	1.05	0.92
sockeye-DEplain-APA	7.27	24.71	0.33	77.3	0.96	1.15
mBART-DEplain-APA	50.56	**44.29**	0.74	70.75	1.04	1.15
mBART-DEplain-APA+web	**55.35**	44.28	**0.79**	64.60	0.97	1.08
mT5-DEplain-APA	28.43	36.93	0.65	67.95	0.80	1.04
mt5-SGC	11.92	28.75	0.55	**78.30**	**0.70**	0.94
BLOOM-zero	28.18	32.15	0.59	67.85	0.87	1.26
custom-decoder-ats	0.77	22.05	0.08	46.55	14.61	**4.76**
Identity baseline	67.12	26.81	0.86	61.50	1.00	1.00
Reference baseline	100.00	100.00	1.00	66.00	0.95	1.32
Truncate baseline	45.39	29.78	0.75	63.80	0.83	1.00

Table 11: Evaluation on GEOlino (n=663) (copied from Stodden (2024)).

	BLEU↑	SARI↑	BS_P↑	FRE↑	Compr. ratio ↓	Sent. splits ↑
hda_LS	20.66	26.92	0.45	33.65	1.00	1.01
sockeye-APA-LHA	0.13	29.87	0.14	**69.05**	0.43	0.97
sockeye-DEplain-APA	0.68	31.79	0.19	65.0	0.51	1.42
mBART-DEplain-APA	13.69	**39.14**	0.50	51.10	0.76	1.57
mBART-DEplain-APA+web	**17.75**	37.37	**0.55**	43.65	0.74	1.29
mT5-DEplain-APA	2.84	35.09	0.40	46.60	0.40	1.14
mt5-SGC	1.05	32.98	0.38	64.40	**0.31**	0.97
BLOOM-zero	9.46	34.96	0.42	45.55	0.78	1.75
custom-decoder-ats	1.73	32.87	0.22	27.70	1.54	**4.22**
Identity baseline	27.31	14.99	0.55	28.10	1.00	1.00
Reference baseline	100.00	100.00	1.00	51.20	0.95	2.04
Truncate baseline	20.17	26.45	0.52	37.65	0.81	1.00

Table 12: Evaluation on TCDE19 (n=250) (copied from Stodden (2024)).

Evaluating the Simplification of Brazilian Legal Rulings in LLMs Using Readability Scores as a Target

Antônio Flávio Castro Torres de Paula[1], Celso Gonçalves Camilo[1],

[1]Institute of Informatics,
Federal University of Goiás (UFG),
Goiânia, Brazil, 74690-900

antonio.castro@discente.ufg.br, celso@inf.ufg.br

Abstract

Legal documents are often characterized by complex language, including jargon and technical terms, making them challenging for Natural Language Processing (NLP) applications. We apply the readability-controlled text modification task with an emphasis on legal texts simplification. Additionally, our work explores an evaluation based on the comparison of word complexity in the documents using Zipf scale, demonstrating the models' ability to simplify text according to the target readability scores, while also identifying a limit to this capability. Our results with Llama-3 and Sabiá-2 show that while the complexity score decreases with higher readability targets, there is a trade-off with reduced semantic similarity.

1 Introduction

Legal documents, in their majority, have a complex language, characterized by the use of jargon and words that are infrequently used in common vocabulary, as well as domain-specific technical terms Cemri et al. (2022a), Collantes et al. (2015). These features hinder access to information for the Brazilian population and pose a challenge that must be addressed by the Brazilian justice system.

Most text simplification approaches require a ground truth, typically provided by human experts Huang and Kochmar (2024). However, the availability of resources and techniques for Brazilian Portuguese is limited, and even more so when considering the specific task of text simplification in the legal domain.

The task of automatic text simplification is a natural language processing task whose objective is to modify the text to make it more understandable.

In this work, we evaluate the simplification of Brazilian legal rulings, using the method proposed by Farajidizaji et al. (2024), and propose an evaluation approach that considers complex words specific to the evaluated domain.

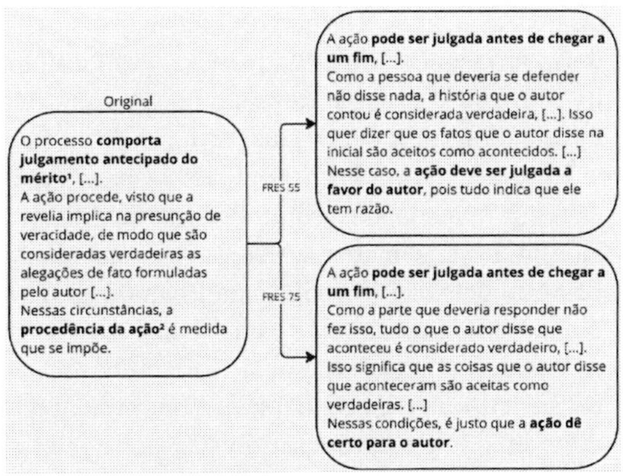

Figure 1: Example of a text simplification selected from the dataset. Highlighted excerpts: **1)** in English, "allows for an early judgment on the merits of the case", simplification could be translated to "can be decided before reaching a conclusion"; **2)** in English, "the claim's success is warranted", simplified to "the case should be decided in favor of the plaintiff" (FRES 55) and "the case goes well for the plaintiff" (FRES 75);

As far as we know, this is the first work evaluating LLMs for text simplification focused on legal documents in Brazilian Portuguese.

2 Related Work

In (Cemri et al., 2022b), the authors present USLT, an unsupervised method that identifies complex words through word frequency and applies measures to quantify complexity. These complex terms are replaced by candidates predicted by a masked language model and ranked based on various word characteristics. Finally, the solution applies sentence splitting, breaking down the original sentence into smaller ones. The results of the study show that the proposed method offers advantages over previous models developed for regular language. Moreover, it demonstrates that using a specific corpus and language models improves text simplification in legal documents.

Proceedings of the Third Workshop on Text Simplification, Accessibility and Readability (TSAR 2024), pages 117–125
November 15, 2024 ©2024 Association for Computational Linguistics

In (Urchs et al., 2022), the authors describe a study on the automatic simplification of legal texts to make them more accessible to people with low literacy levels. The study focuses on South Korean legislation, comparing the original version with its official simplified version and exploring the differences between them in terms of sentence length, use of passive voice, and modal verbs, among other factors. The first model used is LSBert, specialized in lexical simplification. The second is a combination of ACCESS and MUSS, which paraphrases the original sentences. The authors conclude that while these models can quantitatively reduce complexity, they may struggle to retain all the important information from the original text.

Recently, Farajidizaji et al., 2024 presented a new task of readability-controlled text modification, along with new metrics. The work evaluates that LLM models like ChatGPT and Llama-2 are capable of paraphrasing texts using readability scores as a target, although the final readability remains correlated with the original text. This work applies the methodology proposed by Farajidizaji et al., 2024, but focuses on higher FRES scores, aiming to evaluate only text simplification given a target score.

3 Methodology

3.1 Readability-controlled text modification task

The readability-controlled text modification task, presented in (Farajidizaji et al., 2024), defines that for each text, 8 variations are generated based on a target readability score. The function chosen to calculate the target score was the Flesch Reading Ease (FRES) index. Each range of the FRES index results in a text variation.

In this work, our goal is to evaluate the simplification capability, i.e., higher scores of FRES. Therefore, we will generate 5 variations of the original text, considering the following target readability scores: $r1$ = 55, $r2$ = 65, $r3$ = 75, $r4$ = 85, and $r5$ = 95. Each value of r represents half of the FRES score range.

3.2 Flesch reading Ease Portuguese Adaptation

The FRES score was originally developed for English and indicates that the higher the score, the easier the text is to read. The score takes into account the number of words, the number of sentences, and the number of syllables.

US	Brazil
5th grade	*5º ano do Ensino Fundamental I*
6th grade	*6º ano do Ensino Fundamental II*
7th grade	*7º ano do Ensino Fundamental II*
8-9th grade	*8º ano ao 9º ano do Ensino Fundamental II*
10-12th grade	*1º ao 3º ano do Ensino Médio*

Table 1: Proposed correspondence between education levels in the US and Brazil for the interpretability of the FRES index.

In this work, we will use an adaptation of the Flesch score for Brazilian Portuguese, presented by (Scarton and Aluísio, 2010).

The formula of the proposed adaptation is indicated by Equation 1.

$$248.835 - (1.015ASL) - (84.6 * ASW) \quad (1)$$

where ASL = average sentence length (the number of words divided by the number of sentences) and ASW = average number of syllables per word (the number of syllables divided by the number of words).

Originally, each FRES score range can be interpreted as an education level and is accompanied by a description that details the meaning of each range. However, these levels and descriptions are applicable to the English language and the education system in the United States. The education level and description will be used in the experiments as text input, which is why we also adapted this information.

Similar to the United States, Brazil also has a 12-year educational system, and the age at each educational level is the same. For this reason, we adapted the corresponding education level for each FRES score range. The level and description will be used as input in the experiments. Table 1 shows the proposed correspondences.

3.3 Evaluation

Originally in (Farajidizaji et al., 2024), three levels of evaluations are performed.

First, at the **individual level**, for each example in the dataset, the model is evaluated on three aspects concerning the expected readability score: ranking, regression, and classification.

In ranking, Spearman's correlation is calculated to measure whether the ranking of the generated rewrites is maintained relative to the target scores. In regression, the root mean square error (RMSE) between the target score and the actual score of the generated text is calculated. The formula is given by Equation 2.

$$rmse = \left[\frac{1}{5}\sum_{r\in R}(F(y_{(r)}) - r)^2\right]^{1/2} \quad (2)$$

where F represent FRES funcion from Equation 1, $y(r)$ is the text generated with target score r. R is the list of target scores to evaluation. Finally, in classification, the accuracy (Equation 3) of the calculated score is checked within the expected FRES score complexity range, given the target.

$$acc = \frac{1}{5}\sum_{r\in R}\mathbf{1}_{A(r)}(F(y_{(r)})) \quad (3)$$

For the three aspects at the individual level, the mean is reported across the dataset.

The second level of evaluation is called **Population-scale readability control**, where a decorrelation between the generated text and its source is expected. However, since this work aims to evaluate text simplification, a dependency on the source text is expected. This level will not be evaluated.

In the third and final level, **paraphrase metrics** are evaluated. The word error rate (WER [1]) is calculated to measure the lexical divergence between the original and generated texts. Another metric evaluated is the BERTScore [2], which assesses the semantic similarity between the generated and original texts, using cosine similarity between the embeddings of each text.

Additionally, we will evaluate the number of complex words in the original text and in the rewritten texts for each target score.

3.4 Using Complex Word Identification as Score

In (Cemri et al., 2022b), part of the proposed lexical simplification system is the identification of complex words (CWI), which is performed automatically without requiring a predetermined list of labeled complex words. The work uses word frequency across two different corpora to determine the list of complex words.

According to Zipf's law, words with lower frequency tend to be longer and more complex than more frequent and shorter words (Quijada and Medero, 2016). Word frequency was also highlighted as the most effective way to determine word complexity in the study conducted in (Paetzold and Specia, 2016).

To allow comparison between two corpora of different sizes, word frequency was calculated based on the Zipf scale (van Heuven et al., 2014). The Zipf scale is logarithmic, ranging from very low (Zipf value 1) to very high (Zipf value 7) frequency words, and can be represented by Equation 4.

$$Zipf = log\left(\left(\frac{wf * 1000000}{corpus\_size}\right) + 3\right) \quad (4)$$

where wf is the word frequency.

For the complex word score, we are interested in words that are more frequent in the domain corpus and less frequent in the Portuguese corpus. For the Brazilian Portuguese corpus, we considered BrWaC Wagner Filho et al. (2018). BrWaC is a large Brazilian corpus created from web pages, containing 2.7 billion tokens.

Based on the normalized frequency (Zipf value) of the two corpora, we can propose a simple metric that creates a complexity ranking of the words in the domain corpus. The score for each word is given by Equation 5.

$$cws = (1+zipf\_domain)*r\_zipf\_brwac) \quad (5)$$

where $zipf\_domain$ is the word's frequency in Zipf value in the domain corpus, and r_zipf_brwac is the word's ranking index in BrWaC.

As we are only interested in the rarest words in the domain corpus, we consider as complex words only those with a frequency higher than the average frequency in the domain corpus.

The complex score evaluated in the results is the sum of the scores of the complex words identified in the evaluated text. This metrics allow us evaluate the generated text automatically, without data annotation.

[1]Implementation available on https://github.com/jitsi/jiwer.

[2]Implementation available on https://huggingface.co/spaces/evaluate-metric/bertscore.

# examples	# words	# sentences	# paragraphs
10000	216.2 ± 18.6	9.9 ± 4.2	5.8 ± 2.5

Table 2: Statistics of the legal text dataset used in the experiments.

$$complexity\_score = \sum_{x \in CWL} (cws) \quad (6)$$

where x is each word in the text that belongs to the list of complex words in the domain (CWL), and cws is the complexity score of each word.

4 Experiments

4.1 Data

In order to conduct experiments in the context of legal sentence simplification, we prepared a specific dataset for evaluation.

The data used in the experiments are a subset of sentence documents downloaded from the São Paulo State Court website. A total of 80,000 public court sentence documents were downloaded from the period of 2021-06-01 to 2024-06-30, from 1,856 different judges. For this work, only judges with 30 or more sentences were considered, resulting in 195 judges.

The documents were pre-processed, segmenting and extracting the reasoning section of the legal sentences. The final dataset consists of 10,000 documents, with each document being either the entire reasoning or a part of it. Table 2 describe the stats.

4.2 Zero-shot

For the evaluations, we used the Llama-3 (Dubey et al., 2024) (`llama3-8b-8192`) and Sabiá-2 (Almeida et al., 2024) (`sabia-2-small`) models. Inferences for both models were performed via API. The Llama-3 model was accessed through the Groq platform [3] (with free credits available until the publication of this work), and the Sabiá-2 model was accessed through the Maritaca AI platform [4], with our own credits. The cost per million tokens is currently `R$` 1.00 for input tokens and `R$` 3.00 for output tokens.

The input prompts were based on the education level and description of the FRES score interpretation adapted for Portuguese, as shown in Table 1. The prompts used are described in Table 3. Appendix A describes original prompts

In addition to the text to be evaluated and the simplification instructions for each FRES score range, a supplementary prompt was added to prevent model hallucination, different language output and unnecessary structure formatting. The supplementary prompt includes:

- **Do not add facts that do not exist in the original text**: In some cases, the model generated facts that could be inferred from the original text but were not explicitly mentioned.
- **Generate only the rewritten text and in Portuguese**: In some cases, the Llama-3 model generated part of the output in English or described what had been done. For example: "Here is the rewritten document..."
- **Do not segment or separate the text**: Since these are parts of a sentence document, in some cases the model generated headers that structured the output into sections commonly found in such documents, such as Reasoning and Decision.

To demonstrate, without considering the complementary prompt, the Llama-3 model generated the following excerpts as part of the text simplification output for some documents in the dataset:

- "*Espero que isso ajude!*" (I hope this helps!);
- "*Espero que isso seja fácil de entender!*" (I hope this is easy to understand!);
- "*Lembre-se de que o texto original é um trecho de um julgamento e foi escrito em um estilo jurídico, então foi necessário adaptá-lo para que fosse mais fácil de entender para um estudante do 7º ano do Ensino Fundamental II.*" (Keep in mind that the original text is an excerpt from a legal ruling and was written in a legal style, so it had to be adapted to make it easier to understand for a 7th-grade student.);

[3]https://groq.com.

[4]API documentation `https://docs.maritaca.ai/pt/modelos`.

Target score	Prompt
55	*Reescreva este documento para o nível escolar do 1º ao 3º ano do Ensino Médio (Brasil). Deve ser relativamente difícil de ler.*
65	*Reescreva este documento para o nível escolar do 8º ano ao 9º ano do Ensino Fundamental II (Brasil). Deve ser em português claro e facilmente compreendido por estudantes de 13 a 15 anos.*
75	*Reescreva este documento para o nível escolar do 7º ano do Ensino Fundamental II (Brasil). Deve ser relativamente fácil de ler.*
85	*Reescreva este documento para o nível escolar do 6º ano do Ensino Fundamental II (Brasil). Deve ser fácil de ler e em portugûes coloquial, adequado para o público em geral.*
95	*Reescreva este documento para o nível escolar do 5º ano do Ensino Fundamental I (Brasil). Deve ser muito fácil de ler e de fácil entendimento para estudantes com média de 11 anos de idade.*

Table 3: Prompts considering each target score, in Brazilian Portuguese, translated from English and aligned with the educational level mentioned in Table 1. Appendix A describes original prompts in English.

Model	p(↑)	rmse(↓)	acc(↑)
Original data	0.0	$44.35_{\pm 14.63}$	$2.24_{\pm 6.52}$
Llama-3	$61.05_{\pm 37.38}$	$24.46_{\pm 10.13}$	$10.89_{\pm 15.32}$
Sabiá-2	$22.76_{\pm 49.64}$	$20.41_{\pm 7.29}$	$16.51_{\pm 15.14}$

Table 4: Mean of the individual-level metrics: p value (%) is the Spearman's rank correlation coefficient, rmse measures regression ability, and accuracy of the generated scores classification.

Target	WER	BERTScore (F1)
55	73,6 ± 34.0	78,1 ± 6.1
65	84,1 ± 39.8	74,4 ± 5.1
75	82,9 ± 11.1	74,4 ± 5.1
85	87,4 ± 10.2	72,1 ± 4.8
95	87,2 ± 33.2	72.0 ± 4.7

Table 5: Lexical divergence metrics (WER) and semantic similarity (BERTScore) between the original and generated texts, to model Llama-3. The mean of all examples with one standard deviation.

Target	WER	BERTScore (F1)
55	90,9 ± 25.0	72,8 ± 7.8
65	102,8 ± 19.2	69,9 ± 5.5
75	98,9 ± 18.2	70,3 ± 5.6
85	102.0 ± 17.6	68,3 ± 5.1
95	101,8 ± 15.4	67,8 ± 4.5

Table 6: Lexical divergence metrics (WER) and semantic similarity (BERTScore) between the original and generated texts, to model Sabiá-2. The mean of all examples with one standard deviation.

5 Results and Discussion

Table 4 presents the evaluation metrics at the individual level. The item described as "Original data" refers to the original text, which was also evaluated in some of the metrics based on the target scores.

When analyzing the correlation coefficient applied to the generated ranking, we observe that in the Llama-3 model, despite the zero-shot implementation not achieving the target scores exactly, it has a moderate correlation of 61.05% with the expected scores. On the other hand, the correlation of the Sabiá-2 model is weak (20.76 %). It is also interesting to note that, despite the Sabiá-2 model being trained in Brazilian Portuguese, Llama-3 achieves 38 points higher based on the target score ranking. On the other hand, when evaluating the mean squared error of the proposed models, we find that both models achieve a lower error than the original data. However, a high error is expected in relation to the original data, as it is repeated when measured against the expected scores.

Tables 5 and 6 present the paraphrase metrics for Llama-3 and Sabiá-2, respectively. It is possible to see that in both models, the word error rate increases with higher target readability scores, in-

Target	Sabiá-2 (%)	Llama-3 (%)
55	0,336 (71,1%)	0,571 (50,9%)
65	0,301 (74,2%)	0,457 (60,8%)
75	0,288 (75,3%)	0,401 (65,5%)
85	0,242 (79,2%)	0,355 (69,5%)
95	0,238 (79,5%)	0,342 (70,6%)

Table 7: The mean of complexity score achieved at each readability target score. The presented percentage represents the reduction compared to the original text score. For example, at the target score of 85, the Sabiá-2 model shows a 79.2% reduction in the complexity score.

dicating that the generated texts have a high degree of lexical divergence. This behavior is expected when simplifying a text. It is also observed that the Sabiá-2 model has an average advantage of 16.24% over Llama-3, considering all scores. On the other hand, it is also expected that the generated text remains semantically similar to the original text. In this case, for all target readability scores, the Llama-3 model outperformed Sabiá-2, achieving a mean F1 score of 74.2%, while the mean F1 score for Sabiá-2 was 69.82%.

Finally, we have the evaluation of complex words presented in Table 7. Both models show a reduction in the complexity of the words used, considering the original complexity of 1.1635. The Sabiá-2 model has a significant advantage, with an average reduction of 75.84% in the complexity score, while the reduction is 63.44% in Llama-3. It can also be observed that the difference between the target scores of 85 and 95 shows no significant reduction in complexity, which can be interpreted as a simplification limit reached by the models.

6 Conclusions

This work applies the task of readability-controlled text modification, focusing on the simplification of legal texts. We explore an approach based on complex word identification to evaluate the a text based on word complexity, indicating that the evaluated models have simplification capabilities and that there is a limit to this capacity, considering the proposed target scores.

In both evaluated models, Llama-3 and Sabiá-2, we observed that the complexity score decreases with higher readability scores, but with a reduction in the semantic similarity metric, highlighting the challenge of balancing simplification while preserving the main points of the original text.

7 Ethics Statement

This work does not raise any ethical concerns.

8 Limitations

We believe that the score based on complex word identification can be improved, as there is improvements for enhancement in the preprocessing of domain-specific texts. Additionally, the creation of a unified metric that considers various aspects of the generated text could simplify the evaluation of results, instead of assessing each metric in isolation.

Finally, adapting the steps into a framework that can be applied to domains beyond justice and legal texts.

9 Lay Summary

This research focuses on evaluating the simplification of Brazilian legal rulings using large language models (LLMs). Legal documents are often complex, making it difficult for the general public to understand their content. The study examines whether modern language models can simplify legal texts while preserving their original meaning, aiming to improve accessibility to legal information. The main question addressed by the study is whether large language models can automatically simplify Brazilian legal texts. The main question addressed by the study is whether large language models can automatically simplify Brazilian legal texts. Most simplification methods are validated by comparing them to human-made simplifications. However, such resources are limited for Brazilian Portuguese, particularly in the legal domain, making this task both challenging and significant for advancing language technologies in this field.

The findings show that the models are capable of simplifying legal sentences, but there is a trade-off. While both models reduce the complexity of the language used, they also decrease the semantic similarity with the original text, highlighting the challenge of simplifying text while maintaining its core meaning.

This work can benefit Brazilian society by making legal documents more accessible, potentially improving public understanding and compliance with legal decisions. Further research and advancements in this field are needed to enhance the balance between simplification and the preservation of original meaning.

References

Thales Sales Almeida, Hugo Abonizio, Rodrigo Nogueira, and Ramon Pires. 2024. Sabiá-2: A new generation of portuguese large language models. *Preprint*, arXiv:2403.09887.

Mert Cemri, Tolga Çukur, and Aykut Koç. 2022a. Unsupervised simplification of legal texts. *arXiv preprint*.

Mert Cemri, Tolga Çukur, and Aykut Koç. 2022b. Unsupervised simplification of legal texts. *arXiv preprint*.

M. Collantes, Maureen Hipe, Juan Lorenzo Sorilla, Laurenz Tolentino, and Briane Paul V. Samson. 2015. Simpatico: A text simplification system for senate and house bills.

Abhimanyu Dubey, Abhinav Jauhri, Abhinav Pandey, Abhishek Kadian, Ahmad Al-Dahle, Aiesha Letman, Akhil Mathur, Alan Schelten, Amy Yang, Angela Fan, Anirudh Goyal, Anthony Hartshorn, Aobo Yang, Archi Mitra, Archie Sravankumar, Artem Korenev, Arthur Hinsvark, Arun Rao, Aston Zhang, Aurelien Rodriguez, Austen Gregerson, Ava Spataru, Baptiste Roziere, Bethany Biron, Binh Tang, Bobbie Chern, Charlotte Caucheteux, Chaya Nayak, Chloe Bi, Chris Marra, Chris McConnell, Christian Keller, Christophe Touret, Chunyang Wu, Corinne Wong, Cristian Canton Ferrer, Cyrus Nikolaidis, Damien Allonsius, Daniel Song, Danielle Pintz, Danny Livshits, David Esiobu, Dhruv Choudhary, Dhruv Mahajan, Diego Garcia-Olano, Diego Perino, Dieuwke Hupkes, Egor Lakomkin, Ehab AlBadawy, Elina Lobanova, Emily Dinan, Eric Michael Smith, Filip Radenovic, Frank Zhang, Gabriel Synnaeve, Gabrielle Lee, Georgia Lewis Anderson, Graeme Nail, Gregoire Mialon, Guan Pang, Guillem Cucurell, Hailey Nguyen, Hannah Korevaar, Hu Xu, Hugo Touvron, Iliyan Zarov, Imanol Arrieta Ibarra, Isabel Kloumann, Ishan Misra, Ivan Evtimov, Jade Copet, Jaewon Lee, Jan Geffert, Jana Vranes, Jason Park, Jay Mahadeokar, Jeet Shah, Jelmer van der Linde, Jennifer Billock, Jenny Hong, Jenya Lee, Jeremy Fu, Jianfeng Chi, Jianyu Huang, Jiawen Liu, Jie Wang, Jiecao Yu, Joanna Bitton, Joe Spisak, Jongsoo Park, Joseph Rocca, Joshua Johnstun, Joshua Saxe, Junteng Jia, Kalyan Vasuden Alwala, Kartikeya Upasani, Kate Plawiak, Ke Li, Kenneth Heafield, Kevin Stone, Khalid El-Arini, Krithika Iyer, Kshitiz Malik, Kuenley Chiu, Kunal Bhalla, Lauren Rantala-Yeary, Laurens van der Maaten, Lawrence Chen, Liang Tan, Liz Jenkins, Louis Martin, Lovish Madaan, Lubo Malo, Lukas Blecher, Lukas Landzaat, Luke de Oliveira, Madeline Muzzi, Mahesh Pasupuleti, Mannat Singh, Manohar Paluri, Marcin Kardas, Mathew Oldham, Mathieu Rita, Maya Pavlova, Melanie Kambadur, Mike Lewis, Min Si, Mitesh Kumar Singh, Mona Hassan, Naman Goyal, Narjes Torabi, Nikolay Bashlykov, Nikolay Bogoychev, Niladri Chatterji, Olivier Duchenne, Onur Çelebi, Patrick Alrassy, Pengchuan Zhang, Pengwei Li, Petar Vasic, Peter Weng, Prajjwal Bhargava, Pratik Dubal, Praveen Krishnan, Punit Singh Koura, Puxin Xu, Qing He, Qingxiao Dong, Ragavan Srinivasan, Raj Ganapathy, Ramon Calderer, Ricardo Silveira Cabral, Robert Stojnic, Roberta Raileanu, Rohit Girdhar, Rohit Patel, Romain Sauvestre, Ronnie Polidoro, Roshan Sumbaly, Ross Taylor, Ruan Silva, Rui Hou, Rui Wang, Saghar Hosseini, Sahana Chennabasappa, Sanjay Singh, Sean Bell, Seohyun Sonia Kim, Sergey Edunov, Shaoliang Nie, Sharan Narang, Sharath Raparthy, Sheng Shen, Shengye Wan, Shruti Bhosale, Shun Zhang, Simon Vandenhende, Soumya Batra, Spencer Whitman, Sten Sootla, Stephane Collot, Suchin Gururangan, Sydney Borodinsky, Tamar Herman, Tara Fowler, Tarek Sheasha, Thomas Georgiou, Thomas Scialom, Tobias Speckbacher, Todor Mihaylov, Tong Xiao, Ujjwal Karn, Vedanuj Goswami, Vibhor Gupta, Vignesh Ramanathan, Viktor Kerkez, Vincent Gonguet, Virginie Do, Vish Vogeti, Vladan Petrovic, Weiwei Chu, Wenhan Xiong, Wenyin Fu, Whitney Meers, Xavier Martinet, Xiaodong Wang, Xiaoqing Ellen Tan, Xinfeng Xie, Xuchao Jia, Xuewei Wang, Yaelle Goldschlag, Yashesh Gaur, Yasmine Babaei, Yi Wen, Yiwen Song, Yuchen Zhang, Yue Li, Yuning Mao, Zacharie Delpierre Coudert, Zheng Yan, Zhengxing Chen, Zoe Papakipos, Aaditya Singh, Aaron Grattafiori, Abha Jain, Adam Kelsey, Adam Shajnfeld, Adithya Gangidi, Adolfo Victoria, Ahuva Goldstand, Ajay Menon, Ajay Sharma, Alex Boesenberg, Alex Vaughan, Alexei Baevski, Allie Feinstein, Amanda Kallet, Amit Sangani, Anam Yunus, Andrei Lupu, Andres Alvarado, Andrew Caples, Andrew Gu, Andrew Ho, Andrew Poulton, Andrew Ryan, Ankit Ramchandani, Annie Franco, Aparajita Saraf, Arkabandhu Chowdhury, Ashley Gabriel, Ashwin Bharambe, Assaf Eisenman, Azadeh Yazdan, Beau James, Ben Maurer, Benjamin Leonhardi, Bernie Huang, Beth Loyd, Beto De Paola, Bhargavi Paranjape, Bing Liu, Bo Wu, Boyu Ni, Braden Hancock, Bram Wasti, Brandon Spence, Brani Stojkovic, Brian Gamido, Britt Montalvo, Carl Parker, Carly Burton, Catalina Mejia, Changhan Wang, Changkyu Kim, Chao Zhou, Chester Hu, Ching-Hsiang Chu, Chris Cai, Chris Tindal, Christoph Feichtenhofer, Damon Civin, Dana Beaty, Daniel Kreymer, Daniel Li, Danny Wyatt, David Adkins, David Xu, Davide Testuggine, Delia David, Devi Parikh, Diana Liskovich, Didem Foss, Dingkang Wang, Duc Le, Dustin Holland, Edward Dowling, Eissa Jamil, Elaine Montgomery, Eleonora Presani, Emily Hahn, Emily Wood, Erik Brinkman, Esteban Arcaute, Evan Dunbar, Evan Smothers, Fei Sun, Felix Kreuk, Feng Tian, Firat Ozgenel, Francesco Caggioni, Francisco Guzmán, Frank Kanayet, Frank Seide, Gabriela Medina Florez, Gabriella Schwarz, Gada Badeer, Georgia Swee, Gil Halpern, Govind Thattai, Grant Herman, Grigory Sizov, Guangyi, Zhang, Guna Lakshminarayanan, Hamid Shojanazeri, Han Zou, Hannah Wang, Hanwen Zha, Haroun Habeeb, Harrison Rudolph, Helen Suk, Henry Aspegren, Hunter Goldman, Ibrahim Damlaj, Igor Molybog, Igor Tufanov, Irina-Elena Veliche, Itai Gat, Jake Weissman, James Geboski, James Kohli, Japhet Asher, Jean-Baptiste Gaya, Jeff Marcus, Jeff Tang, Jennifer Chan, Jenny Zhen, Jeremy Reizenstein, Jeremy Teboul, Jessica Zhong, Jian Jin, Jingyi Yang, Joe Cummings, Jon Carvill, Jon Shepard, Jonathan McPhie, Jonathan Torres,

Josh Ginsburg, Junjie Wang, Kai Wu, Kam Hou U, Karan Saxena, Karthik Prasad, Kartikay Khandelwal, Katayoun Zand, Kathy Matosich, Kaushik Veeraraghavan, Kelly Michelena, Keqian Li, Kun Huang, Kunal Chawla, Kushal Lakhotia, Kyle Huang, Lailin Chen, Lakshya Garg, Lavender A, Leandro Silva, Lee Bell, Lei Zhang, Liangpeng Guo, Licheng Yu, Liron Moshkovich, Luca Wehrstedt, Madian Khabsa, Manav Avalani, Manish Bhatt, Maria Tsimpoukelli, Martynas Mankus, Matan Hasson, Matthew Lennie, Matthias Reso, Maxim Groshev, Maxim Naumov, Maya Lathi, Meghan Keneally, Michael L. Seltzer, Michal Valko, Michelle Restrepo, Mihir Patel, Mik Vyatskov, Mikayel Samvelyan, Mike Clark, Mike Macey, Mike Wang, Miquel Jubert Hermoso, Mo Metanat, Mohammad Rastegari, Munish Bansal, Nandhini Santhanam, Natascha Parks, Natasha White, Navyata Bawa, Nayan Singhal, Nick Egebo, Nicolas Usunier, Nikolay Pavlovich Laptev, Ning Dong, Ning Zhang, Norman Cheng, Oleg Chernoguz, Olivia Hart, Omkar Salpekar, Ozlem Kalinli, Parkin Kent, Parth Parekh, Paul Saab, Pavan Balaji, Pedro Rittner, Philip Bontrager, Pierre Roux, Piotr Dollar, Polina Zvyagina, Prashant Ratanchandani, Pritish Yuvraj, Qian Liang, Rachad Alao, Rachel Rodriguez, Rafi Ayub, Raghotham Murthy, Raghu Nayani, Rahul Mitra, Raymond Li, Rebekkah Hogan, Robin Battey, Rocky Wang, Rohan Maheswari, Russ Howes, Ruty Rinott, Sai Jayesh Bondu, Samyak Datta, Sara Chugh, Sara Hunt, Sargun Dhillon, Sasha Sidorov, Satadru Pan, Saurabh Verma, Seiji Yamamoto, Sharadh Ramaswamy, Shaun Lindsay, Shaun Lindsay, Sheng Feng, Shenghao Lin, Shengxin Cindy Zha, Shiva Shankar, Shuqiang Zhang, Shuqiang Zhang, Sinong Wang, Sneha Agarwal, Soji Sajuyigbe, Soumith Chintala, Stephanie Max, Stephen Chen, Steve Kehoe, Steve Satterfield, Sudarshan Govindaprasad, Sumit Gupta, Sungmin Cho, Sunny Virk, Suraj Subramanian, Sy Choudhury, Sydney Goldman, Tal Remez, Tamar Glaser, Tamara Best, Thilo Kohler, Thomas Robinson, Tianhe Li, Tianjun Zhang, Tim Matthews, Timothy Chou, Tzook Shaked, Varun Vontimitta, Victoria Ajayi, Victoria Montanez, Vijai Mohan, Vinay Satish Kumar, Vishal Mangla, Vítor Albiero, Vlad Ionescu, Vlad Poenaru, Vlad Tiberiu Mihailescu, Vladimir Ivanov, Wei Li, Wenchen Wang, Wenwen Jiang, Wes Bouaziz, Will Constable, Xiaocheng Tang, Xiaofang Wang, Xiaojian Wu, Xiaolan Wang, Xide Xia, Xilun Wu, Xinbo Gao, Yanjun Chen, Ye Hu, Ye Jia, Ye Qi, Yenda Li, Yilin Zhang, Ying Zhang, Yossi Adi, Youngjin Nam, Yu, Wang, Yuchen Hao, Yundi Qian, Yuzi He, Zach Rait, Zachary DeVito, Zef Rosnbrick, Zhaoduo Wen, Zhenyu Yang, and Zhiwei Zhao. 2024. The llama 3 herd of models. *Preprint*, arXiv:2407.21783.

Asma Farajidizaji, Vatsal Raina, and Mark Gales. 2024. Is it possible to modify text to a target readability level? an initial investigation using zero-shot large language models. *Preprint*, arXiv:2309.12551.

Yichen Huang and Ekaterina Kochmar. 2024. Referee: A reference-free model-based metric for text simplification. *Preprint*, arXiv:2403.17640.

Gustavo Paetzold and Lucia Specia. 2016. Semeval 2016 task 11: Complex word identification. In *Proceedings of the 10th International Workshop on Semantic Evaluation (SemEval-2016)*, pages 560–569.

Maury Quijada and Julie Medero. 2016. HMC at SemEval-2016 task 11: Identifying complex words using depth-limited decision trees. In *Proceedings of the 10th International Workshop on Semantic Evaluation (SemEval-2016)*, pages 1034–1037, San Diego, California. Association for Computational Linguistics.

Carolina Evaristo Scarton and Sandra Maria Aluísio. 2010. Análise da inteligibilidade de textos via ferramentas de processamento de língua natural: adaptando as métricas do coh-metrix para o português. *Linguamática*, 2(1):45–61.

Stefanie Urchs, Akshaya Muralidharan, and Florian Matthes. 2022. How to simplify law automatically? a study on south korean legislation and its simplified version. In *ICAART: PROCEEDINGS OF THE 14TH INTERNATIONAL CONFERENCE ON AGENTS AND ARTIFICIAL INTELLIGENCE - VOL 3*, ICAART, pages 697–704. 14th International Conference on Agents and Artificial Intelligence (ICAART), ELECTR NETWORK, FEB 03-05, 2022.

Walter van Heuven, Paweł Mandera, Emmanuel Keuleers, and Marc Brysbaert. 2014. Subtlex-uk: a new and improved word frequency database for british english. *Quarterly journal of experimental psychology (2006)*, 67.

Jorge A. Wagner Filho, Rodrigo Wilkens, Marco Idiart, and Aline Villavicencio. 2018. The brWaC corpus: A new open resource for Brazilian Portuguese. In *Proceedings of the Eleventh International Conference on Language Resources and Evaluation (LREC 2018)*, Miyazaki, Japan. European Language Resources Association (ELRA).

A Appendix: Original prompts

This appendix provides the original list of prompts in English for each target score used. The prompts below were translated into Brazilian Portuguese, and the school grade levels were adapted to match the Brazilian education system.

A.1 FRES Target 55

Paraphrase this document for 10th-12th grade school level (US). It should be fairly difficult to read.

A.2 FRES Target 65

Paraphrase this document for 8th/9th grade school level (US). It should be plain English and easily understood by 13- to 15-year-old students.

A.3 FRES Target 75

Paraphrase this document for 7th grade school level (US). It should be fairly easy to read.

A.4 FRES Target 85

Paraphrase this document for 6th grade school level (US). It should be easy to read and conversational English for consumers.

A.5 FRES Target 95

Paraphrase this document for 5th grade school level (US). It should be very easy to read and easily understood by an average 11-year old student.

Measuring and Modifying the Readability of English Texts with GPT-4

Sean Trott and **Pamela D. Rivière**
Department of Cognitive Science, UC San Diego
{sttrott, pdrivier}@ucsd.edu

Abstract

The success of Large Language Models (LLMs) in other domains has raised the question of whether LLMs can reliably assess and manipulate the *readability* of text. We approach this question empirically. First, using a published corpus of 4,724 English text excerpts, we find that readability estimates produced "zero-shot" from GPT-4 Turbo and GPT-4o mini exhibit relatively high correlation with human judgments ($r = 0.76$ and $r = 0.74$, respectively), out-performing estimates derived from traditional readability formulas and various psycholinguistic indices. Then, in a pre-registered human experiment ($N = 59$), we ask whether Turbo can reliably make text easier or harder to read. We find evidence to support this hypothesis, though considerable variance in human judgments remains unexplained. We conclude by discussing the limitations of this approach, including limited scope, as well as the validity of the "readability" construct and its dependence on context, audience, and goal.

1 Introduction

The ease with which a text can be read or understood is called *readability*. Measuring and modifying readability has been a topic of interest for decades (Lively and Pressey, 1923; Flesch, 1948; Crossley et al., 2023b), with potential applications ranging from selecting and curating educational materials (Solnyshkina et al., 2017; Creutz, 2024; Liu and Lee, 2023) to making legal, medical, or other technical documents more accessible (Ghosh et al., 2022; Rosati, 2023; Chen et al., 2023). Methods for *assessing* readability, in turn, include: tests of reading comprehension, formulas incorporating basic text features (Lively and Pressey, 1923; Flesch, 1948) or psycholinguistic variables (Kyle and Crossley, 2015), and approaches using supervised learning to estimate readability from labeled text data (Schwarm and Ostendorf, 2005; Martinc et al., 2021).

Recent advances in Large Language Models (LLMs) (Brown et al., 2020) has led to interest in exploring the capacities and applications of these systems—including measuring and modifying the readability of text (Ribeiro et al., 2023; Li et al., 2023; Crossley et al., 2023a; Patel et al., 2023; Farajidizaji et al., 2023). In the current work, we approach this question empirically.

In Section 2, we describe in more detail past work on measuring and modifying readability of text automatically. Then, in Section 3, we empirically assess the ability of a state-of-the-art LLM (GPT-4 Turbo) to measure readability "zero-shot". Next, in a pre-registered human experiment, we ask whether GPT-4 Turbo can be used to modify text readability (Section 4). Finally, we conclude by discussing the implications of the current work (Section 5), as well as its limitations (Section 6). Note that all code and data can be found on GitHub: `https://github.com/seantrott/llm_readability`.

2 Related Work

As described in Section 1, efforts to quantify the readability of text date back at least a century (Lively and Pressey, 1923). For many decades, approaches relied on hand-crafted features thought to correlate with (or be causally implicated in) text readability, such as the average length of words or sentences (Flesch, 1948). As Vajjala (2022) describe, dominant approaches have gradually shifted towards treating readability assessment as a supervised machine learning problem, i.e., training a system to produce representations that facilitate the prediction of "gold standard" human readability judgments—though researchers continue to test the viability of hand-crafted features as an alternative or complementary approach (Deutsch et al., 2020; Wilkens et al., 2024). Pre-trained language models seem potentially well-suited to this task;

Proceedings of the Third Workshop on Text Simplification, Accessibility and Readability (TSAR 2024), pages 126–134
November 15, 2024

indeed, past work (Crossley et al., 2023b) suggests that fine-tuning these models can produce estimates that align with human readability judgments.

Modifying readability is also of considerable interest, with most research focusing on making text easier to read, e.g., for journal abstracts (Li et al., 2023) or math assessments (Patel et al., 2023). Cardon and Bibal (2023) provide a useful overview of the distinct *operations* used in Automatic Text Simplification (ATS), including splitting up long sentences (Nomoto, 2023) and simplifying or substituting individual words (Paetzold and Specia, 2017). As with work on measuring readability, this research has gradually shifted from explicit, rule-based approaches to systems that "learn" appropriate transformations using an annotated corpus (Cardon and Bibal, 2023), sometimes tailored with psycholinguistic features (Qiao et al., 2022).

Recent research has used *prompt engineering* approaches to ask whether Large Language Models (LLMs) can modify text (Farajidizaji et al., 2023; Ribeiro et al., 2023; Liu et al., 2023; Creutz, 2024; Imperial and Tayyar Madabushi, 2023; Pu and Demberg, 2023; Luo et al., 2022; Kew et al., 2023), with some studies asking whether text can be modified to some *target readability level*, e.g., a target Flesch score (Flesch, 1948). Even with "zero-shot" prompting (i.e., no examples provided), LLMs appear to be surprisingly successful at modifying text readability in the desired direction—though not necessarily to the desired text level (Liu et al., 2023). In some cases, a residual correlation is found between the readability of the original text and the modified text (Farajidizaji et al., 2023).

3 Study 1: Measuring Readability

In Study 1, we focused on the ability of LLMs to estimate the readability of text excerpts "zero-shot" (i.e., without any labeled examples in the prompt). We asked: given a corpus of human readability estimates (Crossley et al., 2023b), how well can an LLM equipped solely with instructions and a definition of readability produce outputs that correlate reliably with human judgments?

3.1 CLEAR Dataset

We used the CommonLit Ease of Readability (CLEAR) Corpus (Crossley et al., 2023b), which contains human estimates of readability for 4,724 text excerpts. The CLEAR Corpus was created by Crossley et al. (2023b) by sampling text excerpts (between 140-200 words) from various databases (e.g., Project Gutenberg). It includes fiction and non-fiction, and spans a range from 1875 to 2020. Excerpts were then normed by asking a sample of teachers to rate pairs of items for their relative readability. These pairwise judgments were then aggregated to create a readability index for each individual passage.

3.2 Models

Our primary goal was assessing the reliability of using a state-of-the-art LLM in estimating readability. To this end, we used two state-of-the-art proprietary OpenAI models: GPT-4 Turbo and GPT-4o mini. We accessed both models using the OpenAI Python API: Turbo (GPT-4-1106-PREVIEW) and 4o mini (GPT-4O-MINI-2024-07-18). Because both models are closed-source, it is unclear how many parameters each model has or how much data it was trained on.

3.3 Zero-shot Annotation Procedure

Both OpenAI models were provided with the same system prompt meant to approximate the context of participants in the original CLEAR corpus (Crossley et al., 2023b) ("You are an experienced teacher, skilled at identifying the readability of different texts."). Each text excerpt was presented to the model in a separate prompt (i.e., rather than in succession), along with instructions explaining that the goal was to rate the excerpt for how easy it was to read and understand, on a scale from 1 (very challenging to understand) to 100 (very easy to understand); the exact instructions can be found in Appendix A.1. Each models' responses were produced using a temperature of 0, with a maximum number of tokens of 3. Response strings were then converted to numeric values in Python.

3.4 Results

We first asked how well ratings from GPT-4 Turbo and GPT-4o mini predicted human readability scores from the CLEAR dataset (Crossley et al., 2023b). Concretely, this was operationalized by asking to what extent LLM-generated ratings correlated with human ratings. We found that ratings from each model were positively correlated with human readability: Turbo ($r = 0.76$) and GPT-4o mini ($r = 0.74$); see also Figure 1 for the Turbo results specifically.[1] For comparison, the correla-

[1]Ratings between Turbo and 4o were also highly correlated ($r = 0.81$).

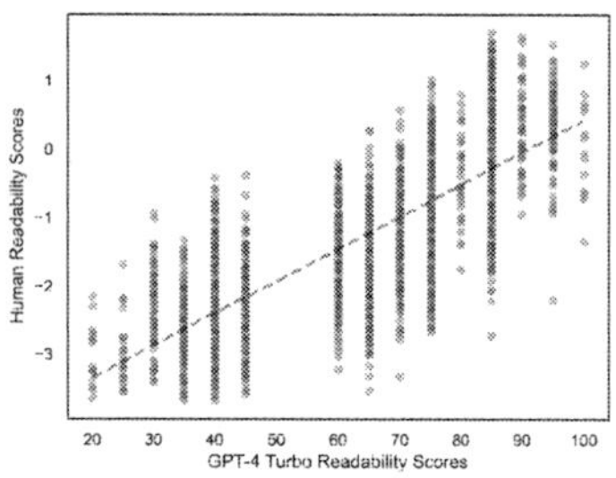

Figure 1: Relationship between ratings elicited by GPT-4 Turbo and average human readability judgments ($R^2 = 0.58$).

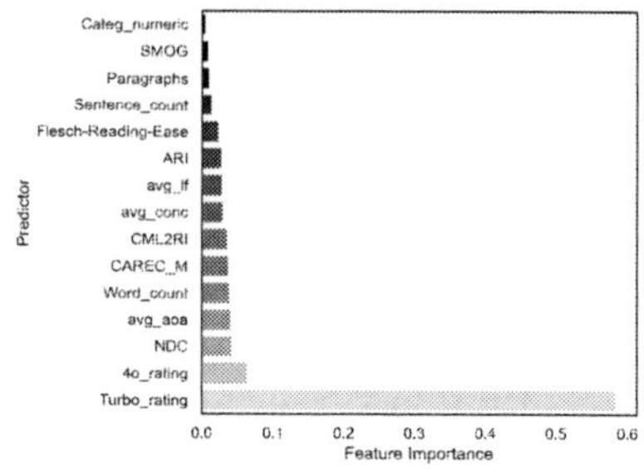

Figure 2: Feature importance scores for each predictor, as determined using a random forest regression. A higher value indicates that this feature was more useful for predicting human readability judgments.

tion between two random splits within the CLEAR corpus was only $r = 0.63$.

In terms of predictive power, these correlation metrics would correspond to an R^2 of .54 (for 4o mini) or .577 (for Turbo). We compared this predictive power to several psycholinguistic variables known to correlate with about readability (Kyle et al., 2018): log word frequency (Brysbaert and New, 2009), word concreteness (Brysbaert et al., 2014), and word age of acquisition (Kuperman et al., 2012). For each variable, we calculated the *average* across all words in a given passage that occurred in the relevant dataset. A linear model including all three psycholinguistic predictors explained approximately 36% of the variance in human readability judgments ($R^2 = 0.36$). Each variable was significantly related: frequency $[\beta = 0.82, SE = 0.13, p < .001]$, concreteness $[\beta = 1.76, SE = 0.11, p < .001]$, and age of acquisition $[\beta = -0.56, SE = 0.06, p < .001]$. Thus, psycholinguistic properties of words in a passage are useful for predicting readability judgments, but under-perform ratings elicited from GPT-4 Turbo and GPT-4o mini.[2]

As a final test of predictive power, we entered the metrics considered above—along with measures like the number of words and sentences, and estimates derived from traditional readability formulas—as predictors in a random forest regression and compared their *feature importance scores*.[3] These scores can be interpreted as reflecting the extent to which the inclusion of a particular feature (e.g., ratings from Turbo) reduce prediction error when predicting human readability. All measures were z-scored before fitting the model. As depicted in Figure 2, Turbo's ratings were assigned the highest importance, followed by the average age of acquisition scores.

4 Study 2: Modifying Readability

In Study 2, we asked whether a state-of-the-art LLM could successfully *modify* (as opposed to simply *measure*) the readability of texts. GPT-4 Turbo performed best in Study 1, so we selected Turbo for modifying text readability as well. We approached this question in the following way: given instructions to make a text excerpt *easier* or *harder*, can an LLM produce a modified version that an independent pool of human judges rate as easier or harder than the original? Although it is unlikely that making texts *harder* to read is a desirable goal, we included this condition as a control (i.e., to ensure that modified passages were not always rated as easier to read). This study was pre-registered on the Open Science Framework (OSF).[4]

4.1 Materials

To make this question empirically tractable, we selected a random sample of 100 excerpts from the original CLEAR corpus. Each excerpt was then presented to GPT-4 Turbo twice, with two different sets of instructions asking Turbo to make the excerpt easier or harder to read (exact prompting and instructions found in Appendix A.1). As in Study 1, Turbo was first provided with a system prompt ("You are an experienced writer, skilled at rewriting texts."); a temperature of 0 was used,

[2]Of course, taking the average of these variables across an entire passage is a relatively coarse measure and likely represents a *lower-bound* on their predictive efficacy.

[3]No maximum depth was used, and the random state was set to 0.

[4]Link to pre-registration for text modification: `https://osf.io/vtwug`. Link to pre-registration for human experiment: `https://osf.io/6hmej`.

and the maximum number of tokens was set to the number of tokens in the original excerpt, plus a "buffer" of 5 tokens. Additionally, we specified that the modified version should be of approximately the same length as the original.

This resulted in 300 items altogether. For the human study, these items were assigned to 6 lists using a Latin Square design, where each list had approximately 50 items. No list contained multiple versions of the same item. Note that in some cases, the modified version produced by Turbo cut-off in mid-sentence; we further modified these excerpts by removing the final sentence fragment. The experiment was designed on the Gorilla experimental design platform (Anwyl-Irvine et al., 2018).

4.2 Participants

Our target N was 60 participants (10 per list). We anticipated a non-zero exclusion rate, so we intended to recruit 70 participants via Prolific; due to an error in the recruiting platform, we recruited only 69. As per our pre-registration, we excluded participants whose readability ratings for the *original* text excerpts exhibited a correlation with the gold standard of $r < .1$; this resulted in the removal of 10 participants. Participants were paid \$6.00 and the median completion time was 34 minutes and 21 seconds (an average rate of \$10.48 per hour). In the final pool of participants, 34 participants identified as female (22 male, 2 non-binary, and 1 preferred not to answer); the average self-reported age was 40.77 (SD = 14). Note that unlike the CLEAR corpus (Crossley et al., 2023b), we did not recruit specifically teachers or other employees in the education sector.

4.3 Procedure

Each participant rated the readability of a series of 50 text excerpts on a scale from 1 (very challenging to understand) to 5 (very easy to understand). Participants were instructed to consider factors such as "sentence structure, vocabulary complexity, and overall clarity"; they were also reminded to try to focus on the readability of the passage itself, as opposed to the complexity of the topic. No participant rated multiple versions of the same item and the order of items was randomized across trials.

4.4 Results

We carried out three pre-registered analyses in R using the *lme4* package (Bates, 2011). In the case of fitting mixed effects models, we began with maximal random effects structure and reduced as needed for model convergence (Barr et al., 2013). Nested model comparisons were conducted by comparing a full model to a reduced model omitting only the variable of interest, using a log-likelihood ratio test (LRT).

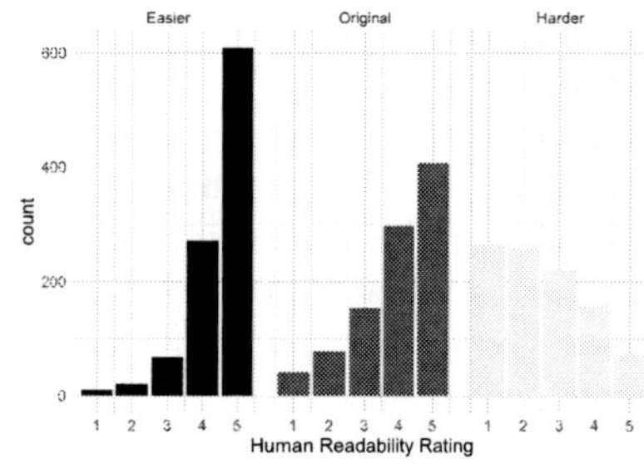

Figure 3: Distribution of human readability judgments for each text condition.

Human readability judgments were predicted by the contrast between *Easy* and *Hard* $[\chi^2(1) = 97.58, p < .001]$, between *Easy* and *Original* $[\chi^2(1) = 32.4, p < .001]$, and between *Hard* and *Original* $[\chi^2(1) = 74.75, p < .001]$. That is, significant variance in human readability judgments was explained by the condition under which a particular passage was produced. As depicted in Figure 3, excerpts in the *Easier* condition were rated as the most readable ($M = 4.48, SD = 0.8$), excerpts in the *Harder* condition were rated as the least readable ($M = 2.5, SD = 1.25$), with excerpts in the *Original* condition between the two ($M = 3.97, SD = 1.13$).

5 Discussion

Our primary question was whether state-of-the-art LLMs could be used to *measure* and *modify* the readability of a text excerpt. In Study 1, we found that ratings from GPT-4 and GPT-4o mini ratings were strongly correlated with gold standard ratings, though Turbo's ratings ($r = 0.76$) were slightly more correlated than ratings from GPT-4o mini; consistent with other recent work using LLMs for text annotation (Trott, 2024a,b), this correlation was higher than the correlation between random splits of human ratings (Cross et al., 2023). Further, Turbo's ratings were the best predictor of human readability judgments of all the variables tested (see Study 3), including several psycholinguistic variables and other readability formula estimates.

In Study 2, we asked Turbo to produce easier

or harder versions of 100 sample excerpts from the same corpus (Crossley et al., 2023b). In a preregistered human study, participants consistently rated the *easier* versions as easier to read, and the *harder* versions as harder to read—though notably, there was a correlation between the readability of the original text passage and the modified passage (see Figure 5).

As with other recent work (Farajidizaji et al., 2023; Liu et al., 2023; Ribeiro et al., 2023), these results provide a proof-of-concept that LLMs may be useful for both measuring and modifying text readability, at least as operationalized here. Unlike past work (Ribeiro et al., 2023; Farajidizaji et al., 2023), we do not investigate the question of modification to *target readability levels*, though we do collect novel human judgments to validate the success of GPT-4 Turbo's modifications (Study 4). Of course, considerable open questions about the viability of this approach remain. These questions are all explored in more detail in the Limitations section below.

6 Limitations

One limitation, particularly of Study 2, is scope: because we planned to collect human annotations for each excerpt, we considered only 100 text excerpts, and compared the performance of only one model (GPT-4 Turbo). The results of this study can be seen as a proof-of-concept, which future work can build on with larger samples and more sophisticated prompt engineering techniques. More generally, a limitation of both studies is that they considered excerpts from a single readability dataset only. Future work ocould explore other readability datasets and benchmarks to ask how well these results generalize. Relatedly, we aimed to use a prompt that would allow fair comparisons to data collected from humans and thus did not explore alternative prompt engineering techniques. However, future work could explore how prompting strategies affect model performance and behavior.

A further limitation of Study 2 is that we did not assess the modified excerpts in terms of their faithfulness to the original text. Evaluating the quality of summaries is notoriously difficult (Wang et al., 2019), though recent work (Liu et al., 2023) has made use of automated metrics like BERTScore (Zhang et al., 2020). Future work would benefit from another human study that asks directly about the *quality* of the modified texts; these results could then be used to validate automated metrics. Relatedly, the evaluators in Study 2 did not have particular experience in assessing readability or linguistics more generally; future work could recruit annotators with more expertise to create more nuanced readability ratings.

A final limitation is the question of what the *construct* of readability means in the first place, and how best to measure it. Construct validity is by no means a new challenge for work in NLP generally (Raji et al., 2021) or readability specifically (Crossley et al., 2008). "Readability" may not be a unitary construct; different stakeholders may construe readability in different ways depending on their goal (e.g., making a product manual accessible vs. curating educational materials) and audience (e.g., school-aged children vs. professionals). Further, different formulas or automated metrics emphasize different properties of a text, making implicit or explicit assumptions about the underlying construct. The current work relied on human judgments of readability as a "gold standard", using both existing corpora (Crossley et al., 2023b) and novel data (Study 2). By these metrics, using Turbo to measure and modify readability was modestly successful. Yet it is unclear whether these results generalize to other texts, contexts, goals, or audiences. Thus, future work could benefit from additional research on "benchmarking" readability itself (Kew et al., 2023) and whether different benchmarks are needed for different senses of readability.

7 Lay Summary

We asked whether Large Language Models (LLMs) were able to measure—and later change—the "readability" of snippets of English-language text taken from the openly available CLEAR Corpus. We presented text excerpts to GPT-4o mini and GPT-4 Turbo, collected their readability ratings on a scale from 1 (very difficult) to 100 (very easy), and found that their ratings were positively correlated with the corresponding human readability judgments. Notably, GPT-4 Turbo outperformed readability estimates from -4o mini, and from a battery of more traditional readability measures. We next instructed GPT-4 Turbo—the best-performing model—to rewrite each text excerpt to make it "easier" or "harder" to read relative to the original, while keeping the length of the rewritten excerpts roughly the same as the original. We then conducted a validation study to determine whether human judges found the rewritten excerpts easier or harder to read. Human judges produced readability ratings for each rewritten text excerpt between 1 (difficult) to 5 (easy). When GPT-4-Turbo rewrote a text to read more easily, human judges did in fact find it easier to read than texts rewritten to seem harder to read. This suggests that off-the-shelf LLMs are capable of assessing text readability, and can modify readability to (coarsely defined) target levels.

8 Ethical Considerations

All data collected from human participants has been fully anonymized before analysis or publication.

One potential risk with research on automatic text simplification is that tools will be deployed in various applied settings (e.g., education) before they are ready. As we discussed in the Limitations section (Section 6), we believe there are a number of open questions remaining with this kind of research and do not intend for these results to signal that LLMs could and should be used for measuring and modifying readability in an applied domain at this time.

Acknowledgments

We are grateful to advice and suggestions from Benjamin Bergen and Cameron Jones. Pamela Rivière was funded by the Chancellor's Postdoctoral Fellowship Program at UC San Diego.

References

Alexander Anwyl-Irvine, Jessica Massonnié, Adam Flitton, Natasha Kirkham, and Jo Evershed. 2018. Gorillas in our midst: Gorilla. sc. *Behavior Research Methods*.

Dale J Barr, Roger Levy, Christoph Scheepers, and Harry J Tily. 2013. Random effects structure for confirmatory hypothesis testing: Keep it maximal. *Journal of memory and language*, 68(3):255–278.

Douglas Bates. 2011. Mixed models in r using the lme4 package part 5: Generalized linear mixed models. *University of Wisconsin: Madison, WI, USA*.

Tom Brown, Benjamin Mann, Nick Ryder, Melanie Subbiah, Jared D Kaplan, Prafulla Dhariwal, Arvind Neelakantan, Pranav Shyam, Girish Sastry, Amanda Askell, et al. 2020. Language models are few-shot learners. *Advances in neural information processing systems*, 33:1877–1901.

Marc Brysbaert and Boris New. 2009. Moving beyond kučera and francis: A critical evaluation of current word frequency norms and the introduction of a new and improved word frequency measure for american english. *Behavior research methods*, 41(4):977–990.

Marc Brysbaert, Amy Beth Warriner, and Victor Kuperman. 2014. Concreteness ratings for 40 thousand generally known english word lemmas. *Behavior research methods*, 46:904–911.

Rémi Cardon and Adrien Bibal. 2023. On operations in automatic text simplification. In *Proceedings of the Second Workshop on Text Simplification, Accessibility and Readability*, pages 116–130, Varna, Bulgaria. INCOMA Ltd., Shoumen, Bulgaria.

Chao-Yi Chen, Jen-Hao Yang, and Lung-Hao Lee. 2023. NCUEE-NLP at BioLaySumm task 2: Readability-controlled summarization of biomedical articles using the PRIMERA models. In *The 22nd Workshop on Biomedical Natural Language Processing and BioNLP Shared Tasks*, pages 586–591, Toronto, Canada. Association for Computational Linguistics.

Mathias Creutz. 2024. Correcting challenging Finnish learner texts with claude, GPT-3.5 and GPT-4 large language models. In *Proceedings of the Ninth Workshop on Noisy and User-generated Text (W-NUT 2024)*, pages 1–10, San Ġiljan, Malta. Association for Computational Linguistics.

Ziggy Cross, Michelle Yun, Ananya Apparaju, Jata MacCabe, Garrett Nicolai, and Miikka Silfverberg. 2023. Glossy bytes: Neural glossing using subword encoding. In *Proceedings of the 20th SIGMORPHON workshop on Computational Research in Phonetics, Phonology, and Morphology*, pages 222–229, Toronto, Canada. Association for Computational Linguistics.

Scott Crossley, Joon Suh Choi, Yanisa Scherber, and Mathis Lucka. 2023a. Using large language models to develop readability formulas for educational settings. In *International Conference on Artificial Intelligence in Education*, pages 422–427. Springer.

Scott Crossley, Aron Heintz, Joon Suh Choi, Jordan Batchelor, Mehrnoush Karimi, and Agnes Malatinszky. 2023b. A large-scaled corpus for assessing text readability. *Behavior Research Methods*, 55(2):491–507.

Scott A Crossley, Jerry Greenfield, and Danielle S McNamara. 2008. Assessing text readability using cognitively based indices. *Tesol Quarterly*, 42(3):475–493.

Tovly Deutsch, Masoud Jasbi, and Stuart Shieber. 2020. Linguistic features for readability assessment. In *Proceedings of the Fifteenth Workshop on Innovative Use of NLP for Building Educational Applications*, pages 1–17, Seattle, WA, USA → Online. Association for Computational Linguistics.

Asma Farajidizaji, Vatsal Raina, and Mark Gales. 2023. Is it possible to modify text to a target readability level? an initial investigation using zero-shot large language models. *arXiv preprint arXiv:2309.12551*.

Rudolph Flesch. 1948. A new readability yardstick. *Journal of applied psychology*, 32(3):221.

Sohom Ghosh, Shovon Sengupta, Sudip Naskar, and Sunny Kumar Singh. 2022. FinRAD: Financial readability assessment dataset - 13,000+ definitions of financial terms for measuring readability. In *Proceedings of the 4th Financial Narrative Processing Workshop @LREC2022*, pages 1–9, Marseille, France. European Language Resources Association.

Joseph Marvin Imperial and Harish Tayyar Madabushi. 2023. Flesch or fumble? evaluating readability standard alignment of instruction-tuned language models. In *Proceedings of the Third Workshop on Natural Language Generation, Evaluation, and Metrics (GEM)*, pages 205–223, Singapore. Association for Computational Linguistics.

Tannon Kew, Alison Chi, Laura Vásquez-Rodríguez, Sweta Agrawal, Dennis Aumiller, Fernando Alva-Manchego, and Matthew Shardlow. 2023. BLESS: Benchmarking large language models on sentence simplification. In *Proceedings of the 2023 Conference on Empirical Methods in Natural Language Processing*, pages 13291–13309, Singapore. Association for Computational Linguistics.

Victor Kuperman, Hans Stadthagen-Gonzalez, and Marc Brysbaert. 2012. Age-of-acquisition ratings for 30,000 english words. *Behavior research methods*, 44:978–990.

Kristopher Kyle, Scott Crossley, and Cynthia Berger. 2018. The tool for the automatic analysis of lexical sophistication (taales): version 2.0. *Behavior research methods*, 50:1030–1046.

Kristopher Kyle and Scott A Crossley. 2015. Automatically assessing lexical sophistication: Indices, tools, findings, and application. *Tesol Quarterly*, 49(4):757–786.

Zihao Li, Samuel Belkadi, Nicolo Micheletti, Lifeng Han, Matthew Shardlow, and Goran Nenadic. 2023. Large language models and control mechanisms improve text readability of biomedical abstracts. *arXiv preprint arXiv:2309.13202*.

Fengkai Liu and John Lee. 2023. Hybrid models for sentence readability assessment. In *Proceedings of the 18th Workshop on Innovative Use of NLP for Building Educational Applications (BEA 2023)*, pages 448–454, Toronto, Canada. Association for Computational Linguistics.

Yixin Liu, Alexander R Fabbri, Jiawen Chen, Yilun Zhao, Simeng Han, Shafiq Joty, Pengfei Liu, Dragomir Radev, Chien-Sheng Wu, and Arman Cohan. 2023. Benchmarking generation and evaluation capabilities of large language models for instruction controllable summarization. *arXiv preprint arXiv:2311.09184*.

Bertha A Lively and SL Pressey. 1923. A method for measuring the" vocabulary burden" of textbooks: Educational administration and supervision,". *A method for measuring the" vocabulary burden" of textbooks: Educational Administration and Supervision*.

Zheheng Luo, Qianqian Xie, and Sophia Ananiadou. 2022. Readability controllable biomedical document summarization. In *Findings of the Association for Computational Linguistics: EMNLP 2022*, pages 4667–4680, Abu Dhabi, United Arab Emirates. Association for Computational Linguistics.

Matej Martinc, Senja Pollak, and Marko Robnik-Šikonja. 2021. Supervised and unsupervised neural approaches to text readability. *Computational Linguistics*, 47(1):141–179.

Hiroki Nomoto. 2023. Issues surrounding the use of ChatGPT in similar languages: The case of Malay and Indonesian. In *Proceedings of the 13th International Joint Conference on Natural Language Processing and the 3rd Conference of the Asia-Pacific Chapter of the Association for Computational Linguistics (Volume 2: Short Papers)*, pages 76–82, Nusa Dua, Bali. Association for Computational Linguistics.

Gustavo Paetzold and Lucia Specia. 2017. Lexical simplification with neural ranking. In *Proceedings of the 15th Conference of the European Chapter of the Association for Computational Linguistics: Volume 2, Short Papers*, pages 34–40, Valencia, Spain. Association for Computational Linguistics.

Nirmal Patel, Pooja Nagpal, Tirth Shah, Aditya Sharma, Shrey Malvi, and Derek Lomas. 2023. Improving mathematics assessment readability: Do large language models help? *Journal of Computer Assisted Learning*, 39(3):804–822.

Dongqi Pu and Vera Demberg. 2023. ChatGPT vs human-authored text: Insights into controllable text summarization and sentence style transfer. In *Proceedings of the 61st Annual Meeting of the Association for Computational Linguistics (Volume 4: Student Research Workshop)*, pages 1–18, Toronto, Canada. Association for Computational Linguistics.

Yu Qiao, Xiaofei Li, Daniel Wiechmann, and Elma Kerz. 2022. (psycho-)linguistic features meet transformer models for improved explainable and controllable text simplification. In *Proceedings of the Workshop on Text Simplification, Accessibility, and Readability (TSAR-2022)*, pages 125–146, Abu Dhabi, United Arab Emirates (Virtual). Association for Computational Linguistics.

Inioluwa Deborah Raji, Emily Denton, Emily M Bender, Alex Hanna, and Amandalynne Paullada. 2021.

AI and the Everything in the Whole Wide World Benchmark. In *Thirty-fifth Conference on Neural Information Processing Systems Datasets and Benchmarks Track (Round 2)*.

Leonardo F. R. Ribeiro, Mohit Bansal, and Markus Dreyer. 2023. Generating summaries with controllable readability levels. In *Proceedings of the 2023 Conference on Empirical Methods in Natural Language Processing*, pages 11669–11687, Singapore. Association for Computational Linguistics.

Domenic Rosati. 2023. GRASUM at BioLaySumm task 1: Background knowledge grounding for readable, relevant, and factual biomedical lay summaries. In *The 22nd Workshop on Biomedical Natural Language Processing and BioNLP Shared Tasks*, pages 483–490, Toronto, Canada. Association for Computational Linguistics.

Sarah E Schwarm and Mari Ostendorf. 2005. Reading level assessment using support vector machines and statistical language models. In *Proceedings of the 43rd annual meeting of the Association for Computational Linguistics (ACL'05)*, pages 523–530.

Marina Solnyshkina, Radif Zamaletdinov, Ludmila Gorodetskaya, and Azat Gabitov. 2017. Evaluating text complexity and flesch-kincaid grade level. *Journal of social studies education research*, 8(3):238–248.

Sean Trott. 2024a. Can large language models help augment english psycholinguistic datasets? *Behavior Research Methods*, pages 1–19.

Sean Trott. 2024b. Large language models and the wisdom of small crowds. *Open Mind*, 8:723–738.

Sowmya Vajjala. 2022. Trends, limitations and open challenges in automatic readability assessment research. In *Proceedings of the Thirteenth Language Resources and Evaluation Conference*, pages 5366–5377, Marseille, France. European Language Resources Association.

Su Wang, Rahul Gupta, Nancy Chang, and Jason Baldridge. 2019. A task in a suit and a tie: paraphrase generation with semantic augmentation. In *Proceedings of the AAAI Conference on Artificial Intelligence*, volume 33, pages 7176–7183.

Rodrigo Wilkens, Patrick Watrin, Rémi Cardon, Alice Pintard, Isabelle Gribomont, and Thomas François. 2024. Exploring hybrid approaches to readability: experiments on the complementarity between linguistic features and transformers. In *Findings of the Association for Computational Linguistics: EACL 2024*, pages 2316–2331, St. Julian's, Malta. Association for Computational Linguistics.

Tianyi Zhang, Varsha Kishore, Felix Wu, Kilian Q. Weinberger, and Yoav Artzi. 2020. Bertscore: Evaluating text generation with bert. In *International Conference on Learning Representations*.

A Appendix

A.1 Instructions for Study 1 and Study 2

In this section, we report the exact prompts used to elicit readability judgments from GPT-4 Turbo. Note that symbols like "EXCERPT" indicate that the text of the excerpt was inserted in this section of the prompt.

Study 1 Instructions:

> Read the text below. Then, indicate the readability of the text, on a scale from 1 (extremely challenging to understand) to 100 (very easy to read and understand). In your assessment, consider factors such as sentence structure, vocabulary complexity, and overall clarity.
>
> <Text>:EXCERPT</Text>
>
> On a scale from 1 (extremely challenging to understand) to 100 (very easy to read and understand), how readable is this text?. Please answer with a single number.

Study 2 Instructions:

> Read the passage below. Then, rewrite the passage so that it is easier/harder to read.
>
> When making the passage more/less readable, consider factors such as sentence structure, vocabulary complexity, and overall clarity. However, make sure that the passage conveys the same content.
>
> Finally, try to make the new version approximately the same length as the original version.
>
> <Text>:EXCERPT</Text>
>
> As described in the instructions, please make this passage easier/harder to read, while keeping the length the same.

A.2 Exploratory Analyses for Study 1

We also constructed a correlation matrix of all the variables considered: see Figure 4).

A.3 Exploratory Analyses for Study 2

In an exploratory analysis, we asked whether the readability of the original text excerpt was correlated with the readability of the modified version.

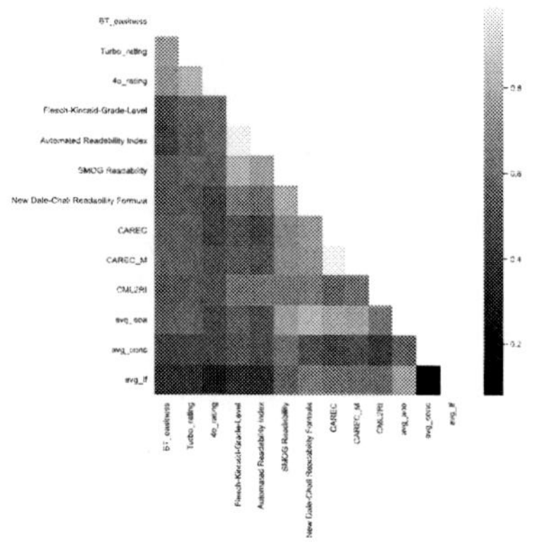

Figure 4: Correlation matrix between all the variables considered in Study 1. Correlation coefficients have all been transformed to absolute values for easier comparison.

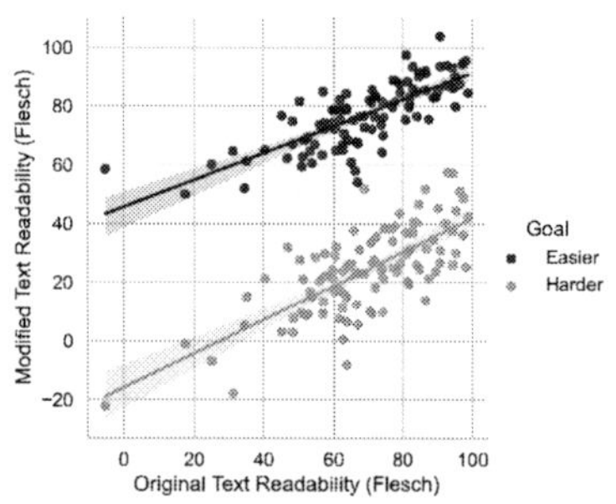

Figure 5: Comparison of Flesch readability for the original version and modified version, according to Turbo's instructions.

Consistent with (Farajidizaji et al., 2023), we found a positive correlation: that is, Turbo successfully modified texts to be easier or harder to read, depending on the instructions, but the readability of the modified text exhibited a residual correlation with the original text's readability (see Figure 5).

Additionally, we calculated the readability of the modified texts using automated readability formulas, e.g., the Flesch Reading Score (Flesch, 1948). We then asked whether the modified versions varied in the expected direction along each metric in question, according to whether Turbo was instructed to make the text easier or harder to read. We found that the modified versions varied in the expected direction according to automated readability metrics as well (see Figure 6).

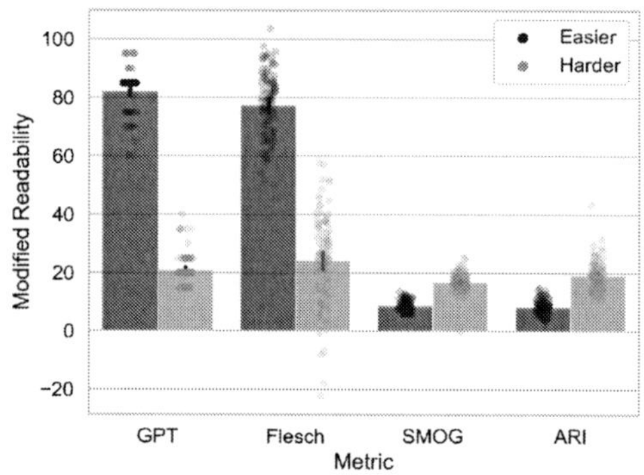

Figure 6: Comparison of automated readability scores for the modified text excerpts.

Author Index

Association for Computational Linguistics
209 N. Eighth Street
Stroudsburg, Pennsylvania 18360

ISBN 979-8-3313-0854-4

9 798331 308544

CURRAN ASSOCIATES INC.
proceedings.com